COLLECTIBLE GLASSWARE from the 40s 50s 60s...

PHOTO LEGENDS INCLUDED

Ninth Edition
an illustrated value guide

Gene & Cathy Florence

COLLECTOR BOOKS
A Division of Schroeder Publishing Co., Inc.

ABOUT THE AUTHOR

Gene Florence, born in Lexington, Kentucky, in 1944, graduated from the University of Kentucky where he held a double major in mathematics and English. He taught for nine years in Kentucky at the junior high and high school levels, one unforgettable year at a school for gifted students, before his glass collecting "hobby" became his full-time job.

Mr. Florence has been interested in collecting since childhood, beginning with baseball cards and progressing through comic books, coins, bottles, and finally, glassware. He first became interested in glass after buying a large set of pink Sharon Depression glass at a garage sale for $5.00… and studying to find out what it was.

By the time this is published, he will have written over 109 books, at least 80 of them on glassware. Titles include the following: *Collector's Encyclopedia of Depression Glass* now in its eighteenth edition; *Kitchen Glassware of the Depression Years*, sixth edition; *Collectible Glassware from the 40s, 50s, 60s*, 9th edition; *Elegant Glassware of the Depression Era*, 12th edition; *The Collector's Encyclopedia of Akro Agate*; *Stemware Identification*; *Glass Candlesticks of the Depression Era*; four volumes of *Pattern Identification*; three editions of *Anchor Hocking's Fire-King & More*; *Very Rare Glassware of the Depression Years, Six Series*; *Treasures of Very Rare Depression Glass*; *The Collector's Encyclopedia of Occupied Japan, Volumes I through V*; *Florences' Ovenware from the 1920s to the Present*; *The Hazel-Atlas Glass Identification and Value Guide*; *Glass Kitchen Shakers, 1930 – 1950s*; *Florences' Big Book of Salt & Pepper Shakers*; *Occupied Japan Collectibles*; *American Pattern Glass Table Sets*; *Pocket Guide to Depression Glass*, fifteen editions. He also wrote six editions of an innovative *Standard Baseball Card Price Guide* and two volumes about Degenhart collectibles.

If you know of any unlisted or unusual pieces of glassware from the examples shown in this book, you may write Mr. Florence at Box 22186, Lexington, KY 40522 or Box 64, Astatula, FL 34705. If you would like a reply, enclose a self-addressed, stamped envelope — and be patient. The volume of mail/e-mail from his web page (www.geneflorence.com) has begun to soar exponentially. He still answers it when time permits, but much of the year is spent writing, traveling, doing research, and sometimes, fishing.

On the Cover:

Front: Clockwise from top left — Moon and Star large jardiniere, page 149; Coin Glass one-handled nappy, page 39; Heirloom squared bowl, page 103; Coin Glass red oval bowl, page 39; Tiara Crown Collection basket, page 49. Center — Fire-King Honeysuckle juice tumbler, page 75.

Back: "Gay Nineties" items, page 95.

Cover design by Beth Summers
Book design by Heather Carvell
Cover photography by Charles R. Lynch

COLLECTOR BOOKS
P.O. Box 3009
Paducah, Kentucky 42002-3009

www.collectorbooks.com

The current values in this book should be used only as a guide. They are not intended to set prices, which vary from one section of the country to another. Auction prices as well as dealer prices vary greatly and are affected by condition as well as demand. Neither the authors nor the publisher assumes responsibility for any losses that might be incurred as a result of consulting this guide.

Searching for a Publisher?

We are always looking for people knowledgeable within their fields. If you feel that there is a real need for a book on your collectible subject and have a large comprehensive collection, contact Collector Books.

Proudly printed and bound in the
United States of America

CONTENTS

ACKNOWLEDGMENTS

We wish to thank friends, readers, collectors, and dealers who have supplied wide-ranging information and suggestions for patterns for this book. There are five extra patterns in this ninth edition of *Collectible Glassware from the 40s, 50s, 60s...* and the book is now 50 percent larger than it was when started in 1990. Were it not for you, sharing with us through writing, e-mailing, calling, and talking to us directly, it could not have grown the way it has. All this has been invaluable to us and to collectors needing what we try to share through our books.

Thanks, particularly to Cathy, my wife, who now shares equal billing as co-author. She has always been the workforce of this job which involves much more than spending 14 – 16 hours a day at the computer writing. There's research and proofing and van loads of glass which need unpacking, packing, labeling, and sorting between photography and show stock. Regrettably, as her work hats have increased, so have her stress levels, which have to be actively "managed" now along with hectic schedules and deadlines for books. We are cutting down, back, and out things we have always done. We are trying to hold our show schedule to two or three a year, partially because of health demands and also in gratitude to certain clubs who have supported and appreciated our efforts over 30 years.

Thanks for this book need to go to Dick and Pat Spencer, Dan and Geri Tucker, Ron and Barbara Marks, and various readers throughout the United States and Canada for glass photos and information provided. There has also been information forthcoming from readers outside of the United States — Australia, New Zealand, England, Canada, and Puerto Rico. Thanks even for information received that we cannot yet use but which is valued, and chronicled, for possible yet-to-come endeavors.

Charles R. Lynch of Kentucky and Daniel Tucker of Ohio took photographs for this book. Most were accomplished during a couple of week sessions; but with digital photos now, we are able to take pictures throughout the two years between books. As we approach retirement, our photo filing system is finally so organized that we wish we could go back a few books.

The customary photo session encompassing tasks of unwrapping, sorting, arranging set-ups, taking measurements, carting, and repacking glass was handled by Cathy Florence, Dick and Pat Spencer, and the guys from the shipping department at Collector Books. Bringing together all this glass for photographs in the time prearranged is a gargantuan task; but with digital photography, the hours of time waiting for Polaroids to develop, film to be loaded, and two days wait to see the final result of pictures taken has mostly been eliminated to where Charlie is looking at the photo immediately and we can determine any problems. The photos are then stored in-house in memory and can usually be found when needed.

Thanks, also, to the members of the editorial department at Collector Books who did design and layout and dutifully worked with our irregular schedules. This book would never become a reality were it not for them. If we've omitted the name of anyone who contributed, please forgive us; know that we, as well as our readers, thank you for your assistance.

If you write us about glassware, please enclose a self-addressed, stamped envelope that is large enough for your photos if you wish them back. Writing books from November through May leaves precious little time for answering the numerous letters that arrive each week. In fact, most received while writing this are in a large container we will take with us to various locations to answer. We wish to thank the thoughtful people who send postcards with the possible answers to their questions for us to check off the correct response. Those are answered immediately when we know the answer without having to research information. We want to inform people who do not include the SASE that they'll not be answered.

We try to respond to e-mails as we have time and you can find the current e-mail address through our website www.gene-florence.com. We wish to encourage you to send pictures or even pencil rubbings of items you hope to have identified, rather than descriptions. We need to explain that our expertise lies in knowledge of the patterns presented in our books. We now have four *Glassware Pattern Identification Guides* that contain almost 2,000 patterns identified by name, date, color, company, and how many different pieces were made. They should save you some searching on your own. We're trying to document those "wonder who made this" type pieces you see at markets but seldom in books.

PREFACE

A few years ago we began a legend numbering system so you can match pieces pictured with the accompanying price list. This will help you with any questions about what exactly is pictured. We have had extremely positive feedback on this concept.

Change is inevitable; and in the 36 years we've been involved with writing about glass, we've seen collectors changing venue from buying in small shops, estate and garage sales, and flea markets to attending Depression glass shows, visiting entire malls filled with antiques and finally, surfing the Internet auctions and websites.

Collectible Glassware from the 40s, 50s, 60s... evolved from our Depression glassware book featuring glass made in the 1920s and 1930s. That type of glass was being found regularly at garage, estate, and rummage sales when we first started buying it in the late 1960s. Now, glassware made during the 40s, 50s, 60s, and even 70s is what is being found, and bought, at those same type sales. Old timers wonder what people see in this "new" glass. It's the same thing Depression glass buyers saw almost two generations ago, things triggering childhood memories — only it's moved forward. When we started with Depression glass, it was frowned upon by antique dealers and was not allowed in many antique shows as it was too "new." In traveling and searching for glass in New England states, you could literally be ushered out of a shop if you asked if they had Depression glass for sale. Of course, those owners would send you down the road to someone who sold it out of their basement or garage, but they didn't allow it in their shop.

Primarily, this 50s book encompasses glassware made after the Depression era that is being bought by today's glass collectors. A few patterns made after 1940 that had been included in *Collector's Encyclopedia of Depression Glass* (e.g., Holiday, Floragold, Moonstone) were transferred into this one comprising glass produced in the 40s, 50s, and 60s…. This has allowed us to both research newer glass being collected and also to significantly increase the number of older patterns in *Collector's Encyclopedia of Depression Glass*. We think everyone has ultimately benefited from this trek into later made wares.

However, this 50s era book didn't materialize overnight. Preparations (i.e. finding the glass) took a few years before launching it; but it has now been so well received that some Depression glass clubs and show promoters are updating contracts first written 30 years ago to include glassware made during this later time span. That's progress. What some show promoters need to realize is that when Depression glass shows began in 1973, the glass was typically about 40 years old; today, glassware from the late 60s is 40 years old.

Both machine-produced and handworked glassware from this era are included in this book inasmuch as both classifications are being collected. A few hand-etched glassware patterns included actually had their beginning near the end of 1930, but their primary production was during 40s and 50s and even some 60s. Several patterns previously listed in our *Elegant Glassware of the Depression Era* book have been relocated to this book because of that.

Our goal has been a book that shows color photos, that will inform you about what is being collected and what is hard or easy to find, that will show you realistic pricing of what glass really sells for, and perhaps entertain you.

Requests and collecting trends have always determined the direction this book has taken and will take in the future. If you have glassware that you think should be included or would be willing to lend for photography purposes or have copies of glass company advertisements listing pieces which you received with your sets, let us hear from you. Keep us updated about new discoveries regarding the wares already listed. We will try to pass your information along to other collectors. Your input is valuable to us and to others. Collectors have repeatedly expressed their gratefulness and have told us numerous times "to thank all those people who help" in putting our books together.

PRICING

All prices in this book are retail prices for mint condition glassware. This book is intended to be only a guide since there are some regional price differences which cannot reasonably be dealt with herein.

In the present market you may expect dealers to pay from 50% to 70% less than the prices quoted. Glass that is in less than mint condition, i.e., chipped, cracked, scratched, or poorly molded, will bring only a small percentage of the price of glass that is in mint condition. Since this book covers glassware made from 1940 onward, you may assume that dealers and collectors will be less charitable of wear marks or imperfections than in glass made earlier.

Pricing this book has been extremely difficult — more so than in the past. We have always tried to price glass by what it is actually selling for and not what one or two sales may have recorded. Right now, glassware from the time period covered in this book is being unearthed in quantities previously not thought possible. There were tons of Depression glass thrown away, discarded, or used as ship's ballast. We had almost 40 years of collecting that before supplies became weaker. This later 50s glassware was acknowledged as collectible in a shorter time span than earlier glass; so tons of it have been rediscovered, and are still being unearthed in attics, basements, garages, and inventories of bankrupt businesses. Supplies of some patterns are overwhelming collectors' demands right now, and thus prices are dropping for items being found. This condition is usually temporary and demand, typically, has eventually caught up to supply.

The next big factor affecting collecting was the introduction of the Internet and stockpiles are being acknowledged and offered for sale by people who had no idea this glassware was of value. Due to this unveiling, items thought scarce or rare are turning out not so hard to find and prices are adjusting — in most cases downward. It may take years for us to actually know what is really rare and hard to find. There are hundreds of examples in this book of items that are now selling regularly for half, and sometimes even less, than they were five years ago. That price is taking into consideration the sometimes extravagant postage and handling rates some sellers are asking just to supplement the prices for which items are selling. We are sure this will not last forever, but glass dealers are going to have to learn to adjust their prices if they are going to be able to continue business in this changing world. We have been forced to lower our expectations and that means that some glass bought for 60% of retail a few years ago is selling for what we paid for it — or less. That expected profit is gone. As collectors, unless you must sell your collections, we'd suggest you just enjoy them and hang onto them now. We could be seeing an over-inflated market suddenly correcting itself, or we could just be seeing an Internet influx of unknown quantities of product — or both. At any rate we don't envision a world where these wares aren't loved, appreciated, and valued.

MEASUREMENTS

All measurements are taken from company catalogs or by actually measuring each piece if no catalog lists are available. Capacities of tumblers, stemware, and pitchers are always measured to the very top edge until nothing more can be added. Heights are measured perpendicular to the bottom of the piece, not up a slanted side. Handles are not included in general measurements unless so stated.

ANNIVERSARY, JEANNETTE GLASS COMPANY, 1947 – 1949; late 1960s – mid 1970s

Colors: crystal, iridescent, pink, and Shell Pink

Pink Anniversary was regarded as Depression glass by collectors for years since earlier authors included it in their books. It was not made until years after the Depression era, and thus we moved it to our first *Collectible Glassware of the 40s, 50s, 60s...* in 1990. Crystal and iridescent could be purchased in boxed sets in glassware outlets as late as 1975. Pink dinner plates are an earlier normal 9" size, but were changed to 10" in crystal and iridescent. Crystal can be found trimmed with either silver (platinum) or gold; but, so far, these trims do not add to the price of the items, but are more of a detraction due to wear than anything else.

Although iridescent Anniversary is regularly found in antique malls, it has been prohibited from being exhibited at some Depression era glass shows since it was made in the 1970s. Iridescent is desirable and prices are actually outperforming those of crystal. Some later carnival glass books actually list it now, though it is doubtful anyone ever pitched pennies in it to win a piece at carnivals before 1970. In spite of that, this identifiable color of Anniversary does create an additional market for it.

Snack plates with a cup indent have been discovered in iridescent and crystal, but not in pink. There was a flurry of interest in collecting snack plates in all patterns for a while; and several people have notified us over the last 10 years they are writing a book on them. Those television tray accoutrements were for dishing up quick nibbles to serve before the "idiot box" which so fascinated people they gave up meals at table. Both square and #2965 round crystal cake plates have been found with an indentation and sometimes covered by an aluminum painted lid displaying a variety of decals.

Challenging to find are the pink Anniversary #2975 butter dish, #2938 pin-up vase, #2963 wine glass, and sandwich plate. Both the 2½ ounce wine and pin-up vase are reasonably priced considering how few of them are ever displayed for sale. Watch for water stains in the pin-up vases. They are nearly impossible to remove and staining will lessen their value.

The 1947 Jeannette catalog describes the open, three-legged candy as a comport rather than a compote. Terminology used for glassware varies from company to company and from time period to time period. For instance, older glassware catalogs usually listed "cream" to describe what we now call a creamer.

An Anniversary vase has been reproduced in India according to a paper label attached. It was pictured in our last book. The "why," of such a production we do not understand, as it is not an expensive item to buy. The newly made vase was priced $4.99 in a major discount store. The satinized frosting actually enhances the appearance. We were rather flabbergasted by the item; but with the demise of so many of the glassmaking companies in the last few years, we in the collecting world are going to have to get used to seeing items reappearing in bizarre fashions.

		Crystal	Pink	Iridescent
7 ▸	Bowl, 4⅞", berry	2.00	7.00	2.00
4 ▸	Bowl, 6¾", soup w/o rim	6.00		
	Bowl, 7⅜", soup w/rim	6.00	18.00	7.00
16 ▸	Bowl, 9", fruit	9.00	20.00	8.00
	Butter dish bottom	7.50	20.00	
	Butter dish top	7.50	20.00	
9 ▸	Butter dish and cover	15.00	40.00	
14 ▸	Candy jar and cover	20.00	40.00	
20 ▸	*Cake plate, 12½"	8.00	15.00	
	Cake plate, round, w/metal cover	12.00		
	Cake plate, 12⅜", square, w/metal cover	15.00		
15 ▸	Candlestick, 4⅞", pr.	15.00		15.00
8 ▸	Comport, open, 3-legged	4.00	12.00	3.00
	Comport, ruffled, 3-legged	5.00		
3 ▸	Creamer, footed	3.00	10.00	3.00
10 ▸	Cup	2.00	6.00	2.00

		Crystal	Pink	Iridescent
	Pickle dish, 9"	5.00	12.00	5.00
	Plate, 6¼", sherbet	1.00	2.00	1.00
6 ▸	Plate, 9", dinner		11.00	
2 ▸	Plate, 10", dinner	4.00		4.00
17 ▸	Plate, 12½", sandwich server	8.00	18.00	6.00
	Relish dish, 8"	6.00	12.00	4.00
	Relish, 4-part, on metal base	12.00		
11 ▸	Saucer	.50	1.00	.50
	Sherbet, ftd.	3.00	7.00	
5 ▸	Sugar	2.00	7.00	4.00
13 ▸	Sugar cover	3.00	9.00	4.00
	Tidbit, berry & fruit bowls w/metal hndl.	10.00		
19 ▸	**Vase, 6½"	12.00	22.00	
	†Vase, wall pin-up	14.00	30.00	
18 ▸	Wine glass, 2½ oz.	7.00	12.00	

*Shell Pink $250.00   **reproduced in crystal   †Shell Pink $350.00

ARGUS, #2770 FOSTORIA GLASS COMPANY, 1960 – 1965; SOME ADDITIONAL STEM PRODUCTION THROUGH 1982

Colors: amber, crystal, cobalt, green, Olive, Ruby, Smoke

After adding Argus to our book, the abundance of stems appearing on the market was quite overwhelming for a while. This small Fostoria pattern is more known for its pieces being made to order and promoted at the Henry Ford Museum gift shop than for any other reason. Items sold there were embossed HFM on each piece; however those sold by the company displayed only a Fostoria paper label.

Admirers concentrate on the Ruby more than any other color which is great since Ruby Argus is being marketed more often than other colors. Red is a popular color, as in most patterns. Crystal and Smoke may be the uncommon colors, but we have never been asked by any collector if we have them for sale.

Compotes and sugars are frequently found topless; but unless priced economically, you might refrain from the temptation to buy them, as lids are rarely seen in this pattern. The original Argus design itself dates from the 1850s though it was only made in crystal at that time.

		Crystal Olive Smoke	Cobalt Ruby
10 ▸	Bowl, 5"	7.00	15.00
5 ▸	Compote w/cover, 8"	40.00	70.00
1 ▸	Creamer, 6"	10.00	20.00
7 ▸	Plate, 8"	9.00	16.00
2 ▸	Stem, 5", 4 oz., wine	8.00	11.00
6 ▸	Stem, 5", 8 oz., sherbet	6.00	10.00
4 ▸	Stem, 6½", 10½ oz., water	7.00	12.00
12 ▸	Sugar, w/lid	20.00	55.00
8 ▸	Tumbler, 2⅞", 4½ oz., juice	5.00	10.00
	Tumbler, 3⅞", 10 oz., old fashioned	6.00	12.00
3 ▸	Tumbler, 5¼", 12 oz., highball	7.00	10.00
11 ▸	Tumbler, 6¾", 13 oz., ftd., tea	7.00	12.00

ATTERBURY SCROLL, IMPERIAL GLASS COMPANY, c. late 1960s

Colors: amber, blue, carnival red, custard, crystal, Dynasty jade, some milk

Atterbury Scroll was originally distributed only as a crystal production, and, though eye-catching, judging by the short run, it obviously did not snare the interest of buyers. In recent years with all the importance placed on collecting jadite colored items, Dynasty Jade items began appearing rather regularly at our show table, having been brought in to be identified.

Regrettably, only five different pieces of Dynasty Jade were made in the "Scroll" as it is generally called by collectors. However, because of its later manufacture, pieces are now beginning to turn up at markets in various production colors. So, if you like this, you need to latch on quickly, for unlike many of Imperial's dinnerware lines, you may have to work at securing pieces of Atterbury Scroll. The jade and other colors were made as a part of various color productions after 1963.

		Crystal	Jade
	Basket	15.00	
6 ▸	Bowl, 3-toed	15.00	
10 ▸	Bowl, cereal	7.00	
9 ▸	Bowl, salad	12.00	
	Bowl, sq., w/ladle	24.00	
	Candle	15.00	
	Candy compote w/lid	22.00	
	Compote	15.00	
	Compote, sm, crimped	12.00	
	Creamer, ftd.	15.00	
	Pitcher	35.00	65.00
	Plate, dessert	6.00	
2 ▸	Plate, lunch	8.00	15.00
	Plate, sq.	12.00	
4 ▸	Shaker	12.00	
5 ▸	Sherbet	6.00	12.00
1 ▸	Stem, water	8.00	12.00
7 ▸	Stem, wine	8.00	
	Sugar, ftd.	15.00	
8 ▸	Tumbler, juice	8.00	
	Tumbler, tea	12.00	
3 ▸	Tumbler, water	10.00	16.00

BALTIMORE PEAR, JEANNETTE GLASS COMPANY, 1950s – 1975

Colors: crystal, crystal with red stain, and Shell Pink

Baltimore Pear is a modern day rendition of an old pattern glass pattern made by Adams and Co. Jeannette made this in the early 1950s and some pieces were listed in their catalog as late as 1975. You will find a capital letter "R" on many of the pieces. We have been told it represents reissue, but we have never been able to ascertain that for absolute truth. It does make a good story though.

Some pieces have appeared in Internet auctions in original Jeannette boxes calling this Double Baltimore Pear, but that was a new name for us. A chip and dip set consisting of the 9" and 4¾" bowls with a metal holder is one of the items found under the "Double" nomenclature.

Luncheon plates are not seen as readily as the creamer, sugar, or butter dish. Sets consisting of the large two-handled tray holding the creamer, sugar with lid, and butter dish turn up occasionally. The lid to the butter is harder to find in mint condition than the sugar. That sugar with lid and creamer were also made in Shell Pink in the later 50s. Again, it is the lid that is often missing as illustrated by our photo. It was getting down to the wire for a photo session; so in order to show the Shell Pink, we had to settle for buying a pair sans lid.

We only found the pictured candy with red stain, so it may not be very common as red stains in that period do have a tendency to disappear if washed regularly. We see goblets occasionally, but they are generally from an older issue and were not made by Jeannette. Of course many of these later Jeannette items are erroneously listed as the older pattern glass in Internet auctions. Be sure to see our new book *American Pattern Glass Table Sets* for a look at the original butter which did not have a pointed knob.

		Crystal	Shell Pink
	Bowl, 4¼"		5.00
	Bowl, 9"		12.00
2 ▸	Butter dish w/lid		30.00
3 ▸	Candy dish w/lid		30.00
1 ▸	Comport		15.00
6 ▸	Creamer	7.00	12.50
7 ▸	Plate. 8¼", luncheon		12.50
4 ▸	Plate, 11¼", 2-hdld		12.50
5 ▸	Sugar	5.00	10.00
8 ▸	Sugar lid	7.00	15.00

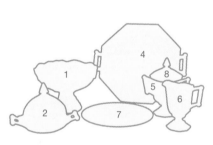

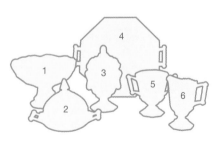

BEADED EDGE, PATTERN #22 MILK GLASS, WESTMORELAND GLASS COMPANY, late 1930s – 1950s

Westmoreland's line number for Beaded Edge was #22, but they did, in at least one catalog, refer to this pattern as Beaded Edge. The majority of glass companies utilized line numbers for patterns and not names as we are used to employing. (Earlier editions of this book have shown an assortment of catalog pages if you wish to refer to them; introduction of new patterns caused space limitations which prevented showing them in the last few books.)

Decorated fruits, flowers, and birds were predominantly made available in sets of eight designs. It took us over 10 years and thousands of miles of travel to find all eight dinner plates with fruit patterns and eight tumblers with different floral decorations. That was long before the Internet auctions existed which would have greatly speeded up the process. Bird decorated items have been harder to find than fruits or flowers. You may also find a random Christmas decoration and additional designs of roosters and chickens. Those pieces seem to disappear into collections as soon as we put them out for sale.

Fruit designs include strawberries, plums, raspberries, grapes, apples, cherries, peaches, and pears. Apples, pears, and peaches occupy most of the 15" torte plates we've encountered. Dinner plates, crimped bowls, and even sherbets can be hard to find; buy them when you get a chance. Be sure to check plates for use and scratch marks. The three-part relish, oval celery, and platter are more arduous to locate than we have previously believed. We have found a few of these undecorated; decorated ones are unusual.

Basic fruit decorated luncheon sets (salad plates, cups, saucers, and tumblers) are found without difficulty and prices are indicating that fact. Pastel-bordered plates present an interesting contrast to those with white backgrounds. We have found these with blue, green, pink, and yellow borders. An entire Beaded Edge set can also be found with red trim. The cup in that set is white with a painted red handle.

The covered creamer and sugar appears with cherries on one side and a depiction of grapes on the opposite side. That sugar and creamer is Westmoreland's Pattern #108 and not #22 Beaded Edge. Many collectors obtain these decorated pieces to enhance their sets.

The reverse side of most 15" plates shows the 12 zodiac symbols. Its opaque white color conceals that design until the plate is turned over.

BEADED EDGE

		Plain	Red Edge	Decorated
15 ▸	Creamer, ftd.	6.00	10.00	14.00
9 ▸	Creamer, ftd., w/lid #108	15.00	20.00	30.00
1 ▸	Cup	3.00	5.00	8.00
4 ▸	Nappy, 5"	3.00	5.00	10.00
11 ▸	Nappy, 6", crimped, oval	6.00	10.00	20.00
	Plate, 6", bread and butter	2.00	4.00	6.00
13 ▸	Plate, 7", salad	4.00	6.00	12.00
5 ▸	Plate, 8½", luncheon	5.00	5.00	10.00
6 ▸	Plate, 10½", dinner	10.00	15.00	30.00
8 ▸	Plate, 15", torte	15.00	20.00	40.00
	Platter, 12", oval w/tab hndls.	25.00	40.00	110.00
	Relish, 3-part	25.00	45.00	90.00
	Salt and pepper, pr.	25.00	35.00	75.00
2 ▸	Saucer	1.00	2.00	2.00
3 ▸	Sherbet, ftd.	7.00	6.00	12.00
14 ▸	Sugar, ftd.	6.00	10.00	14.00
10 ▸	Sugar, ftd., w/lid #108	12.00	18.00	28.00
7 ▸	Tumbler, 8 oz., ftd.	5.00	7.00	10.00

BEADED EDGE

BEEHIVE, LINE #350S, HAZEL-ATLAS, late 1930s – 1950s

Colors: crystal, pink, and some Platonite

First of all, we need to call attention to the 84-ounce pitcher and 15-ounce footed iced teas that are bought regularly as Beehive. Actually, they are an Anchor Hocking product and not, in reality, Hazel-Atlas Beehive. They are superb "go-with" pieces and have fooled collectors for years.

The flat nine-ounce tumbler pictured is truly Beehive. Hazel-Atlas Beehive has a single ribbon of glass between the grooved areas. Hocking's pitcher and tumblers have multiple bands between the grooves. The resemblance is so close that it's very reasonable for collectors to combine them to increase their pattern items.

To date, the only Platonite pieces we have seen include the creamer and sugar with lid. There may be other pieces to be found.

		Crystal	White	Pink
5 ▸	Bowl, 4⅞", berry, 2-hdld.	2.00		5.00
8 ▸	Bowl, 8⅝", berry, 2-hdld.	10.00		15.00
1 ▸	Bowl, 19½ oz., utility, Cat. #355	9.00		
	Butter w/cover, 6", Cat. #355½	18.00		
3 ▸	Creamer, 9½ oz., Cat. #351	4.00	3.00	
	Cup	5.00		
7 ▸	Sherbet, 3¾", flat	5.00		7.00
2 ▸	Sugar, 11½ oz.	3.00	4.00	
	Sugar lid	3.00	4.00	
4 ▸	Tray, 12¼", serving	10.00		15.00
9 ▸	Tumbler, 9 oz., flat			25.00

"BOUQUET," ETCHING #342, FOSTORIA GLASS COMPANY, 1950s

Color: crystal

Fostoria's lovely Bouquet pattern is found on the #2630 Century line and stems and tumblers are on line #6033. You may find additional pieces. Let us know if you do.

	Basket, 10¼", reed hdld.	65.00
	Bowl, 4½", 1-hdld.	11.00
	Bowl, 5", fruit	10.00
	Bowl, 6", cereal	16.00
	Bowl, 9", 2-hdld, oval, serving	28.00
	Bowl, 9", 2-hdld, serving	28.00
	Bowl, 9½", oval	28.00
	Bowl, 10½", salad	35.00
	Bowl, 10¾", ftd.	35.00
	Bowl, 11¼", lily pond	30.00
	Bowl, 11", ftd., rolled edge	30.00
	Bowl, 12", flared	30.00
	Butter w/cover, ¼ lb.	30.00
	Cake plate, 2-hdld.	22.00
	Candlestick, 4½"	15.00
9 ▸	Candlestick, 7", duo	25.00
	Candlestick, 7¾", trindle	40.00
	Candy w/cover, 7"	35.00
	Cheese comport, 2½" high	15.00
4 ▸	Comport, 4⅜"	17.00
6 ▸	Creamer, ftd.	10.00
	Creamer, individual, ftd.	10.00
2 ▸	Cup, ftd.	8.00
	Ice bucket	60.00
	Mayonnaise, plate and spoon	30.00
	Mustard, 4", w/cover and spoon	25.00
	Oil bottle, 5 oz.	30.00
	Pickle, 8¾"	15.00
	Pitcher, 6⅛", 1 pint	50.00
	Pitcher, 9½", 3 pint	110.00
	Plate, 6½", bread and butter	4.00
	Plate, 7½, crescent salad	30.00
8 ▸	Plate, 7½", salad	8.00
	Plate, 8", party w/indent	15.00
	Plate, 8½", luncheon	10.00

	Plate, 9½", dinner	22.00
	Plate, 10¾", cracker	20.00
7 ▸	Plate, 14", torte	28.00
	Platter, 12"	42.00
	Preserve w/cover	30.00
	Relish, 7⅜", 2-part	15.00
	Relish, 11⅛", 3-part	20.00
	Salver, 12¼", 2⅛" high	45.00
3 ▸	Saucer	2.00
	Shaker, pr.	20.00
	Stem, 3¾", 4 oz., oyster cocktail	12.00
11 ▸	Stem, 3⅝", 1 oz., cordial #6033	40.00
10 ▸	Stem, 4¼", 4 oz., cocktail #6033	15.00
	Stem, 4", 6 oz., low sherbet #6033	12.00
12 ▸	Stem, 4¾", 4 oz., claret-wine #6033	18.00
1 ▸	Stem, 4¾", 6 oz., saucer champagne #6033	14.00
	Stem, 5⅝", 6 oz., parfait #6033	14.00
	Stem, 6¼", 10 oz., water #6033	18.00
5 ▸	Sugar, ftd.	10.00
	Sugar, individual, ftd.	10.00
	Tidbit, 8⅛", 3-toed	15.00
	Tray, 7⅛" for ind. cr/sug	10.00
	Tray, 9½", 2-hdld., muffin	28.00
	Tray, 9⅛", 2-hdld., utility	28.00
	Tumbler, 4½", 5 oz., juice #6033	12.00
	Tumbler, 5⅞", 13 oz., tea #6033	15.00
	Vase, 5", #4121	60.00
	Vase, 6", ftd. bud, #6021	35.00
	Vase, 6", ftd., #4143	35.00
	Vase, 7½", 2-hdld	60.00
	Vase, 8¼", oval	60.00
	Vase, 8", flip, #2660	95.00
	Vase, 8", ftd. bud, #5092	75.00
	Vase, 10", ftd. #2470	110.00

"BUBBLE," "BULLSEYE," PROVINCIAL, ANCHOR HOCKING GLASS COMPANY, 1940 – 1965

Colors: pink, Sapphire blue, Forest Green, Royal Ruby, crystal, iridized, Vitrock, and any known Hocking color

"Bubble" is the name collectors have always called this pattern, but original labels found on crystal "Bubble" only say "Heat Proof." A 1942 advertisement (referring to Sapphire blue) guaranteed this Fire-King tableware to be "heat-proof," indeed a "tableware that can be used in the oven, on the table, in the refrigerator." This added feature is exclusive to Fire-King since earlier Depression glass patterns do not permit sudden changes in temperature without breaking. However, later Forest Green or Royal Ruby "Bubble" stickers do not declare these heat-proof abilities. Be forewarned.

Should you find original factory labels on "Bubble" pieces, it will be for the color and not the name "Bubble" which collectors have assigned to it. Forest Green (dark) and Royal Ruby (red) "Bubble" dinner plates have both become challenging to find in mint condition (without scratches or knife marks on the surface). There are two styles of green and crystal dinner plates. The first plate is ⅛" larger than the customarily found dinner plate. The center of this plate is smaller and there are four rows of bubbles outside the center. Notice the Forest Green ones pictured. One collector remembered the larger diameter, smaller centered crystal plates were given as a flour premium and offered as a cake plate. The typically found dinner plate has three rows of bubbles. The plates with four rows (cake?) are in shorter supply than those with three. Today's collectors do not make as much distinction between these as we did in the past.

"Bubble" is one of Anchor Hocking's most collected patterns from this era. There is still an ample supply of most pieces in all colors; and even new collectors can readily identify the simple, circular design called "Bullseye" by early Depression glass collectors. Few items are hard to find, and even those are appearing more regularly than in the past. Blue creamers have always been in shorter supply than sugars, and the 9" flanged bowl has for all intents and purposes disappeared from the collecting field, even though it has turned up in two different styles. Both styles are shown in our *Anchor Hocking's Fire-King & More* book. You will search long and hard for blue grill plates and 4" berry bowls without inner rim damage. Grill plates are divided into three sections and were mainly used in restaurants to keep the food separated and to permit smaller servings to fill the plate.

A few collectors regularly use red and green "Bubble" for Christmas settings. One devotee mentioned she also used her Royal Ruby for Valentine parties. Green and red water goblets are frequently found with advertising, suggesting they were premium items. Ruby and Forest Green "Bubble" stemware was originally called "Early American." Another stemware line sold along with "Bubble," sometimes called "Boopie," was actually named Berwick and sells for about 20 percent less in green. Both stemware lines were manufactured after production of blue "Bubble" had ceased; thus, no blue "Bubble" stems are found.

A small number of pieces of amber and iridescent "Bubble" are found. Those few iridized pieces we found a few years ago have now been absorbed into several collections. That small set included dinner plates, cups, saucers, soup, and salad bowls. Iridized items have turned out to be rare although few collectors seem to know they exist.

Pink "Bubble" is difficult to find except for the 8⅛" bowl that sells in the $10.00 to $12.00 range. That large berry bowl can be found in almost any color that Anchor Hocking made including all the opaque and iridescent colors. The recent demand for the jadite "Bubble" bowl has it selling in the $20.00+ range. Milk white bowls were listed only in the 1959 – 1960 catalog. The inside depths of these bowls vary. Price all other colors of "Bubble" as you would crystal.

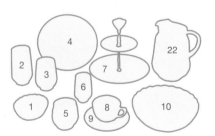

"BUBBLE"

		Crystal	Forest Green	Light Blue	Royal Ruby
17 ▸	Bowl, 4", berry	3.00		15.00	
	Bowl, 4½" with tab	4.00			
1 ▸	Bowl, 4½", fruit	3.50	9.00	12.00	7.00
12 ▸	Bowl, 5¼", cereal	6.00	14.00	14.00	
	Bowl, 6", deep	25.00			
18 ▸	Bowl, 7¾", flat soup	10.00		14.00	
16 ▸	Bowl, 8⅜", large berry (Pink – $8.00)	9.00	15.00	15.00	22.00
	Bowl, 9", flanged			495.00	
13 ▸	Candlesticks, pr.	20.00	110.00	250.00 (black)	
11 ▸	Creamer	5.00	10.00	30.00	
8 ▸	*Cup	2.50	6.00	4.00	6.00
	Lamp, 3 styles	40.00			
22 ▸	Pitcher, 64 oz., ice lip	150.00			55.00
21 ▸	Plate, 6½"			6.00	
10 ▸	Plate, 6¾", bread and butter	2.00	16.00	2.50	
20 ▸	Plate, 9⅜", grill			20.00	
4 ▸	Plate, 9⅜", dinner	5.00	18.00	5.00	18.00
15 ▸	Plate, 9½" (4 rows)	8.00	25.00		
19 ▸	Platter, 12", oval	12.00		14.00	

		Crystal	Forest Green	Light Blue	Royal Ruby
9 ▸	**Saucer	1.00	3.00	1.00	3.00
	†Stem, 3½ oz., cocktail	3.00	12.00		12.00
	†Stem, 4 oz., juice	3.50	14.00		14.00
	Stem, 4½ oz., cocktail	3.00	12.00		14.00
	Stem, 5½ oz., juice	4.00	12.00		16.00
	†Stem, 6 oz., sherbet	2.00	8.00		10.00
	Stem, 6 oz., sherbet	2.50	8.00		10.00
	†Stem, 9 oz., goblet	5.00	14.00		15.00
	Stem, 10¾ oz., goblet	5.00	13.00		14.00
	†Stem, 14 oz., iced tea	8.00	16.00		
14 ▸	Sugar	5.00	10.00	22.00	
7 ▸	Tidbit, 2-tier				75.00
6 ▸	Tumbler, 5 oz., 4", juice	3.00			7.00
5 ▸	Tumbler, 8 oz., 3¼", old fashioned	8.00			14.00
	Tumbler, 9 oz., water	4.00			8.00
3 ▸	Tumbler, 12 oz., 4½", iced tea	10.00			10.00
2 ▸	Tumbler, 16 oz., 5⅞", lemonade	12.00			16.00

*Pink – $125.00   **Pink – $40.00   †Berwick

18

BUTTERCUP, ETCHING #340, FOSTORIA GLASS COMPANY, 1941 – 1960

Color: crystal

Sets of Fostoria's Buttercup are beginning to find their way into the marketplace; but, so far, there are few collectors gathering these flowers. People, especially brides, who chose this as their crystal pattern in the 1940s, are now dispersing it due to retirement or downsizing. Often, as families reduce or sell estates, glassware is either brought into the collectible market or shared within the family and either situation may create new collectors. The flowers depicted in the pattern may be buttercups, but Buttercup was also a term of endearment made famous in Hollywood movies.

More collectors are noticing this pattern which is not as bountiful as other Fostoria patterns. Perhaps its introduction near the start of WWII may have been inopportune. Although there were many new brides, it is doubtful that crystal and entertaining were foremost in their minds.

Prices are declining somewhat as more Buttercup is being offered for sale.

Vases are difficult pieces to find in almost all Fostoria crystal patterns, and Buttercup is no exception. Stemware is more plentiful than other Buttercup items since many brides bought only stems to go with their china and did not purchase glass serving dishes. Should you like the look of older stemware, this pattern is available and reasonably priced — for now.

We usually point out the small items in this pattern, but due to our "legend" format, that is no longer necessary. That small cigarette holder is more often used as a toothpick holder, today. Smoking items have fallen somewhat out of favor with collectors, just as has smoking in today's world.

Stemware, salad plates, and luncheon plates were in matching service catalogs as late as 1960 and that is why those items are easier to find today than many of the other Buttercup serving pieces. Buttercup also had a corresponding Gorham silver pattern that could be purchased to use with this Fostoria crystal. That might be another possibility to pursue if you fancy Buttercup.

2 ▸	Ashtray, #2364, 2⅝", individual	18.00
	Bottle, #2083, salad dressing	275.00
	Bowl, #2364, 6", baked apple	16.00
	Bowl, #2364, 9", salad	35.00
12 ▸	Bowl, #2364, 10½", salad	40.00
	Bowl, #2364, 11", salad	40.00
	Bowl, #2364, 12", flared	40.00
	Bowl, #2364, 12", lily pond	38.00
	Bowl, #2364, 13", fruit	45.00
	Bowl, #2594, 10", 2 hndl.	45.00
	Candlestick, #2324, 4"	16.00
	Candlestick, #2324, 6"	20.00
7 ▸	Candlestick, #2594, 5½"	20.00
	Candlestick, #2594, 8", trindle	40.00
	Candlestick, #6023, 5½", duo	40.00
	Candy w/cover, #2364, 3¾" diameter	110.00
	Celery, #2350, 11"	18.00
	Cheese stand, #2364, 5¾" x 2⅞"	15.00
1 ▸	Cigarette holder, #2364, 2" high	30.00
3 ▸	Coaster	15.00
	Comport, #2364, 8"	30.00
	Comport, #6030, 5"	30.00
	Creamer, #2350½, 3¼", ftd.	12.00
10 ▸	Cup, #2350½, ftd.	10.00
	Mayonnaise, #2364, 5"	22.00
	Pickle, #2350, 8"	16.00
	Pitcher, #6011, 8⅞", 53 oz.	250.00
	Plate, #2337, 6"	4.00
6 ▸	Plate, #2337, 7½"	9.00

	Plate, #2337, 8½"	10.00
9 ▸	Plate, #2337, 9½"	28.00
	Plate, #2364, 6¾", mayonnaise	5.00
	Plate, #2364, 7¼" x 4½", crescent salad	30.00
	Plate, #2364, 11¼", cracker	25.00
	Plate, #2364, 11", sandwich	25.00
	Plate, #2364, 14", torte	40.00
	Plate, #2364, 16", torte	75.00
	Relish, #2364, 6½" x 5", 2-part	20.00
	Relish, #2364, 10" x 7¼", 3-part	25.00
11 ▸	Saucer, #2350	2.00
	Shaker, #2364, 2⅝"	25.00
	Stem, #6030, 3¾", 4 oz., oyster cocktail	14.00
	Stem, #6030, 3⅞", 1 oz., cordial	35.00
	Stem, #6030, 4⅜", 6 oz., low sherbet	9.00
	Stem, #6030, 5¼", 3½ oz., cocktail	10.00
8 ▸	Stem, #6030, 5⅝", 6 oz., high sherbet	10.00
	Stem, #6030, 6", 3½ oz., claret-wine	18.00
	Stem, #6030, 6⅜", 10 oz., low goblet	18.00
5 ▸	Stem, #6030, 7⅞", 10 oz., water goblet	20.00
	Sugar, #2350½, 3⅛", ftd.	12.00
	Syrup, #2586, sani-cut	275.00
	Tray, #2364, 11¼", center handled	25.00
	Tumbler, #6030, 4⅝", 5 oz., ftd. juice	12.00
4 ▸	Tumbler, #6030, 6", 12 oz., ftd. iced tea	15.00
	Vase, 6", ftd., #4143	75.00
	Vase, 6", ftd., #6021	75.00
	Vase, 7½", ftd., #4143	110.00
	Vase, 10", #2614	110.00

CABOCHON, A.H. HEISEY & COMPANY, 1950 – 1957

Colors: amber, crystal, and Dawn

A Cabochon is a gem cut in a convex curve with no facets, and therefore Cabochon was an appropriate name for this Heisey pattern. Evidently, the original creators of Cabochon expected the design to stand on its own... as a "gem" of glassware. This down-to-earth pattern lures a few Heisey collectors; but average collectors reject it as too plain.

Crystal Cabochon is found easily, but amber or Dawn colors are rarely spotted outside a major Heisey glass show. Only the base of a footed tumbler is amber, so these are often ignored by unperceptive consumers. Although rare, amber tumblers are regularly purchased reasonably due to this non-recognition factor. Dawn is easier to find than amber, but it is typically identified and rarely a bargain.

Prices overall remain tolerable for this pattern produced in the latter years before the Heisey plant closed in 1957. Inexpensive pricing causes many Heisey dealers to not stock Cabochon for shows. However, you can remedy that by shopping on the Internet.

Our listing is taken from a 1953 catalog. Many patterns made in the waning years of the factory are more difficult to find than those manufactured during the prime years of the 30s and 40s. Production runs were smaller and shorter as sales were declining; so there is not as much available to be found.

You may find a few pieces of Cabochon that are cut or etched, but Orchid and Rose etchings on Cabochon are the items most sought. We recently found a candy with the Orchid etching that sold lightning fast. It was only the second we had seen. The cordial pictured here has Heisey's Debutante cut which is a cordial collector's dream.

		Dawn	Crystal
2 ▸	Advertising sign (Cabochon), frosted, #50		190.00
16 ▸	Bonbon, 6¼", hndl. (sides sloped w/squared hndl.), #1951		24.00
11 ▸	Bottle, oil, w/#101 stopper, #1951		50.00
	Bowl, 4½", dessert, #1951		4.00
	Bowl, 5", dessert, #1951		5.00
	Bowl, 7", cereal, #1951		6.00
	Bowl, 13", floral or salad, #1951		18.00
	Bowl, 13", gardenia (low w/edge cupped irregularly), #1951		18.00
	Butter dish, ¼ lb., #1951	175.00	30.00
	Cake salver, ftd., #1951		75.00
	Candleholder, 2 lite, ground bottom, pr., #1951		110.00
15 ▸	Candlette, 1 lite (like bowl), pr., #1951		38.00
	Candy, 6¼", w/lid (bowl w/lid), #1951	300.00	38.00
7 ▸	Cheese, 5¾", ftd., compote for cracker plate		17.50
14 ▸	Creamer, #1951	40.00	13.00
	Creamer, cereal, 12 oz., #1951		50.00
13 ▸	Cup, #1951		6.00
	Jelly, 6", hndl. (sides and hndl. rounded), #1951		20.00
4, 5 ▸	Mayonnaise, 3-pc. (plate, bowl, ladle), #1951		35.00
6 ▸	Mint, 5¾", ftd. (sides slanted), #1951		20.00
	Pickle tray, 8½", #1951		15.00
3 ▸	Plate, 8", salad, #1951		6.00
	†Plate, 13", center hndl., #1951		50.00
	Plate, 14", cracker w/center ring, #1951		18.00
	Plate, 14", party (edge cupped irregularly), #1951		18.00
	Plate, 14", sandwich, #1951		18.00
1 ▸	Relish, 9", three-part, oblong, #1951		22.00
	Relish, 9", three-part, square, #1951	100.00	20.00
	Salt and pepper, square, w/#60 silver-plated tops, pr., #1951		80.00
	Saucer, #1951		1.50
	Sherbet, 6 oz., #1951 (pressed)		6.00
	Sherbet, 6 oz., #6092 (blown)		4.00

		Dawn	Crystal
17 ▶	Stemware, 1 oz., cordial, #6091		30.00
	Stemware, 3 oz., oyster cocktail, #6091		4.00
9 ▶	Stemware, 3 oz., wine, #6091		8.00
	Stemware, 4 oz., cocktail, #6091		5.00
10 ▶	Stemware, 5½ oz., sherbet, #6091		6.00
8 ▶	*Stemware, 10 oz., goblet, #6091		8.00
12 ▶	Sugar, w/cover, #1951	55.00	18.00
	Tidbit, 7½" (bowl w/sloped outsides), #1951		12.50
	Tray, 9", for cream and sugar, #1951		35.00
	Tumbler, 5 oz., #1951 (pressed)		7.00
	Tumbler, 5 oz., juice, flat bottomed, #6092 (blown)	10.00	
	Tumbler, 5 oz., juice, ftd., #6091		10.00
	Tumbler, 10 oz., beverage, #6092 (blown)		8.00
	Tumbler, 10 oz., tumbler, #6092 (blown)		8.00
	Tumbler, 12 oz., #1951 (pressed)		25.00
	**Tumbler, 12 oz., iced tea, #6092 (blown)		12.50
	Tumbler, 12 oz., iced tea, ftd., #6091		10.00
	Tumbler, 14 oz., soda, #6092 (blown)		11.00
	Vase, 3½", flared, #1951		24.00

* with Southwind cutting $12.00

** with amber foot $65.00

† Amber $50.00

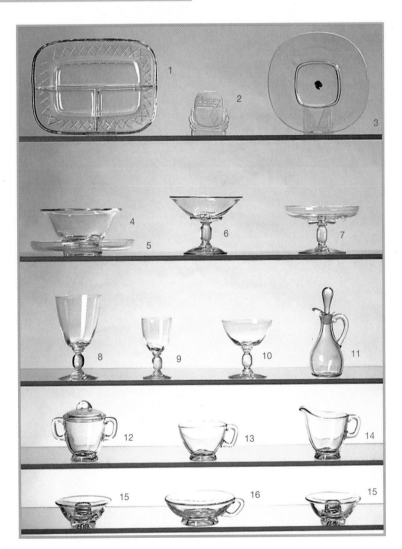

CAMELLIA, PLATE ETCHING #344, FOSTORIA GLASS COMPANY, 1952 – 1976

Color: crystal

"Camellia Rose" is the name that is more familiar to collectors, but Fostoria omitted the rose when they were naming it in the early 1950s. This pattern was Fostoria's answer to Heisey's Rose, Cambridge's Rose Point, and Tiffin's Cherokee Rose. Even though Fostoria's Camellia production outlasted all the other companies' rose patterns, it never achieved the vast acceptance of the Heisey or Cambridge patterns. Camellia is repeatedly mistaken by collectors first starting out with the more desirable Heisey Rose pattern.

Regrettably, it is routine in this business to have pieces misidentified as being more expensive wares. Years of dealing with the public have shown us that people nearly always believe that they find the most expensive piece or (desirable) pattern instead of lesser ones. Whether this is done erroneously or on purpose, the buyer of mislabeled items is ultimately upset and "put off" buying collectibles. The reason items are expensive is usually due to rarity or high demand. Lest you not know, most stemware found will not be expensive cordials or clarets — but usually the more common and cheaper sherbets or champagnes.

Many items are found misidentified at antique malls where you take for it granted that dealers are informed. Have you noticed that all antique malls have signs posted — "No Refunds or Returns?" Just because an item is bought in an antique mall does not make it an antique. We often visit shops where the only old thing in it is the proprietor. You need to know what you are buying. If you buy it, and it is not what it was supposed to be, you are still the owner whether you like it or not.

All pieces in the listing below that have no line numbers were made on Fostoria's #2630 blank, better known as Century. (See page 32.) All stems and tumblers are etched on Fostoria's #6036 line.

16 ▶	Ashtray, 6"	15.00
	Basket, 10¼" x 6½", wicker hndl.	75.00
	Bowl, 4½", hndl.	10.00
	Bowl, 5", fruit	11.00
	Bowl, 6", cereal	20.00
	Bowl, 6¼", snack, ftd.	15.00
17 ▶	Bowl, 7¼", bonbon, 3-ftd.	18.00
	Bowl, 7⅛", 3-ftd., triangular	16.00
	Bowl, 8", flared	25.00
	Bowl, 8½", salad	28.00
	Bowl, 9", lily pond	28.00
14 ▶	Bowl, 9½", hndl., serving bowl	30.00
	Bowl, 9½", oval, serving bowl	40.00
	Bowl, 10", oval, hndl.	35.00
	Bowl, 10½", salad	40.00
	Bowl, 10¾", ftd., flared	40.00
	Bowl, 11, ftd., rolled edge	45.00
	Bowl, 11¼", lily pond	40.00
	Bowl, 12", flared	45.00
	Butter, w/cover, ¼ lb.	38.00
3 ▶	Candlestick, 4½"	18.00
	Candlestick, 7", double	28.00
	Candlestick, 7¾", triple	40.00
2 ▶	Candy, w/cover, 7"	40.00
	Comport, 2¾", cheese	15.00
	Comport, 4⅜"	18.00
	Cracker plate, 10¾"	20.00
9 ▶	Creamer, 4¼"	12.00
	Creamer, individual	10.00
12 ▶	Cup, 6 oz., ftd.	12.00
	Ice bucket	60.00

	Mayonnaise, 3-pc.	30.00
	Mayonnaise, 4-pc., div. w/2 ladles	35.00
	Mustard, w/spoon, cover	25.00
	Oil, w/stopper, 5 oz.	35.00
	Pickle, 8¾"	20.00
	Pitcher, 6⅛", 16 oz.	55.00
	Pitcher, 7⅛", 48 oz.	150.00
	Plate, 6½", bread/butter	4.00
	Plate, 7½", crescent salad	35.00
	Plate, 7½", salad	7.00
	Plate, 8", party, w/indent for cup	20.00
	Plate, 8½", luncheon	11.00
8 ▶	Plate, 9½", small dinner	22.00
	Plate, 10", hndl., cake	25.00
	Plate, 10¼", dinner	35.00
	Plate, 10½", snack, small center	20.00
7 ▶	Plate, 14", torte	40.00
	Plate, 16", torte	75.00
	Platter, 12"	40.00
	Preserve, w/cover, 6"	50.00
10 ▶	Relish, 7⅜", 2-part	15.00
	Relish, 11⅛", 3-part	40.00
	Salt and pepper, 3⅛", pr.	40.00
	Salver, 12¼", ftd. (like cake stand)	55.00
13 ▶	Saucer	3.00
	Stem, #6036, 3¼", 1 oz., cordial	35.00
	Stem, #6036, 3¾", 4 oz., oyster cocktail	12.00
	Stem, #6036, 4⅛", 3½ oz., cocktail	13.00
11 ▶	Stem, #6036, 4⅛", 6 oz., low sherbet	8.00
	Stem, #6036, 4¾", 3¼ oz., claret-wine	18.00
	Stem, #6036, 4¾", 6 oz., high sherbet	10.00

	Stem, #6036, 5⅞", 5½ oz., parfait		20.00
6 ▸	Stem, #6036, 6⅞", 9½ oz., water		18.00
1 ▸	Sugar, 4", ftd.		12.00
	Sugar, individual		9.00
	Tidbit, 8⅛", 3 ftd., upturned edge		20.00
	Tidbit, 10¼", 2 tier, metal hndl.		35.00
	Tray, 4¼", for ind. salt/pepper		12.00
	Tray, 7⅛", for ind. sugar/creamer		12.00
15 ▸	Tray, 9½", hndl., muffin		25.00
	Tray, 9⅛", hndl., utility		22.00
	Tray, 11½", center hndl.		30.00
5 ▸	Tumbler, #6036, 4⅝", 5 oz., ftd. juice		14.00
4 ▸	Tumbler, #6036, 6⅛", 12 oz., ftd. iced tea		20.00
	Vase, 5", #4121		50.00
	Vase, 6", bud		25.00
	Vase, 6", ftd., #4143		65.00
	Vase, 6", ftd., #6021		50.00
	Vase, 7½", hndl.		65.00
	Vase, 8", flip, #2660		65.00
	Vase, 8", ftd., #5092		60.00
	Vase, 8½", oval		65.00
	Vase, 10", ftd., #2470		95.00
	Vase, 10½", ftd., #2657		95.00

CAMELLIA, JEANNETTE GLASS COMPANY, 1950s

Colors: crystal, crystal with gold trim, iridized, flashed red and blue

Jeannette's Camellia is a small pattern whose design is impressed into the glass itself. A newly found Camellia bowl has a ruffled top and is 11½" in diameter which an e-mail picture confirmed.

The punch set includes a 9⅛" bowl which is 4¼" deep. It is normally found surrounded by a metal rack with extended metal hooks from which hang eight cups. You may find this on a gold or black stand or without a stand. It is one of the few punch sets marketed with only eight cups. The punch bowl is also found iridized which sells for about 50% more than the crystal bowl. This bowl also turns up with gold lettering proclaiming it an eggnog set. All Camellia pieces appear to come with or without the 22K gold trim that disappears with use. Don't put these gold-trimmed pieces in the dishwasher if you want the trim to remain, especially if you have lemon in your dishwasher soap.

Most often the creamer and sugar are found with gold trim, but without the impressed flower on the bottom. However, we've finally found a creamer with the flower, but no sugar as yet. Price those with the impressed flower about 50% more than the price listed for the plain renditions.

Notice the sprayed electric blue Camellia relish tray with the original label still attached. We've also found this piece sprayed with a red color. The sprayed-on colors are easily removed — whether you wish them removed or not.

	Crystal			Crystal
9 ▸ Bowl, 5"	5.00		Cup	1.00
3 ▸ Bowl, 1-hndl., nappy	7.00	6 ▸	Plate, 8", luncheon	3.00
10 ▸ Bowl, 8⅞", vegetable	10.00	7 ▸	Plate, 12", sandwich	7.00
Bowl, 9⅜", 4¼" deep, punch	16.00	1 ▸	Powder box	25.00
Bowl, 10⅛", 3½" deep, salad	16.00	8 ▸	Relish, 6¾" x 11¾"	10.00
4 ▸ Bowl, 11", rolled edge	15.00		Saucer	.50
2 ▸ Candleholder	10.00		Sugar, ftd.	5.00
Creamer, ftd.	5.00		Sugar, ftd. (with design)	12.00
Creamer, ftd. (with design)	12.00	11 ▸	Tidbit, 2-tier	15.00
		5 ▸	Tray, two-handled	12.00

CAPRI, "SEASHELL," "SWIRL COLONIAL," "COLONIAL," "ALPINE,"
HAZEL WARE, DIVISION OF CONTINENTAL CAN, 1960s

Color: Azure blue

Capri refers to the blue color of this ware. All other colors with shapes like those of Capri are not Capri. Several different mould lines and shapes exist for this color, but any found with original labels have all stated CAPRI. This electric blue coloring was popular in the 1960s and can be seen in glassware from other companies as well. You will note some price declines in most of the basic pieces. This has come about from the massive amount of pieces being made available outpacing the number of new collectors as well as overwhelming older ones. It appears that more new collectors began accumulating Anchor Hockings' Fire-King wares than Hazel-Atlas's Capri. Lack of demand always diminishes price.

You can find a more detailed listing and pictures of Hazel-Atlas wares in our book *The Hazel-Atlas Glass Identification and Value Guide*.

We have organized various Capri designs into a form of reference for collectors. The bottom of this page shows the designs known as "Seashell" and "Tulip." The "Seashell" (swirled) pattern is the most commonly found design in Capri and "Tulip" (petal edged with circular dotted center) the most sparsely distributed. Ashtrays are the same moulds as Moroccan Amethyst. That intaglio floral ashtray seems to be unusual in both Capri and Moroccan. The coaster is Capri, but not of any particular design.

Pictured on the bottom of page 28 is octagonal dinnerware. Only Capri labels have been found on these pieces so far. Boxed sets also only say Capri when found.

On the top of page 29 is the "Dots" and "Hobnails" Capri. The patterned glasses on the right are Skol Swedish-style glasses according to a boxed set we have, but collectors have always called them "Dots." The three sizes of tumblers in this boxed set were priced 12¢, 15¢, and 18¢. Maybe the whole design is Skol, but we can only say the glasses were named that for sure. Skol is a toasting phrase meaning "to your health," and perhaps that's what this name implied. The "Hobnails" design is shown on the left side of the photo. The cup, creamer, and sugar have the hobs on the base of those respective pieces. A "Simplicity" label on crystal pieces may indicate the Hazel-Atlas designation for crystal.

Pictured on the bottom of page 29 are Colony "Square," and octagonal. The Colony name comes from actual labels on the square based items; square, hexagonal, and octagonal are descriptions coming from the shapes. Shape names seemed the only easy way to describe these. The square-based tumbler is the only item that will fit the square indentation plate. There may be a square-based cup, but we haven't heard of one.

Pentagonal flat tumblers, hexagonal stems, and octagonal dinnerware items make this a very geometric ware to collect should you so desire. Importantly, they are reasonably priced in today's market.

CAPRI

2 ▸	Ashtray, 3¼", triangular	5.00
	Ashtray, 3¼", round	5.00
4 ▸	Ashtray, 3½", square, embossed flower	15.00
	Ashtray, 3½", square w/ads	10.00
	Ashtray, 5", round	6.00
1 ▸	Ashtray, 6⅝", triangular	10.00
	Bowl, 4¾", octagonal	5.00
5 ▸	Bowl, 4¾", swirled	5.00
28 ▸	Bowl, 4⅞", round, Dots	4.00
19 ▸	Bowl, 5⅜", salad, round, Hobnails	5.00
47 ▸	Bowl, 5⅝, Colony Swirl	5.00
40 ▸	Bowl, 5¾", square, deep, Colony	6.00
11 ▸	Bowl, 6", round, Tulip	7.00
	Bowl, 6", round, Dots	5.00
38 ▸	Bowl, 6", round, sq. bottom, Colony	5.00
	Bowl, 6¹⁄₁₆", round, Colony Swirl	5.00
	Bowl, 7¾", oval, Colony	9.00
39 ▸	Bowl, 7¾", rectangular, Colony	10.00
6 ▸	Bowl, 8¾", swirled	9.00
	Bowl, 9⅛" x 3" high	15.00
	Bowl, 9½" x 2⅞" high	15.00
	Bowl, 9½" oval, 1½" high	7.00
37 ▸	Bowl, 10¾", salad, Colony	16.00
10 ▸	Bowl, 12", tulip	20.00
44 ▸	Candy jar, w/cover, ftd.	25.00
	Chip and dip, 2 swirled bowls (8¾" and 4¾" on metal rack)	20.00
3 ▸	Coaster	4.00
20 ▸	Creamer, round	12.50
	Creamer, round, Colony Swirl	12.00
14 ▸	Cup, octagonal	3.00
21 ▸	Cup, round, Hobnails or Dots	3.00
	Cup, round, Colony Swirl	3.00
8 ▸	Cup, round, Tulip	5.00
	Cup, swirled	2.00
	Plate, 5¾", bread and butter, octagonal	3.00
	Plate, 7", salad, round, Colony Swirl	4.00
	Plate, 7⅛", round, salad, Colony Swirl	4.00
17 ▸	Plate, 7¼", salad, Hobnails	4.00
12 ▸	Plate, 7¼", salad, octagonal	4.00
48 ▸	Plate, 8", square	6.00
41 ▸	Plate, 8", square, w/square cup rest	6.00
43 ▸	Plate, 8⅞", square	6.00
42 ▸	Plate, 8⅞", square, w/round cup rest	6.00
9 ▸	Plate, 9½", round, snack w/cup rest, Tulip	6.00
13 ▸	Plate, 9¾", dinner, octagonal	7.00
23 ▸	Plate, 9⅞", dinner, round, Hobnails	6.00
	Plate, 10", snack, fan shaped w/cup rest	5.00

	Saucer, 5½", square	1.00
22 ▸	Saucer, 6", round, Hobnails or Dots	1.00
15 ▸	Saucer, octagonal	1.00
	Saucer, Tulip	1.50
	Sherbet, 2¾" high, round footed, Dots	4.00
45 ▸	Stem, 4½", sherbet	6.00
46 ▸	Stem, 5½", water	7.00
18 ▸	Sugar, round	6.00
18 ▸	Sugar lid	10.00
24 ▸	Tidbit, 3-tier (round 9⅞" plate, 7⅛" plate, 5¾" bowl)	20.00
	Tumbler, 2¾", 4 oz., Colony Swirl	4.00
29 ▸	Tumbler, 3", 4 oz., fruit, Dots	3.00
33 ▸	Tumbler, 3", 5 oz., pentagonal bottom	4.00
	Tumbler, 3¹⁄₁₆", Colony or Colony Swirl	4.00
	Tumbler, 3⅛", 5 oz., pentagonal	4.00
27 ▸	Tumbler, 3¼", 8 oz., old fashioned, Dots	5.00
26 ▸	Tumbler, 3⅝", 6 oz., Dots	3.00
25 ▸	Tumbler, 3⅞", Dots	3.00
30 ▸	Tumbler, 4", Dots	3.00
	Tumbler, 4¼", 9 oz., Colony Swirl	4.00
34 ▸	Tumbler, 4¼", 9 oz., water, pentagonal bottom	4.00
	Tumbler, 5", 12 oz., Colony Swirl	5.00
35 ▸	Tumbler, 5", 12 oz., tea, pentagonal bottom	5.00
31 ▸	Tumbler, 5¼", Dots	3.00
	Tumbler, 5½", 12 oz., tea, Colony Swirl	5.00
36 ▸	Tumbler, 6", pentagonal bottom	6.00
	Tumbler, 6", 10 oz., Dots	3.00
32 ▸	Vase, 8", Dots	18.00
7 ▸	Vase, 8½", ruffled	28.00

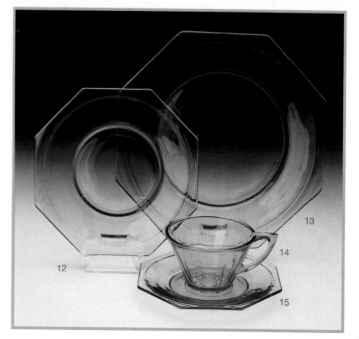

28

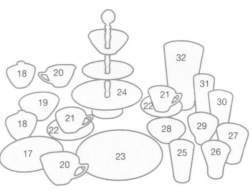

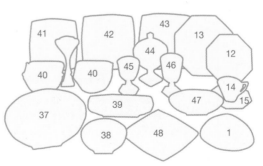

CASCADE, 4000 LINE, CAMBRIDGE GLASS COMPANY, 1950s

Colors: crystal; some Emerald Green, Mandarin Gold, and Milk White — infrequently Tahoe Blue, Crown Tuscan, and Carmen

Cascade remains an attractive Cambridge pattern with startling few collectors. Its heavy, bold design should be appealing. However, it is also heavy in the weight department which you will notice if you ever pick up a box of it. There is enough Emerald Green or Mandarin Gold available to complete a small set, or those colors could be used to add splashes of color to a crystal set.

There are two styles of stems on the water goblets — something to scrutinize if you are attracted to this pattern. One stem design is turned upside-down from the other. It actually is not so conspicuous until you place each style side by side, and then, it's perceptible. A collector wrote that he had been buying Cascade for several years and had not even noticed he had two stem styles until he read it in our book and checked his 11 stems. He had four of one and seven of the other.

A Cascade 8" ashtray had a number of functions. In addition to a lamp base and its conventional use, it also served as the punch bowl base when turned upside-down. Then, too, it held up the 21" plate to make a buffet set. That 21" plate also became the punch bowl liner in the punch set. It was a judicious use of expensive moulds at a time when Cambridge was headed toward closing for good.

Cascade items usually detected at the markets are bowls of assorted sizes. Unfortunately, Cascade tends to be found water stained here in Florida, and water stains are not as easily discerned at outdoor markets if the glass is wet from dew or an occasional frost. If you run across an ice tub, tumblers, or colored items, you may want to buy those. Some unusual pieces and colors are shown in *Treasures of Very Rare Depression Glass.*

	Crystal	Green	Yellow
Ashtray, 4½"	5.00		
Ashtray, 6"	6.00		
Ashtray, 8"	10.00		
Bowl, 4½", fruit	6.00		
2 ▸ Bowl, 6½", relish	10.00		

	Crystal	Green	Yellow
Bowl, 6½", relish, 2-pt.	10.00		
Bowl, 6", 4-ftd., bonbon	10.00		
Bowl, 7", 2 hndl., ftd., bonbon	10.00		
15 ▸ Bowl, 10", 3-pt., celery	15.00		
Bowl, 10", 4-ftd., flared	25.00		
Bowl, 10½", 4-ftd., shallow	25.00		
18 ▸ Bowl, 12", 4-ftd., oval	25.00		
Bowl, 12½", 4-ftd., flared	25.00		
Bowl, 13", 4-ftd., shallow	25.00		
Buffet set (21" plate w/8" ashtray)	60.00		

		Crystal	Green	Yellow
	Candlestick, 5"	10.00	20.00	20.00
	Candlestick, 6", 2-lite	20.00		
6 ▸	Candy box, w/cover	25.00	45.00	45.00
	Cigarette box w/cover	18.00		
	Comport, 5½"	14.00		
7 ▸	Creamer	7.00	15.00	15.00
4 ▸	Cup	5.00		
3 ▸	Ice tub, tab hndl.	28.00		
	Mayonnaise spoon	5.00		
	Mayonnaise, w/liner	14.00	50.00	50.00
12 ▸	Plate, 6½", bread & butter	4.00		
11 ▸	Plate, 8½", salad	7.00		
1 ▸	Plate, 8", 2 hndl., ftd., bonbon	11.00		
9 ▸	Plate, 11½", 4-ftd.	20.00		
	Plate, 14", 4-ftd., torte	25.00		
	Plate, 21"	50.00		
	Punch base (same as 8" ashtray)	16.00		

		Crystal	Green	Yellow
	Punch bowl liner, 21"	50.00		
	Punch bowl, 15"	110.00		
	Punch cup	5.00		
5 ▸	Saucer	1.50		
	Shaker, pr.	16.00		
13 ▸	Stem, cocktail	9.00		
17 ▸	Stem, sherbet	8.00		
16 ▸	Stem, water goblet	12.00		
8 ▸	Sugar	5.00	15.00	15.00
	Tumbler, 5 oz., flat	7.00		
14 ▸	Tumbler, 5 oz., ftd.	7.00		
10 ▸	Tumbler, 12 oz., ftd.	10.00		
	Tumbler, 12 oz., flat	10.00		
	*Vase 9½"	30.00	40.00	40.00
	Vase, 9½", oval	35.00		

*Milk White $35.00

31

CENTURY, LINE #2630, FOSTORIA GLASS COMPANY, 1950 – 1982

Color: crystal, rare in pink

Manufacture of Fostoria's Century began in 1950 and it was still being produced when Fostoria closed in the early 1980s. Century's mould line was used for many of Fostoria's crystal etchings as was Fairfax during the earlier years of color production. Heather, Bouquet, and Camellia are the most collected patterns found on this #2630 shape. Some collectors having difficulty finding those etched patterns are buying Century to fill in missing pieces for their sets.

Prices for Century pieces have stalled, but those of stemware and tumblers have nosedived. Wines, water goblets, and footed iced teas have turned up in such quantities on the Internet that most collectors have found all they need for now. Nationally, prices are fairly uniform in a downward mode. While shopping on the West Coast, we found prices there are similar to those we are seeing in Florida. Right now, there are dealers willing to sell and those wanting customers to see what they own. Collectors are comparing prices more than ever. If your items are priced too high, you can be certain someone else will get your business.

Sizes in Fostoria catalog listings for Century plates differ from the actual measurements by up to ½". Of course, that is true for most Fostoria plate measurements in catalogs since the 1920s, as they consistently used whole inches without regard to fractions. We have tried to use actual measurements for Fostoria patterns in this book. We recognize that this has been a never-ending problem for people ordering through the mail or via dealer lists on the Internet.

The ice bucket has two glass tabs for attaching a metal handle. The 8½" oval vase is shaped similar to the ice bucket, but without those tabs. Some damaged ice buckets (sans handles) with those tabs ground off by a glass repairer have changed hands as vases. Be wary of those.

		Crystal				Crystal
	Ashtray, 2¾"	8.00			Bowl, 9", lily pond	22.00
	Basket, 10¼" x 6½", wicker hndl.	50.00			Bowl, 9½", hndl., serving bowl	22.00
1 ▶	Bowl, 4½", hndl.	9.00	13 ▶	Bowl, 9½", oval, serving bowl	28.00
9 ▶	Bowl, 5", fruit	12.00	22 ▶	Bowl, 10", oval, hndl.	25.00
	Bowl, 6", cereal	18.00			Bowl, 10½", salad	22.00
	Bowl, 6¼", snack, ftd.	12.00			Bowl, 10¾", ftd., flared	28.00
	Bowl, 7⅛", 3-ftd., triangular	12.00			Bowl, 11, ftd., rolled edge	28.00
21 ▶	Bowl, 7¼", bonbon, 3-ftd.	16.00			Bowl, 11¼", lily pond	24.00
	Bowl, 8", flared	20.00			Bowl, 12", flared	25.00
	Bowl, 8½", salad	15.00			Butter, w/cover, ¼ lb.	25.00
					Candy, w/cover, 7"	30.00

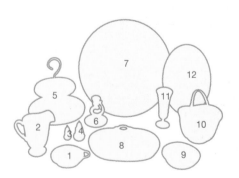

	Crystal			Crystal
6 ▶ Candlestick, 4½"	12.00		Relish, 7⅜", 2-part	14.00
Candlestick, 7", double	20.00	8 ▶	Relish, 11⅛", 3-part	15.00
Candlestick, 7¾", triple	28.00	3 ▶	Salt and pepper, 2⅜" (individual), pr.	10.00
Comport, 2¾", cheese	12.00	4 ▶	Salt and pepper, 3⅛", pr.	14.00
Comport, 4⅜"	14.00		Salver, 12¼", ftd. (like cake stand)	40.00
Cracker plate, 10¾"	30.00		Saucer	2.00
Creamer, 4¼"	5.00	20 ▶	Stem, 3½ oz., cocktail, 4⅛"	12.00
Creamer, individual	5.00		Stem, 3½ oz., wine, 4½"	15.00
25 ▶ Cup, 6 oz., ftd.	6.00		Stem, 4½ oz., oyster cocktail, 3¾"	10.00
10 ▶ Ice bucket	50.00		Stem, 5½" oz., sherbet, 4½"	6.00
Mayonnaise, 3-pc.	22.00	16 ▶	Stem, 10 oz., goblet, 5¾"	10.00
Mayonnaise, 4-pc., div. w/2 ladles	25.00		Sugar, 4", ftd.	5.00
Mustard, w/spoon, cover	20.00	15 ▶	Sugar, individual	5.00
26 ▶ Oil, w/stopper, 5 oz.	22.00	23 ▶	Tidbit, 8⅛", 3-ftd., upturned edge	12.00
Pickle, 8¾"	12.00	5 ▶	Tidbit, 10¼", 2 tier, metal hndl.	22.00
2 ▶ Pitcher, 6⅛", 16 oz.	40.00		Tray, 4¼", for ind. salt/pepper	10.00
28 ▶ Pitcher, 7⅛", 48 oz.	75.00	14 ▶	Tray, 7⅛", for ind. sugar/creamer	8.00
Plate, 6½", bread/butter	5.00		Tray, 9⅛", hndl., utility	22.00
18 ▶ Plate, 7½", salad	5.00		Tray, 9½", hndl., muffin	20.00
Plate, 7½", crescent salad	20.00		Tray, 11½", center hndl.	25.00
24 ▶ Plate, 8", party, w/indent for cup	10.00		Tumbler, 5 oz., ftd., juice, 4¾"	12.00
19 ▶ Plate, 8½", luncheon	10.00	17 ▶	Tumbler, 12 oz., ftd., tea, 5⅞"	16.00
27 ▶ Plate, 9½", small dinner	15.00	11 ▶	Vase, 6", bud	14.00
Plate, 10", hndl., cake	16.00		Vase, 7½", hndl.	40.00
Plate, 10½", dinner	25.00		Vase, 8½", oval	40.00
7 ▶ Plate, 14", torte	25.00			
12 ▶ Platter, 12"	30.00			
Preserve, w/cover, 6"	25.00			

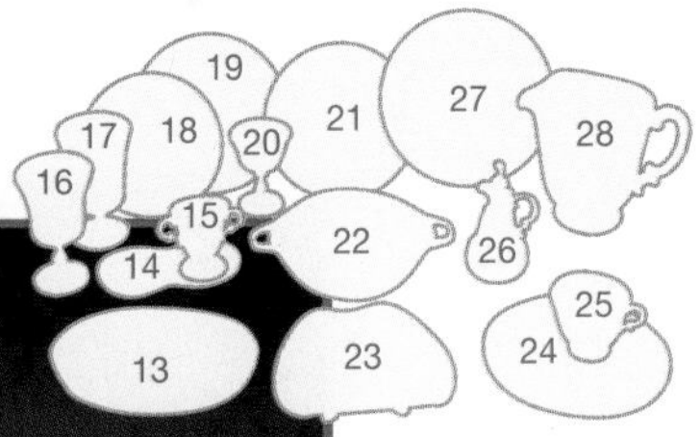

CHINTZ, PLATE ETCHING #338, FOSTORIA GLASS COMPANY, 1940 – 1977

Color: crystal

Fostoria's Chintz pattern is actually an Elegant glassware pattern, but it was transferred to this 50s book because it was made entirely during the time frame of this book. Chintz, as well as Fostoria's Century pattern, were both relocated from *Elegant Glassware of the Depression Era* where they were first listed before this book was envisioned.

Chintz stemware is abundant, a common happening for most Elegant patterns from this time as it was bought to accompany china patterns. People in the 1950s purchased stemware and did without serving pieces — as did their 1930s counterparts. As a matter of fact, glass company advertisements show they went to great pains to "sell" the use of glassware as complete table settings. Almost all serving pieces are harder to acquire now than stems since stemware was bought to use with "good" china sets; glass serving pieces were superfluous and didn't sell well. We might mention that the original water goblets are being bought for wine today. People seem to like their wine in eight or nine ounce goblets rather than the traditional three or four ounce wine goblets of the period. Dealers are having to adjust to prices of water goblets increasing due to demand while the prices for wines and clarets are decreasing for the same reason. Even though wines and clarets are much harder to find, there is a surplus becoming available since so many customers are not interested in owning them.

Pieces of Chintz that are in short supply include the syrup pitcher (Sani-cut metal top) and the footed 9¼" bowl. Further, the cream soup, finger bowl, oval vegetable, and all vases are missing in many collections, although a few more 9½" oval bowls are being stumbled upon than in the past. Fostoria called the 8" oval bowl a sauce dish. These came divided or not. Many collectors refer to them as gravy boats. The oval sauce dish liner came with both, but a pamphlet listed it as a tray instead of liner. Trays are not found as often as the sauce dishes. These used to fall into the "hard to find" category, but, since the Internet, not anymore.

Chintz has only one size dinner plate, which is different from other Fostoria patterns. There was no service plate (usually an inch larger which was considered a dinner plate by most users). You have to accept a 9½" plate although catalogs list it at 9". Scratched and worn plates are a problem and sadly, the rule rather than the exception. Prices listed are for mint condition plates.

That 11" celery on the #2496 (Baroque) mould blank does exist according to several collectors who have written to correct our omitting it in earlier editions. It is not unusual for dyed-in-the-wool collectors who concentrate on only one or two patterns to know specifics about those patterns more thoroughly than we do. Bear in mind that our books cover hundreds of patterns, and it's difficult to keep up with all peculiarities of each pattern; but we try. We freely acknowedge learning from collectors.

(For novice collectors, a fleur-de-lis in relief is the design on the Baroque #2496 blank.)

34

1 ▸	Bell, dinner	100.00
	Bowl, #869, 4½", finger	50.00
	Bowl, #2496, 4⅝", tri-cornered	16.00
6 ▸	Bowl, #2496, cream soup	65.00
	Bowl, #2496, 5", fruit	22.00
	Bowl, #2496, 5", hndl.	20.00
	Bowl, #2496, 7⅝", bonbon	22.00
	Bowl, #2496, 8½", hndl.	50.00
	Bowl, #2496, 9¼", ftd.	195.00
8 ▸	Bowl, #2496, 9½", oval vegetable	95.00
	Bowl, #2496, 9½", vegetable	60.00
	Bowl, #2484, 10", hndl.	55.00
	Bowl, #2496, 10½", hndl.	55.00
	Bowl, #2496, 11½", flared	55.00
	Bowl, #6023, ftd.	40.00
	Candlestick, #2496, 4"	15.00
	Candlestick, #2496, 4½", double	25.00
	Candlestick, #2496, 5½"	25.00
	Candlestick, #2496, 6", triple	40.00
	Candlestick, #6023, double	40.00
4 ▸	Candy, w/cover, #2496, 3-part	110.00
	Comport, #2496, 3¼", cheese	22.00
	Comport, #2496, 4¾"	25.00
	Comport, #2496, 5½"	30.00
	Creamer, #2496, 3¾", ftd.	13.00
	Creamer, #2496½, individual	15.00
	Cup, #2496, ftd.	20.00
	Ice bucket, #2496	80.00
9 ▸	Jelly, w/cover, #2496, 7½"	60.00
	Mayonnaise, #2496½, 3-piece	42.00
7 ▸	Oil, w/stopper, #2496, 3½ oz.	85.00
	Pickle, #2496, 8"	25.00
	Pitcher, #5000, 48 oz., ftd.	295.00
	Plate, #2496, 6", bread/butter	6.00
	Plate, #2496, 7½", salad	9.00
	Plate, #2496, 8½", luncheon	12.00

5 ▸	Plate, #2496, 9½", dinner	30.00
	Plate, #2496, 10½", hndl., cake	38.00
	Plate, #2496, 11", cracker	30.00
	Plate, #2496, 14", upturned edge	45.00
	Plate, #2496, 16", torte, plain edge	100.00
	Plate, 17½", upturned edge	110.00
	Platter, #2496, 12"	60.00
	Relish, #2496, 6", 2 part, square	22.00
	Relish, #2496, 10" x 7½", 3 part	25.00
	Relish, #2419, 5 part	30.00
	Salad dressing bottle, #2083, 6½"	350.00
	Salt and pepper, #2496, 2¾", flat, pr.	75.00
2 ▸	Sauce boat, #2496, oval	30.00
	Sauce boat, #2496, oval, divided	30.00
	Sauce boat liner, #2496, oblong, 8"	15.00
	Saucer, #2496	3.00
	Stem, #6026, 1 oz., cordial, 3⅞"	40.00
	Stem, #6026, 4 oz., cocktail, 5"	13.00
10 ▸	Stem, #6026, 4 oz., oyster cocktail, 3⅜"	15.00
	Stem, #6026, 4½ oz., claret-wine, 5⅜"	28.00
	Stem, #6026, 6 oz., low sherbet, 4⅜"	10.00
	Stem, #6026, 6 oz., saucer champagne, 5½"	12.00
3 ▸	Stem, #6026, 9 oz., water goblet, 7⅝"	15.00
	Sugar, #2496, 3½", ftd.	13.00
	Sugar, #2496½, individual	15.00
	Syrup, #2586, Sani-cut	395.00
	Tidbit, #2496, 8¼", 3 ftd., upturned edge	20.00
	Tray, #2496½, 6½", for ind. sugar/creamer	18.00
	Tray, #2375, 11", center hndl.	25.00
	Tumbler, #6026, 5 oz., juice, ftd.	16.00
	Tumbler, #6026, 9 oz., water or low goblet	15.00
	Tumbler, #6026, 13 oz., tea, ftd.	18.00
	Vase, #4108, 5"	90.00
	Vase, #4128, 5"	90.00
	Vase, #4143, 6", ftd.	125.00
	Vase, #4143, 7½", ftd.	175.00

Left to right: water goblet, water tumbler, claret-wine, cocktail, low sherbet, cordial, tea, juice, oyster cocktail.

"CHRISTMAS CANDY," NO. 624, INDIANA GLASS COMPANY, 1937 – early 1950s

Colors: Terrace Green (teal) and crystal

Indiana's #624 line has been called "Christmas Candy" by collectors. Indiana called the popular teal color Terrace Green. The rarely seen Terrace Green 9½" round vegetable bowl price has continued an upward trend, while other prices have declined somewhat. That bowl has not been found in crystal and only one teal one has reared it head in all these years. Patterns that have made fast price hikes or are already highly priced are often avoided by new collectors. That leaves a shortage of collectors buying common items (cups, saucers, plates, creamers, and sugars). The collectors who have those pieces are still searching for and buying the harder to find items which cause them to continue escalating in price unless supply overtakes demand. Crystal "Christmas Candy" collectors are in short supply even though the prices are fairly inexpensive compared to most patterns. That bowl on top of the crystal tidbit measures 5¼". That bowl without a drilled hole is taxing to find and has never been found in Terrace Green.

Teal supplies were exhausted before everyone completed their collections. That short resource is what drove the price up in the first place. Of course, pricing is relative. Years from now, we may think these were very reasonable prices for uncommon items.

Normally, teal "Christmas Candy" is found in large groupings rather than a piece here and there. Glassware made in the 1950s, or later, is often found as sets — having been stored unused in someone's attic, garage, or basement. Sets may even be discovered in unopened boxes. It used to be in bad taste to return gifts, even duplicate ones, unlike today. The Internet has opened up many previously unknown supplies of glassware, but teal "Christmas Candy" is not one of them.

A few years ago we received a copy of a letter from a lady who had written Indiana Glass Company about this pattern. They told her it was made in the late 1930s and the 1950s, which partially confirmed information found on a boxed set, i.e. "15 pc. Luncheon set (Terrace Green) To F W Newburger & Co. New Albany Ind Dept M 1346; From Pitman Dretzer Dunkirk Ind 4-3-52." We never quite believed in the 1930s production as this color never appeared in any pattern known to have been made at Indiana in the 1930s. However, this box gave invaluable documentation because this color had only been attributed to those earlier production dates in previously published material.

We used to see groupings in Florida when we first moved here in 1990, but that hasn't been true lately. One of the problems with teal in Florida comes from well water (and dishwasher) usage which fogs or clouds the glass. No, there is no miracle cure for this cloudiness. We're told the cloudiness is in the glass, not just on the surface; and only polishing it out will remove it. This is an expensive process, but it can be done.

One good thing about buying glassware in Florida, besides shopping outside in winter, is that "snow birds" (northerners in the local vernacular) yearly bring glass to sell from all over the country. You never know what will show up. Retirees also bring glassware south with them, and as they downsize or leave this world, much of that glass becomes available to collectors. Today, glassware from the 1950s and 1960s is more the norm than older wares from the Depression era.

		Crystal	Teal
	Bowl, 5¾"	3.00	
2 ▸	Bowl, 7⅜", soup	5.00	45.00
9 ▸	Bowl, 9½", vegetable		650.00
1 ▸	Creamer	5.00	22.00
7 ▸	Cup	2.00	18.00
	Mayonnaise, w/ladle, liner	14.00	
6 ▸	Plate, 6", bread and butter	2.00	6.00

		Crystal	Teal
3 ▸	Plate, 8¼", luncheon	3.00	20.00
	Plate, 9⅝", dinner	6.00	38.00
5 ▸	Plate, 11¼", sandwich	10.00	45.00
8 ▸	Saucer	1.00	5.00
4 ▸	Sugar	5.00	22.00
10 ▸	Tidbit, 2-tier	15.00	

CHROMA, No. 123, IMPERIAL GLASS COMPANY, c. 1957

Colors: crystal, Burgundy, Evergreen, Indigo, and Madeira; some canary, custard, slag, and iridized

Imperial first made Chroma in 1938, but then it was called Coronet; by 1942, its name was promoted as Victorian. Both of these were made in crystal and ruby and production was terminated by the end of WWII. The first goblets had one rough and one smooth ball on the stem; this was later made into just the rough patterned stem. The eight ounce water goblet and six ounce sherbet have two such balls; the 12 ounce footed tea goblet has only one. The water and juice tumblers are flat.

We have been able to acquire some new colors and pieces to show. Unfortunately, we keep running into groupings that are priced as a lot instead of pieces priced individually and we do not need large groupings. As dealers, it seems to us there are a lot more customers looking for a piece or two rather than groupings of six to 20 diverse pieces. Basically, only dealers buy assorted lots and they don't pay retail. We have watched a small grouping of nearly 20 pieces in an Ohio antique mall for several years. The artificial lights have faded the price sticker so much it is now unreadable, yet the owner obviously can't figure out why it is not selling.

		*All Colors
4 ▸	Cake stand	50.00
	Compote, open	15.00
	Compote w/lid (Banquet)	50.00
2 ▸	Goblet, 8 oz., water	15.00
6 ▸	Goblet, 12 oz., tea	15.00
5 ▸	Plate, 8"	8.00
1 ▸	Sherbet, 6 oz.	8.00
8 ▸	Tumbler, 5½ oz., juice	12.00
3 ▸	Tumbler, 8 oz., water	13.00
7 ▸	Tumbler, 12 oz., tea	18.00

*deduct 25% for crystal

"CHROMA" Burgundy 53/123

8 oz. Goblet   6 oz. Sherbet   5½ oz. Juice   12 oz. Tumbler   12 oz. Footed Ice Tea

CLOVER BLOSSOM, DECORATION NO. 105, FEDERAL GLASS COMPANY, c. 1960

Colors: milk glass white/pink and gray decoration

There has been little attention devoted to Federal's heat-proof wares from the 1950s – 1970s, so check out our new *Florences' Ovenware from the 1920s to the Present* which covers some of Federal's heat-proof patterns. These were in direct competition with Anchor Hocking's Fire-King and obviously Federal lost this contest.

Clover Blossom is one of those patterns where we show some original catalog documentation in our Ovenware book. In the catalog, Clover Blossom was promoted as "heat-proof and durable," "practically chip-proof" with "detergent resistant decoration." Regarding that last claim, there seems to be a substantial amount of this pattern showing up not having full-color decoration. Those claims do not appear to have been as true as Federal would have had you believe. The catalogs also publicized a "full size, 10" dinner plate." The set was packaged four ways: a five-piece place setting, a 16-piece starter set, a 35-piece dinnerware set, and a 53-piece dinnerware set. This was a contemporary of Golden Glory and the ever-present Rosecrest Snack set often encountered at markets. These sets are 40 years old and now is the time to pick them up as that generation begins to downsize.

If you have additional information, please let us know. Write to our mailing address in the front of the book or e-mail us through our web page, www.geneflorence.com.

8 ▸	Bowl, 4⅞", dessert	2.50
4 ▸	Bowl, 8", rim soup	7.00
	Bowl, 8½"	10.00
1 ▸	Creamer	3.00
6 ▸	Cup	2.00
	Plate, 7⅝", coupe	4.00
5 ▸	Plate, 10", coupe	5.00
3 ▸	Plate, 11¼", coupe chop	7.00
7 ▸	Saucer	.50
2 ▸	Sugar w/cover	7.00

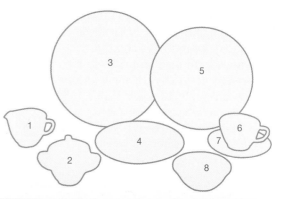

COIN GLASS, LINE #1372, FOSTORIA GLASS COMPANY, 1958 – 1982

Colors: amber, blue, crystal, green, Olive, and red

Fostoria's Coin pattern has had some significant price alterations, mostly lower, in the last few years. Rare pieces and most non-reproduced items are selling, albeit slowly. Blue and red colors are still sought, but the reproductions that Lancaster Colony (who now owns these Fostoria moulds) produced have resulted in a conspicuous decline in sales for other items. It was considered by some to be a continuance of the pattern since the original moulds are being used, but Lancaster Colony's blue and green pieces were a different color hue.

Long-time collectors who treasure Fostoria's Coin continue to search for rarely seen items, bargains, and mistakes in pricing by uninformed sellers. Lack of collectors starting the pattern holds down sales of commonly found items. We originally included Coin in this book because it was becoming a very desirable collectible — so desirable, in fact, that it became profitable enough to remake. We do not mean merely moulding a few pieces, but that Lancaster Colony produced a whole line in many of the original colors. These colors deviate slightly from the original cherished Coin in amber, blue, and green; but there is virtually no way for new collectors to distinguish the red or crystal made a few years ago from that made in the late 1950s and 1960s; so, many won't even consider buying it. Much of this later made ware was sold at outlet stores without frosted coins, but not all. We formerly told collectors to accept only frosted coins as a way to distinguish older Coin; but, today, anyone can buy an acid for satinizing glassware at a crafters' store. Thus, frosted coins cannot always be believed a true indication of older Coin glassware.

The small jelly, often referred to as a small comport, was made in crystal for Avon; an astonishing number of those are offered through Internet auctions. Not everyone seems to be informed of that, so once in a while, one of these sells for a highly inflated price. We had a local dealer approach us about buying a couple of these which he had been unable to sell. He was surprised to learn why he was not receiving any bids on his auctions.

Coins as glassware designs began on early American pattern glass around the late 1880s. Actually, Congress made it unlawful to reproduce actual coin images at some point and glass companies had to revamp their moulds for this popular type ware.

There is an asterisk (*) in the listing by all pieces that were manufactured in last 15 years. Obviously, this has caused chaos in pricing. Large quantities of all sizes of crystal tumblers have reached the market which created price declines on those.

The good news is that prices for the later made items were so expensive initially that dealers were able to boost the prices on older pieces. Who can blame them? Why sell an older piece for $50.00 when the newer item sells for $40.00?

Olive green is sometimes referred to as avocado, but Olive was the official name. Collectors often call the brighter, most desired green "emerald," although it was issued as green.

39

COIN GLASS

		Amber	Blue	Crystal	Green	Olive	Ruby
17 ▸	Ashtray, 5", #1372/123	15.00	25.00	15.00	30.00	15.00	22.50
16 ▸	Ashtray, 7½", center coin, #1372/119	18.00		20.00	35.00		25.00
	Ashtray, 7½", round, #1372/114	20.00	40.00	20.00	45.00	25.00	20.00
	Ashtray, 10", #1372/124	25.00	50.00	22.00	65.00	25.00	
	Ashtray, oblong, #1372/115	15.00	20.00	10.00	25.00	25.00	
	Ashtray/cover, 3", #1372/110	20.00	25.00	25.00	30.00		
1 ▸	Bowl, 4"	10.00		10.00			
	Bowl, 8", round, #1372/179	30.00	50.00	25.00	70.00	25.00	45.00
	Bowl, 8½", ftd., #1372/199	60.00	90.00	50.00	125.00	55.00	75.00
	Bowl, 8½", ftd. w/cover, #1372/212	100.00	175.00	85.00	225.00		
8 ▸	**Bowl, 9", oval, #1372/189	30.00	48.00	30.00	70.00	33.00	35.00
	*Bowl, wedding w/cover, #1372/162	70.00	90.00	55.00	150.00	55.00	87.50
	Candleholder, 4½", pr., #1372/316	30.00	55.00	40.00	50.00	30.00	50.00
15 ▸	Candleholder, 8", pr., #1372/326	50.00		50.00		50.00	100.00
4 ▸	Candy box w/cover, 4⅛", #1372/354	30.00	60.00	30.00	100.00	33.00	60.00
	*Candy jar w/cover, 6⁵⁄₁₆", #1372/347	30.00	50.00	28.00	150.00	20.00	50.00
	*Cigarette box w/cover, 5¾" x 4½", #1372/374	50.00	80.00	40.00	115.00		
	Cigarette holder w/ashtray cover, #1372/372	50.00	75.00	45.00	90.00		
	Cigarette urn, 3⅜", ftd., #1372/381	25.00	45.00	20.00	50.00	22.00	40.00
	Condiment set, 4 pc. (tray, 2 shakers and cruet), #1372/737	225.00	335.00	135.00	250.00		
	Condiment tray, 9⅝", #1372/738	60.00	75.00	40.00		75.00	
6 ▸	*Creamer, #1372/680	11.00	16.00	10.00	35.00	15.00	20.00
	Cruet, 7 oz., w/stopper, #1372/531	65.00	125.00	55.00	210.00	80.00	
	*Decanter w/stopper, pint, 10³⁄₁₆", #1372/400	110.00	265.00	95.00	325.00	165.00	
	*Jelly, #1372/448	17.50	25.00	15.00	35.00	15.00	25.00
	Lamp chimney, coach or patio, #1372/461	50.00	60.00	40.00			

**Blue is late production, note color.

Experimental item.

		Amber	Blue	Crystal	Green	Olive	Ruby
	Lamp chimney, hndl., courting, #1372/292	45.00	65.00				
	Lamp, 9¾", hndl., courting, oil, #1372/310	60.00	190.00				
	Lamp, 10⅛", hndl., courting, electric, #1372/311	65.00	210.00				
	Lamp, 13½", coach, electric, #1372/321	90.00	250.00	100.00			
10 ▸	Lamp, 13½", coach, oil, #1372/320	90.00	250.00	100.00			
	Lamp, 16⅝", patio, electric, #1372/466	100.00	295.00	145.00			
	Lamp, 16⅝", patio, oil, #1372/459	100.00	295.00	145.00			
	Nappy, 4½", #1372/495			22.00			
18 ▸	*Nappy, 5⅜", w/hndl., #1372/499	20.00	28.00	15.00	38.00	18.00	25.00
7 ▸	Pitcher, 32 oz., 6³⁄₁₆", #1372/453	38.00	145.00	48.00	195.00	45.00	120.00
	Plate, 8", #1372/550			20.00		20.00	40.00
	Punch bowl base, #1372/602			140.00			
	Punch bowl, 14", 1½ gal., #1372/600			110.00			
	Punch cup, #1372/615			20.00			
	*Salver, ftd., 6½" tall, #1372/630	110.00	225.00	75.00	295.00	125.00	
5 ▸	Shaker, 3¼", pr. w/chrome top, #1372/652	30.00	65.00	18.00	90.00	22.00	45.00
11 ▸	Stem, 4", 5 oz., wine, #1372/26			22.00		35.00	75.00
	Stem, 5¼", 9 oz., sherbet, #1372/7			14.00		20.00	50.00
12 ▸	Stem, 10½ oz., goblet, #1372/2			22.00		35.00	75.00
9 ▸	*Sugar w/cover, #1372/673	35.00	40.00	25.00	65.00	20.00	32.00
2 ▸	Tumbler, 3⅝", 9 oz., juice/old fashioned, #1372/81			15.00			
	Tumbler, 4¼", 9 oz., water, scotch & soda, #1372/73			15.00			
	Tumbler, 5⅛", 12 oz., iced tea/highball, #1372/64			18.00			
	Tumbler, 5⅜", 10 oz., double old fashioned, #1372/23			15.00			
3 ▸	Tumbler, 5³⁄₁₆", 14 oz., iced tea, #1372/58			18.00		40.00	75.00
14 ▸	*Urn, 12¾", ftd., w/cover, #1372/829	80.00	140.00	60.00	200.00	40.00	100.00
13 ▸	Vase, 8", bud, #1372/799	16.00	30.00	20.00	60.00	16.00	45.00
	Vase, 10", ftd., #1372/818			45.00			

"COLONIAL COUPLE," HAZEL-ATLAS GLASS, c. 1940

Color: Platonite w/trims

"Colonial Couple" has brought quantities of questions through our e-mail. Please notice that our books predominantly deal with glass and not china or pottery. We do not know or admit to knowing anything about the many "Colonial Couple" designs on any china, pottery, or porcelain. We have received several hundred questions on pottery and china; so please, be cautioned; we cannot answer questions on items other than glass and that means furniture and other collectibles also.

We have had several inquires wanting to know where to buy "Colonial Couple." Truthfully, we don't know. We had a chance to buy a larger set, but chose only to buy one of each piece for photography. It gets rather expensive buying a whole set for photography when you only need one representative piece. In hindsight, we could have sold the extra items many times over had we bought them all.

We are still looking for a cup for our saucer. Notice that several Hazel-Atlas mould lines were used including those of Ovide and Moderntone. "Colonial Couple" also crosses over into the Kitchenware collectible field with shakers, mixing bowls, and stacking refrigerator sets. In that respect, it was competing with Anchor Hocking which used the same patterns for dinnerware and kitchenware. The refrigerator bowl with lid was part of a four-piece stacking set that could be used individually if needed. Lids are therefore at a premium today as there were at least three dishes made for each lid. The milk pitcher can be found with a beater.

Most likely other pieces can be found in this charming ware made by Hazel-Atlas Glass Company around 1940. It is possible that almost any Platonite piece could be found with "Colonial Couple." We are only listing pieces verified, however. If you should find additional pieces with this decoration, we'd appreciate hearing about what you've discovered.

Though Hazel-Atlas had first come out with a line of Platonite in the early 1930s, much of their early ware had translucent edges and was presented as white ware. Toward the late 1930s and early 1940s, when color trims were taking the glass world by storm (see Rainbow pattern by Anchor Hocking), they started affixing various designs to their white Platonite which by now had wonderful, full white coloring and was a perfect background on which to display images of nursery rhymes, Dutch children, windmills, Hopalong Cassidy, Tom and Jerry, red birds, forget-me-nots, black and red stripes — or a "Colonial Couple" as we see here. You may check out these numerous designs in our *Hazel-Atlas Glass Identification and Value Guide*.

7 ▶	Bowl w/lid, round, refrigerator	32.00
1 ▶	Bowl, 5"	15.00
	Cup	12.00
5 ▶	Egg cup	20.00
4 ▶	Pitcher, 16 oz., milk	40.00
2 ▶	Plate, dessert	10.00
	Saucer	4.00
3 ▶	Shaker, kitchen, pr.	70.00
6 ▶	Tumbler, 8 oz., flat	15.00

CONSTELLATION, PATTERN #300, INDIANA GLASS COMPANY, c. 1940;
YELLOW MIST AND SUNSET CONSTELLATION, TIARA HOME PRODUCTS, 1980s

Colors: crystal; amber; amberina, yellow mist, red, and green

We are seeing more and more Constellation available for sale as we travel the country. However, most of what we are spying is colored wares made by Indiana for Tiara Home Products.

Constellation cake stands appear readily available for all those collectors participating in the latest craze of decorating with cake stands. Luckily, we have recently only seen a couple priced over $100.00 calling them 1900s production. Before we included Constellation in this book, we saw these cake stands regularly highly priced in markets in Georgia and Texas.

Indiana made a few flat pieces with intaglio fruit centers and these appear less frequently than the plain ones. They should be priced at 10% to 20% more, but there seems to be few searching for them. Note the intaglio platter and salad plate pictured in the photo below.

In a quirk of fate that everyone thinks "only happens to them," we started gathering Constellation to put in this book about 10 years ago. We found it a piece or two at a time, and it typically was not priced economically. After garnering enough for a book photo, Constellation pieces magically were being displayed for sale at every market we shopped — and in glittering colored stock. Yes, Indiana had decided to revive this line for their Tiara Home Products division. We decided to incorporate it anyway, since Tiara has finally stopped production. All colored pieces priced below are most likely Tiara products.

		Crystal	Colors
	Basket, 11", lg. centerpiece	25.00	
	Basket, sm. centerpiece	18.00	22.00
	Bowl, 6", nut, cupped	8.00	
6 ▸	Bowl, 7½", deep	14.00	
13 ▸	Bowl, jumbo salad	20.00	
	Bowl, 11", 2-hndl., oval	15.00	
	Bowl, 11½", flat rim, ftd. console, belled	20.00	18.00
12 ▸	Bowl, nappy, 3-toe	10.00	
	Bowl, punch, flat	35.00	
16 ▸	Cake stand, round	30.00	
9 ▸	Cake, sq. pedestal. ft.	30.00	
	Candle, triangle, pr.	16.00	20.00
	Candy w/lid, 5½", 3-toe	18.00	15.00
1 ▸	Celery, oval, compote, low centerpiece	18.00	
	Cookie jar & lid, 9"	25.00	25.00
3 ▸	Creamer	8.00	

		Crystal	Colors
2 ▸	Mayonnaise bowl, flat, w/ladle	20.00	
11 ▸	Mug	10.00	
	Pickle, oval, 2-hndl.	12.00	
5 ▸	Pitcher, 7½", ½ gal.	30.00	40.00
14 ▸	Plate, dessert	3.00	
15 ▸	Plate, lunch	5.00	
	Plate, mayonnaise liner	3.00	
7 ▸	Plate, salad	6.00	
	Plate, 13½", serving/cake	15.00	20.00
	Plate, 18", buffet	25.00	
8 ▸	Platter, oval	18.00	
	Relish, 6", 3 pt.	12.00	
	Stem, 6¼", 8 oz., water	9.00	10.00
4 ▸	Sugar	8.00	
	Tumbler, flat, 8 oz.	8.00	
10 ▸	Vase, 3 ftd.	12.00	

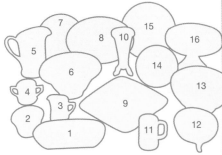

CORSAGE, PLATE ETCHING #325, FOSTORIA GLASS COMPANY, 1935 – 1960

Color: crystal

Fostoria's Corsage pattern is another pattern where quantities are beginning to appear on the market due to the age of the original buyers. Unfortunately, there are more pieces becoming available than there are collectors seeking it and prices have declined to some extent. As with other Elegant patterns, stems and tumblers abound; if you find them attractive it would be a wonderful time to remove your share from all those being offered for sale.

The cone-shaped floral corsage motif resonates of floral designs from the 1920s. One collector remarked that he memorized this pattern by the "ice cream cone" design holding the flowers. Many confuse Corsage with Fostoria's Mayflower which has a cornucopia of flowers in its design. At present, there is still enough Corsage available to collect a substantial set.

Corsage is one Fostoria dinnerware line etched on several mould blanks. Few patterns allow such a diversity of shapes; and variety is supposedly the spice of life. One collector told us she chose the pattern because of the variety of styles. There are three lines portrayed in the picture. The regular size creamer and sugar are Line #2440, or Lafayette blank with its fancy curlicue handles. The ice bucket, three-part relish, and individual creamer, sugar, and tray are found on Line #2496 which is known as Baroque. It has several embossed fleurs-de-lis on each piece. We can't think of any other Fostoria pattern that has different lines for separate sizes of sugar and creamers. Oddly enough, the basic plates are from the #2337 line that has plain, round plates like those found in Buttercup. Stems and tumblers are Fostoria's #6014 line.

All these different lines were intriguing as we researched listings for the book. Was Fostoria etching surplus inventory, a practice at factories which often resulted in highly collectible, short supplied pieces?

12 ▸	Bowl, #869, finger	25.00
	Bowl, 4", #4119, ftd.	18.00
	Bowl, 4⅝", 3-corner, #2496	15.00
	Bowl, 7⅜", 3-ftd., bonbon, #2496	18.00
6 ▸	Bowl, 9", hndl., #2536	50.00
	Bowl, 9½", ftd., #2537	125.00
	Bowl, 10", hndl., #2484	45.00
	Bowl, 12", flared, #2496	45.00
	Bowl, 12½", oval, #2545, Flame	50.00
	Candelabra, 2 light w/prisms, #2527	100.00
	Candlestick, 5½", #2496	20.00
18 ▸	Candlestick, 5½", #2535	28.00
22 ▸	Candlestick, 6¾", duo, #2545, Flame	50.00
	Candlestick, duo, #2496	35.00
11 ▸	Candlestick, trindle, #2496	45.00
	Candy, w/lid, 3-part, #2496	95.00
	Celery, #2440	25.00
	Comport, 3¼", cheese	16.00
	Comport, 5½", #2496	20.00
16 ▸	Creamer, #2440	11.00
14 ▸	Creamer, ind., #2496	9.00
	Cup, #2440	14.00
20 ▸	Ice bucket, #2496	75.00
	Mayonnaise, 2-part, #2440	20.00
	Mayonnaise, 3-pc., #2496½	35.00
	Pickle, #2440	22.00
	Pitcher	265.00
	Plate, 6½", #2337	5.00
3 ▸	Plate, 7½", #2337	8.00
	Plate, 8½"	10.00

8 ▸	Plate, 9½", #2337	28.00
	Plate, 10", cake, hndl., #2496	30.00
	Plate, 10½", cake, hndl., #2440	30.00
	Plate, 11", cracker, #2496	22.00
	Plate, 13", torte, #2440	40.00
	Plate, 16", #2364	75.00

	Relish, 2-part, #2440	20.00
	Relish, 2-part, #2496	18.00
19 ▸	Relish, 3-part, #2440	22.00
	Relish, 3-part, #2496	22.00
	Relish, 4-part, #2419	30.00
21 ▸	Relish, 4-part, #2496	30.00
	Relish, 5-part, #2419	40.00
	Sauce bowl, 6½", oval, #2440	50.00
	Sauce tray, 8½", oval, #2440	20.00
	Saucer, #2440	3.00
	Stem, #6014, 3¾", 1 oz., cordial	35.00
	Stem, #6014, 3¾", 4 oz., oyster cocktail	10.00
9 ▸	Stem, #6014, 4½", 5½ oz., low sherbet	8.00
5 ▸	Stem, #6014, 5¼", 3 oz., wine	20.00

2 ▸	Stem, #6014, 5⅜", 5½ oz., high sherbet	12.00
4 ▸	Stem, #6014, 5", 3½ oz., cocktail	14.00
1 ▸	Stem, #6014, 7⅜", 9 oz., water	18.00
	Stem, #6014, 7⅞", 4 oz., claret	20.00
17 ▸	Sugar, #2440	11.00
13 ▸	Sugar, ind., #2496	9.00
	Tidbit, 3-footed, #2496	14.00
15 ▸	Tray, 6½", ind. sug/cr., #2496½	12.00
7 ▸	Tumbler, #6014, 4¾", 5 oz., ftd. juice	14.00
	Tumbler, #6014, 5½", 9 oz., ftd. water	15.00
10 ▸	Tumbler, #6014, 6", 12 oz., ftd. iced tea	18.00
	Vase, 8", bud, #5092	55.00
	Vase, 10", ftd., #2470	125.00

CRINKLE, #1962, MORGANTOWN GLASS GUILD, 1962 – 1971

Colors: amberina, amethyst, black, blue, Bristol Blue, crystal, green, Moss Green, Nutmeg Green, Peacock Blue, pink, Ruby, Steel Blue, Topaz, Violet, and white

Crinkle was a rejuvenation of Morgantown's earlier pattern El Mexicano that was made in opaque ware. Crinkle was typically made as transparent colors except for some rarely seen colors such as the light blue sherbet pictured. Not all pieces are found in the colors listed, nor are all listed pieces made in one color. For the present, we will register one price as a middle of the road idea. Realize that commonly found colors such as pink, green, topaz, and amethyst will bring at least 20% less than prices shown and Ruby and black will fetch up to 50% more.

Many collectors are just becoming aware of Crinkle; and thus, it will take a while to establish firmer pricing. Dealers who specialize or display quantities of Morgantown's patterns tend to price it higher than those who sell it occasionally. It seems those who sell it occasionally sell it faster as it is still a specialized market with fewer avid collectors.

	*All colors			*All colors
Bowl, 4"	9.00		Tumbler, 10 oz.	9.00
Bowl, 5"	9.00		Tumbler, 11 oz., roly poly	10.00
Cocktail, 5½ oz.	10.00		Tumbler, 12 oz., double old fashioned	10.00
Creamer	25.00		Tumbler, 13 oz., ftd.	12.00
Icer w/insert	30.00	4 ▶	Tumbler, 14 oz.	12.00
Pilsner, 16 oz.	15.00		Tumbler, 20 oz., tea	10.00
8 ▶ Pitcher, 34 oz.	40.00		Vase, 5"	25.00
Pitcher, 54 oz.	50.00		Vase, 7"	30.00
Pitcher, martini	65.00			
3 ▶ Pitcher, squared base	75.00			
Plate, 6½"	6.00			
5 ▶ Plate, 7½"	7.00			
Plate, 9¼"	15.00			
Relish, 3-part	50.00			
6 ▶ Sherbet, 6 oz., ftd.	7.00			
Sugar	25.00			
Tumbler, 3 oz.	9.00			
Tumbler, 4 oz., ftd.	14.00			
Tumbler, 5 oz., juice, ftd.	12.00			
2 ▶ Tumbler, 6 oz.	7.00			
7 ▶ Tumbler, 7 oz., old fashioned	8.00			
1 ▶ Tumbler, 8 oz.	8.00			

*Crystal 25% less, Ruby, black, and white up to 25% more

46

CROCHETED CRYSTAL, IMPERIAL GLASS COMPANY, 1943 – early 1950s

Color: crystal

We first became aware of Crocheted Crystal because the shapes and styles were reminiscent of colored Laced Edge, also made by Imperial. We observed several collectors eagerly buying it, and started watching for it in our travels. You will happen upon a number of "go-with" pieces for this pattern as several companies made similar ones.

The most abundant piece of Crocheted Crystal is the double candle which proliferates. Maybe it was a premium, but in any case it was very well distributed as we have seen it from coast to coast. The punch bowl can be obtained with closed or open handle cups. Open handled cups are preferred. There is no punch liner cataloged as such, but the 14" or 17" plate could serve as such.

Purchasing pieces of Crocheted Crystal is a hit or miss proposition when it comes to prices. The uninformed often have inflated prices because it is "pretty good glass" or "elegant looking glass." One individual we chanced upon before we first added this to our book insisted that her epergne set was Heisey and was illustrated in the Heisey book as rare. Parenthetically, Heisey and Cambridge did not make every elegant looking piece of expensive glass in the country.

We have always been informed by Imperial glass authorities that Crocheted Crystal was made by Imperial solely for Sears, Roebuck, and Company. On the other hand, we found pieces bought at an auction in Florida, where a large set of floral cut mixed wares was sold with labels decreeing it to be "CRYSTALWARE, Genuine Hand Cut Open Stock Pattern by R. G. Sherriff, Toronto." The major portion of the cutting was on Viking's Princess pattern; but the rest was Imperial's Crocheted Crystal. Evidently, this cutting company came by these pieces some way, either from Imperial or Sears. Crocheted Crystal was listed in Sears' catalogs for years. The listing below is mainly from the fall 1943 Sears catalog with some supplementary pieces that were not in that specific catalog.

We have pictured an elusive stem (page 48). No one seems to recognize this as Crocheted Crystal. Be sure to study it since collectors of this pattern really have paid the prices listed below to acquire them. We sold some at a show recently and the people buying them asked my wife if she had "any *idea*" what a trial they'd had trying to find a set for 12. After our pictures in the last book, these stems started appearing in Internet auctions taking them out of the scarce category real fast.

Twice we have found Crocheted Crystal stems in California and had them shipped back to us. Both times, most were battered and broken by the post office. We've had really good luck shipping by wrapping the items themselves three times, once with paper, second with bubble wrap, and third with paper again. This gives the items padding enough to separate them from bouncing into each other in the box when they're dropped from heights to conveyor belts at the distribution centers.

The cake stand, 12" basket, flat creamer and sugar, and narcissus bowl are not abundant. The normally found footed creamer and sugar have the open lace work of the other pieces. You may find that many of the pieces in this pattern will turn light amethyst from exposure to the sun. This is known as SCA (sun colored amethyst) and is becoming somewhat collectible for that reason alone — except in pattern glassware where it is viewed with abhorrence.

	Basket, 6"	25.00
	Basket, 9"	40.00
	Basket, 12"	65.00
	Bowl, 7", narcissus	30.00
	Bowl, 10½", salad	24.00
	Bowl, 11", console	24.00
16 ▸	Bowl, 12", salad	24.00
	Buffet set, 14" plate, ftd. sauce bowl, ladle	40.00
	Cake stand, 12", ftd.	35.00
3 ▸	Candleholder, 4½" high, double	12.00
1 ▸	Candleholder, 6" wide, single	15.00
2 ▸	Candleholder (narcissus bowl shape)	30.00
	Celery, 10", oval	22.00
	Cheese & cracker, 12" plate, ftd. dish	30.00
	Creamer, flat	30.00
12 ▸	Creamer, ftd.	15.00
4 ▸	Epergne, 11", ftd. bowl, center vase	95.00
	Hors d'oeuvre dish, 10½", 4-pt., round	25.00
	Lamp, 11", hurricane	60.00
11 ▸	Mayonnaise bowl, 5¼", flat or ftd.	10.00
	Mayonnaise ladle	5.00
6 ▸	Mayonnaise plate, 7½"	6.00

	Plate, 8", salad	7.50
	Plate, 9½"	10.00
15 ▸	Plate, 13", salad bowl liner	20.00
	Plate, 14"	20.00
	Plate, 17"	30.00
13 ▸	Punch bowl, 14"	50.00
14 ▸	Punch cup, closed hndl.	3.00
	Punch cup, open hndl.	6.00
9 ▸	Relish, 11½", 4 pt.	22.00
	Stem, 4½", 3½ oz., cocktail	18.00
	Stem, 5½", 4½ oz., wine	20.00
	Stem, 5", 6 oz., sherbet	15.00
7 ▸	Stem, 7⅛", 9 oz., water goblet	20.00
	Sugar, flat	30.00
10 ▸	Sugar, ftd.	15.00
8 ▸	Sundae, ftd.	10.00
	Tumbler, 6", 6 oz., ftd. fruit juice	25.00
	Tumbler, 7⅛", 12 oz., ftd. iced tea	20.00
	*Vase, 5", 4-ftd.	25.00
5 ▸	Vase, 8" (2 styles)	30.00
	*made into lamp, 40.00	

CROCHETED CRYSTAL

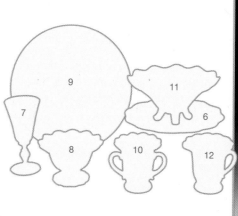

CROWN COLLECTION, FOSTORIA GLASS COMPANY c. 1961 – 1965; INDIANA GLASS CO.
FOR TIARA HOME PRODUCTS, late 1980s

Colors: crystal, Royal blue, gold, and Ruby in Fostoria; red, yellow mist, and green in Indiana Glass

Fostoria's Crown Collection was dealt a big blow when Indiana reproduced the Hapsburg for Tiara. The green basket pictured below is from that later production. It was the only piece we could find to represent the #2750 line for our book.

The Navarre Crown is represented by the blue compote with the fleur-de-lis knobbed lid and the Windsor Crown line by the bottles and the square knobbed lid, small candy bowls with pointed edging. All covered pieces were also sold without covers.

Most collectors pursue the Windsor #2749 line and the #2766 Luxemburg tri-candle. That candleholder is shown in yellow in the top row although it was placed too high to display the three candle cups contained within. That candle is rare in any other color than yellow. The bottle with stopper is being hunted by collectors of colognes and perfumes and minus stopper by candle collectors. The bottles without stoppers used to be difficult to sell until it was discovered that many were sold sans stopper as candles.

According to Fostoria's advertising campaign, the very elegant Fostoria Crown Collection was fashioned on existing crowns for heads of state. These four crown lines came with as few as one item in the Luxemburg line to six in the Windsor Crown line; and nearly all items in each line were produced in every color. Should you wish, at the present, to capture them all, you'd have less than 60 items. If you decide to add the Hapsburg chalice and lid, candy, or the basket that Indiana produced after Fostoria's closing in 1986, you'd have a little over 60. Not counting the Indiana pieces, probably none can be purchased for less than $50.00 unless you get lucky. Prices below are for Fostoria's Crown and not Indiana's Tiara.

#2749 Windsor	Crystal	Blue/Ruby	Gold
2▶ Bottle w/stopper	75.00	125.00	100.00
Candleholder, 3½"	35.00	50.00	45.00
Candy, 3¾"	35.00	45.00	35.00
5▶ Candy & lid, 5½"	50.00	75.00	60.00
Chalice, 6¾", ftd.	40.00	60.00	50.00
4▶ Chalice & lid, 8½", ftd.	65.00	90.00	80.00

#2766 Luxemburg	Crystal	Blue/Ruby	Gold
3▶ Bowl, 7¼", tri-candle	75.00	100.00	90.00

#2752 Navarre	Crystal	Blue/Ruby	Gold
1▶ Bowl, 9"	40.00	60.00	55.00
Bowl & lid, 10½"	60.00	80.00	75.00
Bowl, 9", ftd.	80.00	100.00	90.00
6▶ Bowl & lid, 12", ftd.	100.00	120.00	110.00

#2749 Windsor	Crystal	Blue/Ruby	Gold
7▶ Basket Tiara, made after			
Candy, 5¾"	35.00	50.00	40.00
Candy & lid, 7¼"	50.00	20.00	55.00
Chalice, 7¼", ftd.	55.00	85.00	70.00
Chalice & lid, 9¼", ftd.	70.00	100.00	90.00

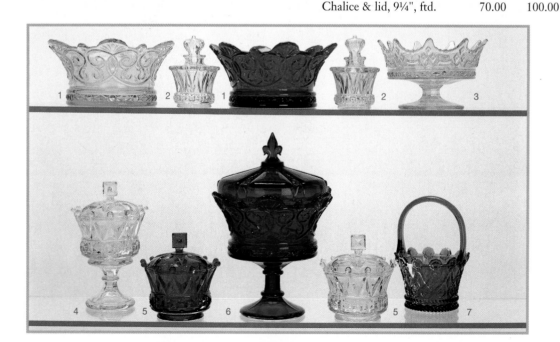

"CUT ROSE," ROSE CUTTING 827, FOSTORIA GLASS COMPANY, 1951 – 1973

Color: crystal w/cut

This smaller Fostoria pattern has an official name of Rose, but most collectors refer to it as "Cut Rose." Rose cuttings are found on Blank #2666 (Contour) and the stems are found on Blank #6036 (Rutledge). Maybe a "bouquet" of these cut roses would be a better gift for a loved one as they will last longer.

"Cut Rose" probably came about from collectors trying to distinguish it from so many other companies' rose patterns. In fact, we had trouble finding a listing in Fostoria catalogs for the pattern when we bought a small set some years ago because we started searching for "Cut Rose" pattern before spotting it as Rose. The people who like it are passionate about it, too, as we once saw two collectors almost come to blows over obtaining it at a flea market.

	Bowl, finger	15.00		Shaker, pr.		35.00
	Bowl, 2¼" high, small salad	16.00	10 ▸	Saucer		3.00
	Bowl, 11", salad	30.00		Stem, 3¼", 1 oz., cordial		25.00
	Celery, 9"	20.00		Stem, 3¾", 4 oz., oyster cocktail		8.00
12 ▸	Creamer	15.00		Stem, 4⅛", 3½ oz., cocktail		8.00
6 ▸	Creamer, individual	15.00	5 ▸	Stem, 4⅛", 6 oz., sherbet		6.00
9 ▸	Cup	10.00	4 ▸	Stem, 4¾", 3¼ oz., claret-wine		12.00
	Mayonnaise	22.00		Stem, 5⅛", 6 oz., saucer champagne		7.00
	Mayonnaise plate	8.00		Stem, 5⅞", 5½ oz., parfait		10.00
	Pickle, 7¼"	16.00	1 ▸	Stem, 6", 4 oz., claret, #6097		11.00
3 ▸	Pitcher, 32 oz., flat	80.00		Stem, 6⅝", 10 oz., #6097		12.00
	Pitcher, 53 oz., ftd.	150.00	2 ▸	Stem, 6⅞", 9½ oz., water		8.00
	Plate, 7"	6.00	11 ▸	Sugar		15.00
8 ▸	Plate, 8"	8.00	7 ▸	Sugar, individual		15.00
	Plate, 14"	30.00		Tray, 7", sugar/creamer		12.00
	Relish, 7⅜", 2-part	18.00		Tumbler, 4⅝", ftd., 5 oz., juice		7.00
	Relish, 10¾", 3-part	20.00		Tumbler, 6⅛", ftd., 12 oz., tea		10.00

"DAISY," NUMBER 620, INDIANA GLASS COMPANY

Colors: crystal, 1933 – 1940; fired-on red, late 1930s; amber, 1940s; dark green and milk glass, 1960s, 1970s, 1980s

"Daisy," as well as Iris, overlaps set time margins between *Collector's Encyclopedia of Depression Glass and Collectible Glassware from the 40s, 50s, 60s....* Since there are more collectors on a quest for amber or green "Daisy," we agreed that it best met the criteria for this book. Crystal "Daisy" was made in 1930s, but there are few collectors buying it today; and it may be harder to gather the crystal daisies than the later colors.

Avocado colored "Daisy" was sold by Indiana under the name Heritage in the 1960s through 1980s and not under the name "Daisy" or No. 620, as it was called when the pattern was first produced in the late 1930s. This has created some confusion in glass collecting circles because Federal Glass Company's Heritage pattern is rare in green (see page 105). Federal's green is the brighter, normally found Depression glass color which glows under ultraviolet light and not the avocado colored green shown here. (Anytime you find avocado colored glassware, you may presume it to have been produced in the late 1960s or early 1970s, when decorators dictated color schemes of Harvest Gold and Avocado Green.) We recently read that some present day collectors are now seeking items in those 70s colors. We associate those colors with the same aghast skepticism our parents did when we told them we were going to write books on Depression glass.

Amber "Daisy" has fewer admirers lately, and prices have dropped due to more people uncovering previously unknown quantities. In that respect, the Internet has hurt the advancement of pricing of many later patterns by illustrating that there really are more resources out there than we could ever have possibly realized.

The indented grill plate is rare, but grill plates are rather unpopular with collectors at the present time. By the way, this grill's indent is for the cream soup and not a cup as is normal. Note how large that ring is. It is much larger than the base of a cup, but fits the base of the cream soup exactly. Conceivably it was touted as a soup and salad set or even a form of snack set so popular at the time.

The 12-ounce footed tea, relish dish, 9⅛" berry, and cereal bowls are all harder to find, but not as sparse as once believed; these have diminished in price over the last few years. Perfect (without inner rim roughness) cereal bowls have become the most troublesome pieces to locate, taking that honor away from the iced tea. It's amazing how many teas appeared from hiding when the price reached $40.00. Unfortunately, so many have materialized that the price has dropped well under that for now and they are becoming rather difficult to sell.

Very few pieces of fired-on red "Daisy" are being stumbled upon. A reader's letter a few years back said that her family had a red set that was acquired in 1935. That helps date this production. There is a pitcher in a fired-on red being found with the No. 618 (Pineapple and Floral) tumblers. This pitcher does not belong to either pattern per se, but was sold with both Indiana patterns. Thus, it's a legitimate go-with pitcher. It has a squared base, if you spot one. Most of the red pieces are rather dull in appearance from years of use.

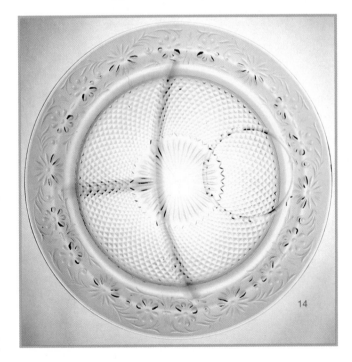

14

		Crystal	Green	Red Amber
8 ▸	Bowl, 4½", berry	3.00	3.00	5.00
12 ▸	Bowl, 4½", cream soup	4.00	3.00	6.00
13 ▸	Bowl, 6", cereal	8.00	7.00	15.00
9 ▸	Bowl, 7⅜", deep berry	7.00	5.00	12.00
10 ▸	Bowl, 9⅜", deep berry	12.00	10.00	15.00
4 ▸	Bowl, 10", oval vegetable	9.00	9.00	12.00
15 ▸	Creamer, footed	4.00	4.00	6.00
2 ▸	Cup	2.00	2.00	3.00
	Plate, 6", sherbet	1.00	1.00	2.00
	Plate, 7⅜", salad	2.00	2.00	5.00
17 ▸	Plate, 8⅜", luncheon	2.00	3.00	5.00
18 ▸	Plate, 9⅜", dinner	4.00	4.00	6.00
	Plate, 10⅜", grill	4.00	5.00	6.00
1 ▸	Plate, 10⅜", grill w/indent		8.00	15.00
19 ▸	Plate, 11½", cake or sandwich	7.00	7.00	12.00
6 ▸	Platter, 10¾"	7.00	7.00	12.00
11 ▸	Relish dish, 8⅜", 3-part	10.00		15.00
3 ▸	Saucer	.50	.50	1.00
14 ▸	Sherbet, ftd.	4.00	4.00	6.00
16 ▸	Sugar, ftd.	4.00	4.00	6.00
5 ▸	Tumbler, 9 oz., ftd.	6.00	7.00	10.00
7 ▸	Tumbler, 12 oz., ftd.	10.00	10.00	25.00

DEWDROP, JEANNETTE GLASS COMPANY, 1953 – 1956

Colors: crystal and iridized

Dewdrop has enticed few new collectors but several items are still in short supply. The tumblers have always been difficult to find, but the candy and butter dishes are also turning out to be few and far between. Most Depression glass dealers do not carry a supply of Dewdrop to shows; it is a pattern you will have to ask for as you travel to shops, malls, and flea markets.

Although finding Dewdrop tumblers remains a challenging task, pitchers are abundant. The tumbler pictured below is the 6" tea and we haven't been able to find a nine ounce water to go with it. Dewdrop was manufactured for four years in the mid-50s, so tumblers should easily be uncovered. We have more requests for Dewdrop tumblers than for any other pieces in this pattern.

In the past, many collectors bought the lazy Susan in Dewdrop to obtain the missing ball bearings for their Shell Pink lazy Susan or for a Candlewick tray because the bearings are the same.

Dewdrop pitchers are continuing to perplex collectors. We believe the true pitcher is the flat one which matches the pointed edges on the other pieces in this pattern. A good case for argument is the creamer which has the same shape and handle style of the pitcher. That said, the footed pitcher has a plain rim which matches the tumblers better, but the handle does not match the shape of any other piece in this pattern. However, pointed edges on the tumblers might make for a better "dribble" glass than one for drinking. The footed pitcher can be a "go-with" type; the iridescent flat one is being sold for $30.00 to $40.00.

We have found several boxed sets of snack trays in our travels. TV tray sets of various types were common in the mid-1950s and there are collectors beginning to accumulate them. Indeed, there is a strong start to collecting many items produced in the 50s, and we understand that some collectors are already looking at things from the 70s such as avocado and gold kitchen appliances, shag carpeting (with rakes to make it stand up again), and plastic, cardboard, and bean bag furnishings. This very well could be the next genre of collectibility, though probably not by us. People collect what they fondly remember and the younger folks remember grandma's chrome dinette set and her Pyrex and Fire-King. Collecting changes with each generation; dealers need to keep that in mind when restocking wares.

Buying Dewdrop will not lead you into bankruptcy and it makes a stunning table setting with added color accoutrements. Many crystal patterns are a delight in large groupings. Dewdrop is heavy and durable, but you'll have to eat from the snack sets, the leaf shaped relish, or the 11½" service plate due to a lack of regular plates.

		Crystal
1 ▸	Bowl, 4¾"	3.00
11 ▸	Bowl, 8½"	12.00
12 ▸	Bowl, 10⅜"	16.00
14 ▸	Butter, w/cover	20.00
10 ▸	Candy dish, w/cover, 7", round, 3 part	18.00
9 ▸	Creamer	6.00
4 ▸	Cup, punch or snack	2.00
7 ▸	Pitcher, ½ gallon, ftd.	18.00
8 ▸	Pitcher, flat	40.00
6 ▸	Plate, 11½"	14.00
3 ▸	Plate, snack, w/indent for cup	3.00
	Punch bowl base	8.00
2 ▸	Punch bowl, 6 qt.	22.00
15 ▸	Relish, leaf shape w/hndl.	3.00
13 ▸	Sugar, w/cover	9.00
16 ▸	Tray, 13", Lazy Susan, complete, 2-pc. w/ball bearing ring	35.00
	Tumbler, 9 oz., water	18.00
5 ▸	Tumbler, 12 oz., flat	6.00
13 ▸	Tumbler, 12 oz., iced tea, 6", ftd.	30.00

DIAMOND POINT, INDIANA GLASS COMPANY, c. 1966; COLORS c. 1980s TIARA HOME PRODUCTS

Colors: crystal, crystal w/ruby stain, crystal w/gold, blue satin, green satin, Cameo/black, yellow, teal, blue, amber, electric blue, carnival, and milk

Diamond Point is one of the patterns we are often asked to identify at shows. Even after we added it to our book we still get pictures sent asking what it is and where can it be found? This is not Depression glass. It is not Miss America or English Hobnail as it is so often labeled in malls or flea markets. It was first cataloged in 1966 by Indiana although we regularly get letters from people who remember it from the 40s or 50s. Time sure flies when you get older. The stories we've heard about the origin of this glass would make a book in itself — particularly about family pieces being over a hundred years old. Colored wares other than the ruby stained items were mostly made for Tiara Home Products during the 1980s and 1990s.

Diamond Point type items have their origins in some "mitered diamond" wares dating back to 1850, various versions of which have been produced by countless companies, including Westmoreland, Kemple, Imperial, and this later production of Indiana. The names have changed from company to company — Diamond, Mitered Diamond, Sawtooth, Diamond Point — and shapes, edge treatments, stems, and clarity of glass have changed, but the four-sided diamond cut has not. This particular diamond shape apparently has ageless appeal for admirers.

It is very likely that we have overlooked some of the Indiana color productions as well as additional pieces. Frankly, we never expected to be adding this pattern in our book when it was appearing all over the markets. A few people are beginning to buy this; and we've heard some wishes for it at shows, though its recent manufacture prohibits its inclusion at most Depression glass shows.

If you have further knowledge regarding this Diamond Point pattern by Indiana, we'd very much appreciate your telling us so we can include it in the future. Prices are those we've encountered and are only specified for the crystal with ruby stain because it is the ruby stained crystal most collectors seek.

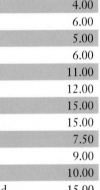

		Crystal w/ruby
	Ashtray, 5½"	4.00
8 ▸	Bowl, 3 toe, crimped	6.00
13 ▸	Bowl, 6", flat rim	5.00
11 ▸	Bowl, 6", scalloped rim	6.00
	Bowl, 9¾", straight side	11.00
	Bowl, 11½", low foot, scalloped	12.00
12 ▸	Bowl, 13½", low foot, flared	15.00
	Cake stand, 10"	15.00
	Candle, ftd.	7.50
17 ▸	Candlelamp	9.00
6 ▸	Candy, 4¾", w/lid	10.00
	Candy, 12" high, 2½" deep, 6" dia., w/lid	15.00
	Candy, 15½" tall, Chalice w/lid	22.00
10 ▸	Compote, 7¼" tall, flat rim	12.50
	Compote, 7¼"tall, crimp rim	12.50
18 ▸	Creamer, ftd.	3.00
1 ▸	Decanter with stopper	20.00
	Duet server, stand w /6" bowls	12.00
2 ▸	Stem, water	6.00
	Ice tub, 11⅝", w/lid (looks like cookie jar)	15.00
4 ▸	Mug	6.00
14 ▸	Pitcher	15.00
5 ▸	Plate, 7"	2.00
	Plate, 14½", serving	12.00
3 ▸	Shaker	10.00
7 ▸	Sherbet, ftd.	5.00
9 ▸	Sugar, ftd.	3.00
15 ▸	Tumbler, 9 oz., water	4.00
	Tumbler, 15 oz., tea	5.00
	Tray, oval for sugar/creamer	3.00
16 ▸	Vase, ftd.	12.00

EARLY AMERICAN PRESCUT, ANCHOR HOCKING GLASS CORPORATION, 1960 – 1999

Colors: crystal, some amber, blue green, red, and black; some with painted designs

Early American Prescut (EAPC) may be the most well-known pattern in this book. Anchor Hocking began its manufacture in 1960 and vases for the florist industry were still being cataloged as late as 2004. People growing up in the 60s and early 70s remember this pattern just as the those growing up in the late 40s and 50s remember Fire-King and Pyrex. When we hold seminars for women's clubs or other groups, we always exhibit a variety of Depression, Elegant, and later glassware. The one pattern readily recognized is a piece of EAPC. Seldom do they know what it is called or who made it, but they do know Mom or Grandma had some of it. It is recognized over Jade-ite, if you can believe that.

All EAPC pieces are listed with a 700 line number in Anchor Hocking's catalogs. There were several Prescut patterns made at Anchor Hocking, a predicament we address on page 60. EAPC has to have the star (often referred to as Star of David) in the design with two exceptions. The double candle has a knob in place of the star. That star was pictured in the catalog where the knob is attached; so probably the mould makers changed the design to better release the piece from the mould. That was an ongoing battle at glass factories — glass designers against mould makers. Also, the cup used with punch and snack sets does not have the star. It was appropriated from the "Oatmeal" line rather than having to make a new cup mould.

Originally, four pieces of EAPC were launched by Anchor Hocking in the 1960 – 1961 catalog. Most pieces were discontinued by 1978, but the creamer, sugar, cruet, and shakers with plastic tops were made as late as 1997. The creamer, sugar, oil bottle, regular shakers, butter dish, gondola bowl, and 13½" plate are difficult to sell due to quantities made which still exist. Moreover, these pieces can occasionally still be found on the shelves of dish barns and closeout stores. We bought eight 5-part relish dishes from such an outlet for $4.99 each a few years ago.

The ever-present punch bowl can be seen at prices ranging from $20.00 to $75.00. For us, they sell slowly at $25.00 and we have been able to move them faster at $22.00. Remember, these were sold for $2.89 a set with an oil and lube job in the middle and late 1960s. Many oil changes were purchased at Marathon gas stations in Ohio, Kentucky, and West Virginia and the punch set was reasonably priced; so one can assume that multitudes were purchased. A large number (over 400 in one group) of Royal Ruby EAPC ashtrays have been discovered, but, so far, that is the only piece of EAPC unearthed in that color. You can also find pieces in laser blue, avocado green, and amber. Colored wares are not common and some are deceiving, having sprayed colors over crystal.

Some items were only made for a year or two. The most difficult, but desirable pieces to own are the oil lamp, 11" four-part relish plate with swirl dividers, and 11¾" paneled bowl. Additionally, the EAPC smooth rim 4½" bowls, 6¾" plates with or without ring, and individual shakers are not as easily obtained. However, prices have dropped quite a bit on all those items due to previously unknown quantities being offered through Internet auctions. There were several seemingly experimental pieces made including a bud vase, footed sherbet, and cocktail shaker. We sold our sherbet and bud vase at the 2000 Fire-King Expo show and have not seen any others since.

There are 4" and 5" round powder jars with a crenulated locking system made in Italy that look like EAPC as well as a three-part small relish and heart-shaped dish. The asking price is in the $15.00 – 20.00 range. These are not EAPC. If you look around the center of the pieces, the word "Italy" will be embossed. It is possible to find two unmarked halves of the covered powders that have been "married" that won't be marked. Realize Hocking did not make these and they are not EAPC. For more detailed information on EAPC, look for our book, *Anchor Hocking's Fire-King & More*.

EARLY AMERICAN PRESCUT

		Crystal
7 ▸	Ashtray, 4", #700/690	3.00
	Ashtray, 5"	8.00
19 ▸	Ashtray, 7¾", #718-G	10.00
3 ▸	Bowl, 4¼", #726 (smooth rim)	16.00
	Bowl, 5¼", #775 (scalloped rim)	7.00
30 ▸	Bowl, 5½", flat	35.00
	Bowl, 6¾", 3-toed, #768	4.50
14 ▸	Bowl, 7¼" (scalloped rim)	16.00
	Bowl, 7¼", round, #767	5.00
	Bowl, 8¾", #787	9.00
	Bowl, 9", console, #797	12.00
4 ▸	Bowl, 9", oval, #776	6.00
9 ▸	Bowl, 9⅜", gondola dish, #752	4.00
13 ▸	Bowl, 10¾", salad, #788	12.00
10 ▸	Bowl, 11¾", paneled, #794	145.00
	Bowl, dessert, 5⅜", #765	2.50
5 ▸	Butter, bottom w/metal handle and knife	12.00
27 ▸	Butter, w/cover, ¼ lb., #705	6.00
	Cake plate, 13½", ftd., #706	26.00
6 ▸	Candlestick, 7" x 5⅝", double, #784	22.00
	Candy, w/lid, 5¼", #744	10.00
	Candy, w/cover, 7¼" x 5½", #792	12.00
8 ▸	Chip & dip, 10¾" bowl, 5¼", brass finish holder #700/733	22.00
12 ▸	Coaster, #700/702	2.50
	Cocktail shaker, 9", 30 oz.	995.00
25 ▸	Creamer, #754	3.00
24 ▸	Cruet, w/stopper, 7¾", #711	5.00
20 ▸	Cup, punch or snack, 6 oz. (no star)	1.50
	Lamp, electric (made from vase)	25.00
	Lazy Susan, 9-pc., #700/713	35.00

		Crystal
	Oil lamp	195.00
	Pitcher, 18 oz., #744	10.00
1 ▸	Pitcher, 40 oz., square	33.00
17 ▸	Pitcher, 60 oz., #791	15.00
2 ▸	Plate, 6¾", no ring	30.00
	Plate, 6¾", w/ring for 6 oz. cup	30.00
	Plate, 10", snack, #780	5.00
	Plate, 11", 4-part w/swirl dividers	125.00
11 ▸	Plate, 11"	10.00
22 ▸	Plate, 11¾", deviled egg/relish, #750	25.00
21 ▸	Plate, 13½", serving, #790	10.00
	Punch base	12.00
	Punch set, 15-pc.	35.00
	Relish, 8½", oval, 2-part, #778	5.00
	Relish, 10", divided, tab hndl., #770	18.00
	Relish, 13½", 5-part	22.00
	Server, 12 oz. (syrup), #707	14.00
28 ▸	Shakers, pr., metal tops, #700/699	5.00
	Shakers, pr., plastic tops, #725	5.00
29 ▸	Shakers, pr., 2¼", individual, #700/736	28.00
	Sherbet, 3½", 6 oz., ftd.	495.00
26 ▸	Sugar, w/lid, #753	4.00
23 ▸	Tray, 6½" x 12", hostess, #750	8.00
	Tray, cr/sug, #700/671	3.00
16 ▸	Tumbler, 5 oz., 4", juice, #730	3.00
15 ▸	Tumbler, 10 oz., 4½", #731	2.50
18 ▸	Tumbler, 15 oz., 6", iced tea, #732	18.00
	Vase, 5", ftd., bud	795.00
	Vase, 6 x 4½", basket/block, #704/205	14.00
	Vase, 8½", #741	6.00
	Vase, 10", #742	11.00

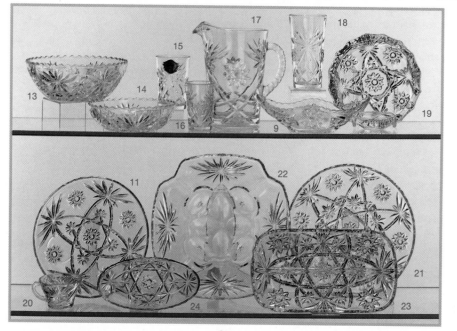

PRESCUT: "OATMEAL" & "PINEAPPLE," ANCHOR HOCKING GLASS CORPORATION, 1941 – 1970s

There has been uncertainty among collectors as to what is and is not EAPC. Read page 57 for what constitutes EAPC. "Oatmeal" is logically identified as EAPC pieces without the "star" and is pictured in the top row below. The "Oatmeal" name subsists since seven of these pieces were packed in boxes of Crystal Wedding Oats. The soap dish may not have been in the oatmeal boxes, but it is the same pattern. You can tell by its price that it is not as commonly found as the others. Like the five pieces of Forest Green Sandwich that were packed in oatmeal, these "Oatmeal" items are bountiful today. "Oatmeal" and "Pineapple" discussed in the next paragraph were both listed in Anchor Hocking catalogs under the general term Prescut and collectors have given them "Oatmeal" and "Pineapple" names over the years, which we are now using so everyone can be on the same page.

The other pattern often mistakenly called EAPC has been labeled "Pineapple" by collectors. It is shown on the second and third rows below. It was first introduced in the 1941 catalog, 20 years before the dawn of EAPC. "Pineapple" is found mostly in crystal with an occasional piece in white. Note the white sugar and creamer decorated with painted flowers. The crystal cigarette box can be found with a Royal Ruby lid and is preferred that way by most collectors.

"Oatmeal"	Crystal		"Pineapple"	Crystal	White
7 ▸ Bowl, 4¼", berry	2.00		Box, 4¾", cigarette or dresser	14.00	10.00
15 ▸ Cup	1.50		16 ▸ Box, 4¾", w/Royal Ruby lid	20.00	
2 ▸ Saucer, 4⅜"	1.00		10 ▸ Butter, round	15.00	
1 ▸ Sherbet, 5 oz.	1.50		17 ▸ Marmalade, w/Royal Ruby lid	20.00	
3 ▸ Soap dish, 5¼" x 3¾"	18.00		11 ▸ Pitcher, 12 oz., milk	7.00	8.00
5 ▸ Tumbler, 4 oz., juice	2.00		14 ▸ Shaker	2.00	
6 ▸ Tumbler, 7 oz., old fashioned	2.50		8 ▸ Sugar w/lid, handled	12.00	
4 ▸ Tumbler, 9 oz., water			9 ▸ Sugar w/lid, no handles	10.00	
			12 ▸ Syrup pitcher	12.00	
			13 ▸ Tumbler, 10 oz., iced tea	5.00	6.00

EMERALD CREST, FENTON ART GLASS COMPANY, 1949 – 1955

Color: white with green edge

Emerald Crest was depicted in Fenton catalogs from 1949 until January 1955. We earlier had a critical letter from a lady who was married in 1957 and was gifted with Emerald Crest. She admonished us that we needed to correct our dates of manufacture as we were wrong. Although production almost certainly ended by 1956 because it was not in that year's catalog, that doesn't mean inventory in stores had been liquidated, just that the retailers could not re-order additional pieces from the Fenton factory.

Emerald Crest followed Aqua Crest (blue trimmed) which started in 1941, and Silver Crest (crystal trimmed) started in 1943. Since Aqua Crest is not in this book, you will find prices for Aqua Crest fall between those of Emerald Crest and Silver Crest (priced on pages 226 and 227).

Some pieces of Emerald Crest have two separate line numbers in the catalogs and in our listing. Initially, Emerald Crest was line #680, and all pieces carried that designation. In July 1952, Fenton began supplying a ware number for each piece rather than the pattern line only; that is why you see two diverse numbers listed for the different sized plates and vases.

Emerald Crest mayonnaise sets are commonly found with crystal spoons, but a green spoon was made. It is occasionally found in mayos and mustards, and the green spoons are desirable and sell in the $30.00 range by themselves. You can observe green spoons in the mustards pictured. The green stopper for the oil bottle is also difficult to locate. Most stoppers for those bottles were offered in crystal. The green adds to the pattern appearance and greatly to its cost.

We do not buy or sell a lot of Fenton; as a result, we are grateful for the help from Fenton collectors and dealers as well as readers who have assisted with listings of Fenton patterns in this book. We appreciate their time and guidance in arriving at price listings for Emerald and Silver Crest.

5 ▸	Basket, 5", #7236	70.00
	Basket, 7", #7237	100.00
22 ▸	Bonbon, 5½", double crimped	25.00
19 ▸	Bowl, 5", finger or deep dessert, #7221	25.00

3 ▸	Bowl, 5½" (heart shaped)	40.00
	Bowl, 5½", soup, #680, #7230	37.50
23 ▸	Bowl, 8½", flared, #680	45.00
11 ▸	Bowl, 9½", #682	60.00
24 ▸	Bowl, 10", salad, #7220	72.50
	Bowl, dessert, shallow, #7222	20.00
	Bowl, ftd., tall, square, #7330	225.00
4 ▸	Bowl, salad, 10½" (heart shaped)	95.00
12 ▸	Cake plate, 13", high ftd., #680, #7213	130.00
13 ▸	Cake plate, low ftd., #5813	120.00

61

EMERALD CREST

	Candleholder, flat saucer base, pr., #680	75.00
6 ▸	Comport, 6", ftd., flared, #206	37.50
18 ▸	Comport, ftd., double crimped	37.50
29 ▸	Creamer, clear reeded hndls., #7231	35.00
16 ▸	Cup, #7208	35.00
8 ▸	Epergne, 4-piece set, #1948	225.00
14 ▸	Flower pot w/attached saucer, #7299	50.00
15 ▸	Jam set	120.00
32 ▸	Mayonnaise bowl, #7203	33.00
34 ▸	Mayonnaise ladle, crystal, #7203	8.00
	Mayonnaise ladle, green, #7203	35.00
33 ▸	Mayonnaise liner, #7203	18.00
	Mayonnaise set, 3-pc., w/crys. ladle, #7203	65.00
	Mayonnaise set, 3-pc., w/gr. ladle, #7203	95.00
	Mustard, w/lid and spoon	85.00
20 ▸	Oil bottle, w/green stopper, #680, #7269	125.00

7 ▸	Pitcher, 6" hndl., beaded melon, #7116	70.00
	Plate, 5½", #680, #7218	15.00
	Plate, 6½", #680, #7219	16.00
28 ▸	Plate, 8½", #680, #7217	22.50
31 ▸	Plate, 8½", handled, #680	27.00
26 ▸	Plate, 10", #680, #7210	50.00
25 ▸	Plate, 12", #680, #7212	47.50
	Plate, 12", #682	55.00
	Plate, 16", torte, #7216	65.00
17 ▸	Saucer, #7208	10.00
27 ▸	Sherbet, ftd., #7226	22.50
30 ▸	Sugar, clear reeded hndls., #7231	35.00
21 ▸	Tidbit, 2-tier bowls, 5½" & 8½"	65.00
	Tidbit, 2-tier bowls, 8½" & 10"	85.00
	Tidbit, 2-tier plates, #7297	60.00
	Tidbit, 3-tier plates, #7298	95.00
10 ▸	Vase, 4½", fan, #36, #7355	30.00
1 ▸	Vase, Tulip, 6", #711	65.00
2 ▸	Vase, 6½", #4517	65.00
9 ▸	Vase, 6¼", fan, #36, #7357	35.00
	Vase, 8", bulbous base, #186	65.00

EMERALD GLO, PADEN CITY and FENTON ART GLASS COMPANY, 1940s – 1950s

Color: Emerald green

Emerald Glo was made predominantly by Paden City Glass Company for Rubel; however, it was also made by Fenton Art Glass Company in the later years of its production. Labeled pieces on metallic accoutrements have been found which state "Cavalier Emerald-Glo Hand-Made." All pieces with "star cut" were made by Paden City, but uncut pieces were made by both companies.

Customarily, the Fenton production pieces are a slightly darker green color. Fenton pieces are more often found with cast-iron accoutrements as opposed to the gold-toned ones. Fenton also made pieces in white from these same moulds, but those are rarely seen. It is the green color that is valued today, no matter which company manufactured it.

Emerald Glo has been a fast seller for us when we have some to sell. Regrettably, we have been able to find very little in recent years. We come across it sporadically, generally with some problem of missing parts or damaged metal pieces. One of the reasons that items bring the prices listed is that collectors are willing to buy mint condition pieces. It is when they are priced as mint and are not that makes a difference.

No.	Item	Price		No.	Item	Price
12 ▸	Bowl, 12"	25.00		9 ▸	Mayonnaise, divided, w/metal underliner & spoons	35.00
11 ▸	Candleholders, pr., ball with metal cups	30.00		2 ▸	Oil bottle	20.00
10 ▸	Casserole w/metal cover on tray	35.00		13 ▸	Relish, 6", divided, w/metal handle	30.00
16 ▸	Cheese dish w/metal top and handle	45.00			Relish, 9", tab hndl., w/metal handle	30.00
	Cocktail shaker, 10", 26 oz.	65.00		3 ▸	Relish, heart shaped	30.00
6 ▸	Condiment set (2 jars, metal lids, spoons & tray)	55.00		17 ▸	Salad bowl w/metal base, fork, and spoon	60.00
5 ▸	Condiment set (3 jars, metal lids, spoons & tray)	60.00			Salad bowl, 10"	22.00
	Condiment set (creamer, sugar, marmalade, shakers on revolving tray)	75.00			Salt & pepper shakers, pr.	20.00
				14 ▸	Server, 5-part, w/metal covered center	50.00
20 ▸	Creamer	12.00		18 ▸	Sugar	12.00
8 ▸	Creamer/sugar, individual (metal), on metal tray	20.00			Sugar w/metal lid & liner	20.00
4 ▸	Creamer/sugar, individual, on metal tray	30.00		15 ▸	Syrup w/metal lid & liner	25.00
	Cruet	20.00			Tidbit, 2-tier (bowls 6" & 8")	40.00
19 ▸	Ice bucket, metal holder & tongs	60.00			Tray, 8½", handled	30.00
1 ▸	Jam jar, w/glass spoon	30.00			Tumbler, 2⅝", 1 oz.	10.00
7 ▸	Marmalade w/metal lid & spoon	30.00				

ENGLISH HOBNAIL, LINE NO. 555, WESTMORELAND GLASS COMPANY, 1920s – 1983

Colors: amber, crystal, and crystal with various color treatments and white

Crystal and amber English Hobnail were made until Westmoreland closed in 1983. Correspondingly, we are now incorporating amber and crystal into this book. We concede that crystal, crystal with amber or black bases or trims, and several shades of amber were made before 1940, but pricing is essentially identical for all crystal or amber no matter when it was made. English Hobnail was one of the patterns originally listed in the first Depression glass book in 1972; now all colors except amber are still listed in it.

Milk glass English Hobnail was only made in this book's constraints. It sells for about the same price as crystal or slightly lower, but fewer people seem to want it unless its priced extremely inexpensively. You can double prices listed for any hand-painted or decorated milk glass English Hobnail. Crystal with ruby flashing on English Hobnail seems difficult to sell at regular crystal prices, but it was a very limited production. There are appreciative patrons buying crystal English Hobnail, but collectors enthusiastically hunting for amber seem in short supply.

The punch set has never been found in color.

		Amber/Crystal			Amber/Crystal			Amber/Crystal
	Ashtray, 3"	5.00		Bowl, 6", round nappy	10.00		Bowl, 8", round nappy	25.00
2 ▸	Ashtray, 4½"	7.00	16 ▸	Bowl, 6", sq. nappy	10.00		Bowl, 9", bell nappy	25.00
	Ashtray, 4½", sq.	7.50		Bowl, 6½", grapefruit	11.00		Bowl, 9", celery	16.00
28 ▸	Basket, 5", hndl.	12.00		Bowl, 6½", round nappy	12.00		Bowl, 9½", round, crimped	28.00
	Basket, 6", tall, hndl.	30.00		Bowl, 6½", sq. nappy	12.50		Bowl, 10", flared	30.00
	Bonbon, 6½", hndl.	10.00		Bowl, 7", 6 pt.	25.00		Bowl, 10", oval, crimped	30.00
	Bottle, toilet, 5 oz.	20.00		Bowl, 7", oblong spoon	15.00		Bowl, 11", bell	30.00
	Bowl, 4", rose	15.00		Bowl, 7", preserve	15.00		Bowl, 11", rolled edge	30.00
22 ▸	Bowl, 4½", finger	7.50		Bowl, 7", round nappy	15.00		Bowl, 12", celery	18.00
	Bowl, 4½", round nappy	7.00		Bowl, 7½", bell nappy	16.00	13 ▸	Bowl, 12", flange or console	25.00
	Bowl, 4½", sq. ftd., finger	9.00		Bowl, 8", 6 pt.	25.00		Bowl, 12", flared	30.00
29 ▸	Bowl, 4½", sq. nappy	7.00		Bowl, 8", cupped, nappy	25.00		Bowl, 12", oval, crimped	32.00
	Bowl, 5", round nappy	9.50		Bowl, 8", ftd.	25.00		Bowl, cream soup	14.00
	Bowl, 5½", bell nappy	11.50		Bowl, 8", hexagonal ftd., 2-hndl.	30.00		Candelabra, 2-lite	22.00
	Bowl, 6", crimped dish	10.00				12 ▸	Candlestick, 3½", rnd. base	8.00
	Bowl, 6", rose	15.00		Bowl, 8", pickle	16.00		Candlestick, 5½", sq. base	12.00

ENGLISH HOBNAIL

Amber/Crystal	
Candlestick, 9", rnd. base	20.00
Candy dish, 3-ftd.	25.00
Candy dish, 9"	50.00
4 ▸ Candy, ½ lb., and cover, cone shaped	22.00
Chandelier, 17", shade w/200+ prisms	250.00
Cheese w/cover, 6"	35.00
Cheese w/cover, 8¾"	45.00
Cigarette box and cover, 4½"x2½"	16.00
Cigarette jar w/cover, rnd.	14.00
Cigarette lighter (milk glass only)	12.00
Coaster, 3"	6.00
Compote, 5", round, rnd. ftd.	10.00
Compote, 5", sq. ftd., round	10.00
Compote, 5½", ball stem, sweetmeat	20.00
Compote, 5½", bell	14.00
Compote, 5½", sq. ftd., bell	14.00
Compote, 6", honey, rnd. ftd.	15.00
Compote, 6", honey, sq. ftd.	15.00
30 ▸ Compote, 8", ball stem, sweetmeat	32.00

Amber/Crystal	
7 ▸ Creamer, hexagonal, ftd.	8.00
Creamer, low, flat	7.00
15 ▸ Creamer, sq. ftd.	8.00
9 ▸ Cup	6.00
Cup, demitasse	12.00
Decanter, 20 oz.	45.00
35 ▸ Egg cup	12.00
Hat, high	20.00
11 ▸ Hat, low	18.00
Ice tub, 4"	25.00
Ice tub, 5½"	40.00
Icer, sq. base, w/patterned insert	50.00
Lamp, 6½", electric	25.00
Lamp, 9½", electric	30.00
37 ▸ Lamp, candlestick (several types)	20.00
Lampshade, 17"	150.00
18 ▸ Marmalade w/cover	18.00
Mayonnaise, 6"	8.00
Mustard, sq. ftd., w/lid	18.00
Nut, individual, ftd.	5.00
Oil bottle, 2 oz., hndl.	18.00
Oil bottle, 6 oz., hndl.	25.00

Amber/Crystal	
Oil-vinegar combination, 6 oz.	30.00
Parfait, rnd. ftd.	12.00
Pitcher, 23 oz., rounded	45.00
Pitcher, 32 oz., straight side	50.00
Pitcher, 38 oz., rounded	55.00
Pitcher, 60 oz., rounded	55.00
Pitcher, 64 oz., straight side	75.00
Plate, 5½", rnd.	3.00
Plate, 6", sq.	4.00
Plate, 6", sq., finger bowl liner	4.00
Plate, 6½", depressed center, rnd.	5.00
Plate, 6½", round	5.00
23 ▸ Plate, 6½, rnd., finger bowl liner	5.00
Plate, 7½", sq.	5.00
14 ▸ Plate, 8", rnd.	6.00
Plate, 8", rnd., 3-ftd.	12.00
Plate, 8½", plain edge	7.00
Plate, 8½", rnd.	7.00

Amber/Crystal

	Item	Price
5 ▸	Plate, 8¾", sq.	12.00
	Plate, 10", rnd.	16.00
	Plate, 10", sq.	16.00
	Plate, 10½", grill, rnd.	16.00
27 ▸	Plate, 12", sq.	22.00
	Plate, 15", sq.	35.00
	Plate, 14", rnd., torte	30.00
	Plate, 20½", rnd., torte	60.00
	Plate, cream soup liner, rnd.	4.00
	Puff box, w/ cover, 6", rnd.	18.00
	Punch bowl	175.00
	Punch bowl stand	60.00
	Punch cup	4.00
	Punch set (bowl, stand, 12 cups, ladle)	295.00
	Relish, 8", 3-part	16.00
	Saucer, demitasse, rnd.	5.00
	Saucer, demitasse, sq.	5.00
34 ▸	Saucer, rnd.	2.00
10 ▸	Saucer, sq.	2.00
6 ▸	Shaker, pr., rnd. ftd.	18.00
	Shaker, pr., sq. ftd.	18.00
33 ▸	Stem, 1 oz., rnd. ftd., cordial	10.00
	Stem, 1 oz., rnd. ball, cordial	12.00
	Stem, 1 oz., sq. ftd., cordial	12.00
	Stem, 2 oz., rnd. ftd., wine	8.00
31 ▸	Stem, 2 oz., sq. ftd., wine	8.00
	Stem, 2¼ oz., rnd. ball, wine	7.00
	Stem, 3 oz., rnd., cocktail	6.00
32 ▸	Stem, 3 oz., sq. ftd., cocktail	6.00

Amber/Crystal

	Item	Price
	Stem, 3½ oz., rnd. ball, cocktail	6.00
	Stem, 5 oz., rnd. claret	10.00
	Stem, 5 oz., sq. ftd., oyster cocktail	7.00
8 ▸	Stem, 8 oz., rnd. ftd., water goblet	8.00
1 ▸	Stem, 8 oz., sq. ftd., water goblet	8.00
	Stem, sherbet, low, one ball, rnd. ftd.	5.00
	Stem, sherbet, rnd. low foot	5.00
36 ▸	Stem, sherbet, sq. ftd., low	5.00
	Stem, champagne, two ball, rnd. ftd.	6.00
	Stem, sherbet, high, two ball, rnd. ftd.	7.00
	Stem, sherbet, rnd. high foot	6.00
	Stem, sherbet, sq. ftd., high	6.00
3 ▸	Sugar, hexagonal, ftd.	7.00
21 ▸	Sugar, low, flat	6.00
	Sugar, sq. ftd.	7.00
	Tidbit, 2-tier	25.00
	Tumbler, 1½ oz., whiskey	10.00
	Tumbler, 3 oz., whiskey	10.00
	Tumbler, 5 oz., ginger ale	6.00
	Tumbler, 5 oz., old fashioned cocktail	10.00
19 ▸	Tumbler, 5 oz., rnd. ftd., ginger ale	6.00

Amber/Crystal

	Item	Price
24 ▸	Tumbler, 5 oz., sq. ftd., ginger ale	6.00
	Tumbler, 7 oz., rnd. ftd., juice	7.00
26 ▸	Tumbler, 7 oz., sq. ftd., juice	7.00
	Tumbler, 8 oz., rnd., ball, water	8.00
17 ▸	Tumbler, 8 oz., water	8.00
	Tumbler, 9 oz., rnd. ball, water	8.00
	Tumbler, 9 oz., rnd. ftd., water	8.00
20 ▸	Tumbler, 9 oz., sq. ftd., water	8.00
	Tumbler, 10 oz., iced tea	10.00
	Tumbler, 11 oz., rnd. ball, iced tea	8.00
25 ▸	Tumbler, 11 oz., sq. ftd., iced tea	10.00
	Tumbler, 12 oz., iced tea	10.00
	Tumbler, 12½ oz., rnd. ftd., iced tea	8.00
	Urn, 11", w/cover	45.00
	Vase, 6½", ivy bowl, sq. ftd., crimp top	25.00
	Vase, 6½", sq. ftd., flower holder	22.00
	Vase, 7½", flip	28.00
	Vase, 7½", flip jar w/cover	40.00
	Vase, 8", sq. ftd.	30.00
	Vase, 8½", flared top	30.00
	Vase, 10" (straw jar)	50.00

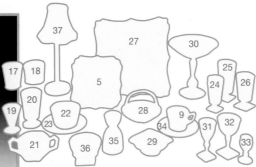

FESTIVE, LINE #155, DUNCAN AND MILLER, c. 1950s

Colors: crystal, Aqua, and Honey

Duncan and Miller's Festive appearance seems to suggest the space age awareness of 1950s by its shape and design. This flame polished glassware captures the attention of more collectors of 50s era than any other Duncan pattern. From the swirling, circle optic in the glassware itself, suggestive of Saturn's rings, to the futuristic shapes contrasted with wooden and metal parts, this glass was an astonishing deviation from the norm. Do not confuse this with Heisey's Saturn pattern which has similar color and shape. Pieces missing the needed wood or metal parts are being ignored by collectors. They want every piece to be original. Notice that Duncan dubbed their yellow color, Honey and the blue, Aqua. Prices are holding up for Festive as hoards of it are not turning up as in other patterns.

		Honey	Aqua
5 ▶	Bowl, 6"	6.00	6.00
2 ▶	Bowl, sauce dish w/ladle	40.00	50.00
	Bowl, 14", flower w/stand, flare	50.00	65.00
4 ▶	Candlestick, 5½"	30.00	35.00
	Candy box w/lid	45.00	55.00
	Cheese tray, oval, w/wood bridge	65.00	75.00
9 ▶	Comport, 7½", high ft.	40.00	50.00
	Comport, 9"	45.00	55.00
3 ▶	Creamer	18.00	20.00
	Cruet, 8"	35.00	45.00
8 ▶	Plate, 16", buffet	60.00	65.00
	Relish, 10", round, 3-pt. hndl.	60.00	65.00
7 ▶	Shaker, 4"	30.00	35.00

		Honey	Aqua
6 ▶	Sugar	18.00	20.00
	Tray for sugar/creamer	20.00	25.00
1 ▶	Twin server, 9½", w/hndl.	35.00	38.00
	Vase, 10"	40.00	45.00

FIRE-KING "ALICE," ANCHOR HOCKING GLASS CORPORATION, early 1940s

Colors: Jade-ite, Vitrock w/trims of blue or red

"Alice" can be purchased in Vitrock, red or blue trimmed Vitrock, or Jade-ite. Finding red-trimmed pieces is challenging at best, but then some of that red tends to fade to pink if used regularly. Not to be bested, there are two shades of blue-trimmed pieces being found. Although not shown here, you can see the red-trimmed "Alice" pictured in our *Anchor Hockings' Fire-King & More* book. Red-trimmed Alice turns out to be the hardest color to find and is absent from almost all collections. We remember seeing the red-trimmed several times in northern Texas about 25 years ago while visiting shops on our way to set up at glass shows. By the time we learned more about the true scarcity of red, those pieces which seemed over priced at the time, had long since been bought by someone who knew a lot more than we did about Fire-King.

The white "Alice" is Vitrock. There are two well-defined hues of Vitrock "Alice." These do not exhibit very well together; so you need to decide whether you like white or the beige/gray shade or both. Neither shade is sufficient for requirements.

"Alice" dinner plates are the pieces to find in this three piece pattern. It appears few people would pay money for the plates to go with those cups and saucers that were free in oatmeal boxes. The quantity of dinner plates we see as we travel in the Missouri area between St. Louis and Joplin makes us believe plates may have been given away as premiums by someone in that region.

		Jade-ite	Vitrock/Blue trim	Vitrock/Red trim	Vitrock
2 ▸	Cup	6.00	8.00	35.00	4.00
1 ▸	Plate, 9½"	24.00	18.00	65.00	12.00
3 ▸	Saucer	3.00	3.00	15.00	1.00

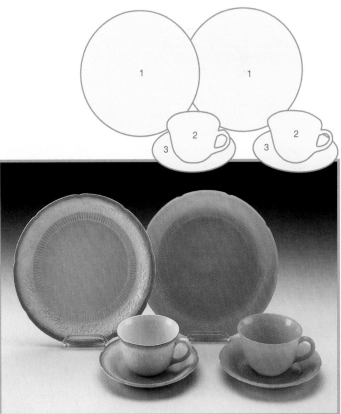

FIRE-KING BLUE MOSAIC, ANCHOR HOCKING GLASS CORPORATION, 1966 – late 1967

Blue Mosaic was made for only two years. This Anchor Hocking pattern is depicted only in the 1966 – 1967 catalog. The sugar, creamer, and cups have solid blue exteriors with a white indented band at the bottom. The sugar is a cup mould with no handles plus a white lid; the creamer is a cup mould with a spout. The sugar lid is a different style than found on most Fire-King patterns. These three pieces are sometimes overlooked as they have no small blue squares in concentric rings which make up the mosaic look on all other pieces.

The identical cup was used for both the saucer and the snack tray, unlike a five or six ounce sized snack cup in other Fire-King patterns. The platter and round vegetable bowl are the most difficult pieces to find. This is one of the decaled patterns that was inclined to grow fainter with use; so keep that in mind.

The Blue Mosaic should be the first snack set that collectors of those items will spot, for an abundance of these are available and surely Florida was a main distribution area for them. We used to see at least one Blue Mosaic snack set every time we went shopping here. The snack tray in this pattern is oval and not rectangular as are most Fire-King lines.

7 ▶	Bowl, 4⅝", dessert	6.00	
8 ▶	Bowl, 6⅝", soup, vegetable	10.00	
5 ▶	Bowl, 8¼", vegetable	15.00	
6 ▶	Creamer	6.00	
10 ▶	Cup, 7½ oz.	4.00	

3 ▶	Plate, 7⅜", salad	6.00	
9 ▶	Plate, 10", dinner	7.00	
4 ▶	Platter, 9" x 12"	15.00	
11 ▶	Saucer, 5¾"	2.00	
1 ▶	Sugar	6.00	
2 ▶	Sugar cover	5.00	
	Tray, 10" x 7½", oval, snack	5.00	

FIRE-KING CHARM, ANCHOR HOCKING GLASS CORPORATION, 1950 – 1954

Colors: Azur-ite, Forest Green, Ivory, Jade-ite, Milk White, pink, and Royal Ruby

Anchor Hocking created Charm from 1950 through 1954. Charm was the original term for the square dishes made in Jade-ite and Azur-ite. These colors were promoted together with their Forest Green and Royal Ruby counterparts; however, the color names of Forest Green and Royal Ruby were used for those squared items instead of the name Charm.

We used to receive numerous letters asking us to list Forest Green and Royal Ruby Charm under Charm instead of the listings under Forest Green and Royal Ruby where they were located. After we surrendered to those wishes, we had gripes about why we didn't list square pieces of Royal Ruby and Forest Green in their listings. It is hard to win every time. When Charm is discussed with Fire-King collectors, red or green does not typically come to mind, Jade-ite and Azure-ite do.

You can only find five different pieces of Royal Ruby Charm. Take note that the large berry bowl has significantly declined in price. An abundance of Internet auctions more than satisfied the current demand, so prices slipped as is typical with more than ample supply.

Jade-ite Charm is one of the hardest Anchor Hocking Jade-ite patterns to accumulate. At present, the platter and dinner plates in Jade-ite are elusive in mint condition. There appears to be an ample supply of Azur-ite except for mint soups, platters, and dinner plates although scratched and mutilated ones do turn up.

		Azur-ite	Forest Green	Jade-ite	Royal Ruby
2 ▶	Bowl, 4¾", dessert	6.00	4.00	18.00	8.00
5 ▶	Bowl, 6", soup	18.00	18.00	42.00	
4 ▶	Bowl, 7⅜", salad	25.00	18.00	50.00	50.00
3 ▶	Creamer	12.00	7.00	22.00	
7 ▶	Cup	4.00	4.00	12.00	6.00
6 ▶	Plate, 6⅝", salad	10.00	8.00	35.00	
10 ▶	Plate, 8⅜", luncheon	14.00	8.00	24.00	10.00
11 ▶	Plate, 9¼", dinner	25.00	22.00	55.00	
9 ▶	Platter, 11" x 8"	28.00	18.00	60.00	
8 ▶	Saucer, 5⅜"	1.50	1.50	5.00	2.50
1 ▶	Sugar	12.00	7.00	22.00	

FIRE-KING FLEURETTE, ANCHOR HOCKING GLASS CORPORATION, 1958 – 1960

Color: white w/decal

Fleurette was first listed in Anchor Hocking's 1959 – 1960 catalog written in April 1958. By the 1960 – 1961 catalog Fleurette seems to have been superseded by Primrose. That should make Fleurette limited to a year of production at most. Finding mint condition Primrose pieces is quite a chore today as the decal wear may have had something to do with dropping the line as quickly as they did. Those decals are washed-out or are very weak on most of the items found today.

Some odd pieces with Fleurette decals have turned up over the years in auctions of former Anchor Hocking employees' estates near Lancaster, Ohio. A Lace Edge candy and Napco vases with Fleurette decals both have been documented. Fleurette is in shorter supply than Primrose which replaced it, but it suffers from a lack of collectors or the price would increase dramatically with the short supply available.

We have only seen the nine ounce Fleurette tumbler, and it is apparently rare.

Most Fire-King sugar lids are interchangeable though they all don't have the same knob design. They are white without decals. Be sure to check these lids while shopping. Sometimes an American Sweetheart lid has been placed on a Fire-King sugar bowl. You get quite a bargain that way, but not such a deal if a Fire-King lid is placed on an American Sweetheart sugar.

3 ▸	Bowl, 4⅝", dessert	2.00
7 ▸	Bowl, 6⅝", soup plate	9.00
	Bowl, 8¼", vegetable	10.00
6 ▸	Creamer	4.00
5 ▸	Cup, 5 oz., snack	2.00
	Cup, 8 oz.	3.00
	Plate, 6¼", bread and butter	5.00
2 ▸	Plate, 7⅜", salad	5.00
	Plate, 9⅛", dinner	3.00
	Platter, 9" x 12"	10.00
	Saucer, 5¾"	.50
1 ▸	Sugar	3.00

	Sugar cover	5.00
	Tumbler, 9 oz., water	125.00
4 ▸	Tray, 11" x 6", snack	3.00

FIRE-KING "GAME BIRD," ANCHOR HOCKING GLASS CORPORATION, 1959

Color: white w/decal

Anchor Hocking had promotional brochures identifying this pattern as "Wild Bird" or "Game Bird." We favored the "Game Bird" designation when we first wrote *Collectible Glassware from the 40s, 50s, 60s...* and those who have followed our footsteps in writing seem to have liked our pick. The following game birds are portrayed on this pattern: Canada goose, ringed-necked pheasant, ruffled grouse, and mallard duck. We only have catalog sheets of mugs, cereals, and ashtrays listed for 1960 – 1961; but, as you can see below, there are many more pieces available than those. The remainder of our listings comes from actual pieces discovered over the years.

We have now found all these wild birds except for three of the juice glasses. We only have found a mallard juice. Note the listing of a nine ounce water tumbler. Up to now, it has only been found with a pheasant, but who knows what is still out there?

That ringed-neck pheasant is the only one you'll find if you are looking for serving pieces. The sugar, creamer, 8¼" vegetable, and platter have appeared only with pheasant decoration. It is possible to gather an entire set of pheasant decorated dinnerware, but no other bird can be collected in an actual set.

Great promotional sales or premiums packed in, or with food, make Missouri and Oklahoma a bird watcher's paradise for "Game Bird." We have encountered dozens of mugs and tumblers on our trips through that area although other items were not as prolific.

We should mention that mugs are microwaveable and first-rate for coffee, tea, or hot chocolate. In fact, mug collecting per se, is catching on, especially in Fire-King circles. You could decorate a whole wall and not use a duplicate mug — actually, maybe a whole room. Obviously they have been very popular as well as durable all these years. We once visited a shop whose outer walls were completely hidden by rows upon rows of different mugs. They even outlined the fence leading up to the shop.

2 ▶	Ashtray, 5¼"	12.00		4 ▶	Plate, 9⅛", dinner	5.00
7 ▶	Bowl, 4⅝", dessert	4.00		6 ▶	Platter, 12" x 9"	65.00
10 ▶	Bowl, 5", soup or cereal	6.00		8 ▶	Sugar	20.00
13 ▶	Bowl, 6⅝", soup	100.00		9 ▶	Sugar cover	5.00
5 ▶	Bowl, 8¼", vegetable	65.00			Tumbler, 5oz., juice	30.00
12 ▶	Creamer	20.00			Tumbler, 9 oz., water	125.00
1 ▶	Mug, 8 oz.	6.00		3 ▶	Tumbler, 11 oz., iced tea	9.00
11 ▶	Plate, 6¼", bread & butter	6.00				

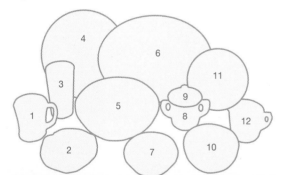

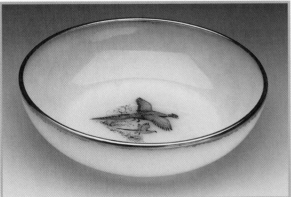

FIRE-KING GRAY LAUREL, ANCHOR HOCKING GLASS CORPORATION, 1952 – 1963

Gray Laurel is listed in a 1953 Anchor Hocking catalog and never again. We purchased our first group of Gray Laurel in a Phoenix antique mall years ago. It was all labeled and like new, so we acquired it for future use. In fact, most of the items photographed here are from that long ago purchase. Gray has turned out to be scarce when compared to the quantity of Peach Lustre (laurel leaf design) found.

The 11" serving plate and 8¼" vegetable bowl are found infrequently, especially with original, excellent color. That is the major shortcoming for Gray Laurel or Peach Lustre — the color wears off and shows white streaks. (A piece of Peach Lustre is in the picture to show the pattern is the same as Gray Laurel.) Dishwashers and abrasive detergents are lethal on both colors as well as many other glassware patterns of this era. With the introduction of the dishwasher, glass companies suddenly had to learn to combat the abusive heat and scouring powders thrust upon their dishes. We've been told that there was much frantic testing of color during this time to get it to stay on the glassware.

Three sizes of tumblers were made to go with Gray Laurel. These tumblers are "complementary decorated" with gray and maroon bands. There is a five ounce juice, nine ounce water, and a 13 ounce iced tea. To date, we have not found any of these to picture.

Crystal stemware, like the Early American Line shown under "Bubble," was also decorated with a laurel cutting and used with this pattern.

9 ▸	Bowl, 4⅞", dessert	5.00		1 ▸	Plate, 7⅜", salad	6.00
4 ▸	Bowl, 7⅝", soup plate	12.00		3 ▸	Plate, 9⅛", dinner	7.00
5 ▸	Bowl, 8¼", vegetable	20.00		2 ▸	Plate, 11", serving	14.00
10 ▸	Creamer, ftd.	4.00		7 ▸	Saucer, 5¾"	2.00
6 ▸	Cup, 8 oz.	3.00		8 ▸	Sugar, ftd.	4.00

FIRE-KING HONEYSUCKLE, ANCHOR HOCKING GLASS CORPORATION, 1959 – 1960

Colors: white w/decal, crystal w/decal

Honeysuckle emerged in the spring 1959 Anchor-Hocking catalog for 1960 – 1961. As with Fleurette, Honeysuckle seems to have been superseded by Primrose almost immediately after its introduction. Honeysuckle survives in smaller quantities than Primrose and more collectors search for it than they do Fleurette. The seemingly non-existent 6¼" bread and butter plate is one item that has been found in significant numbers of late resulting in its value dropping to a shadow of its former price. However, don't pass by any Honeysuckle mugs. They are selling in the $40.00 to $50.00 range if you can unearth one.

Be cautious regarding washed-out or missing designs on all decaled lines. There were three sizes of tumblers listed for Honeysuckle, but we have located only two. These are pictured below. These tumblers are crystal with Honeysuckle decoration and not white as other pieces.

As with most of Anchor-Hocking's decaled lines, the platter and round vegetable bowl are difficult to locate. They were sold only with the largest sized sets; and evidently, smaller sized sets sold much better.

	Item	Price
4 ▸	Bowl, 4⅝", dessert	4.00
3 ▸	Bowl, 6⅝", soup plate	9.00
	Bowl, 8¼", vegetable	14.00
12 ▸	Creamer	5.00
9 ▸	Cup, 8 oz.	4.00
7 ▸	Mug	50.00
	Plate, 6¼", bread and butter	4.00
13 ▸	Plate, 7⅜", salad	4.00
6 ▸	Plate, 9⅛", dinner	5.00
5 ▸	Platter, 9" x 12"	12.00
8 ▸	Saucer, 5¾"	1.50
10 ▸	Sugar	5.00
11 ▸	Sugar cover	5.00
1 ▸	Tumbler, 5 oz., juice	15.00
	Tumbler, 9 oz., water	15.00
2 ▸	Tumbler, 12 oz., iced tea	18.00

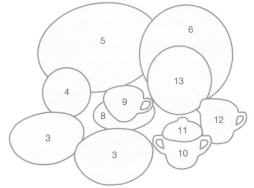

FIRE-KING "JANE RAY," ANCHOR HOCKING GLASS CORPORATION, 1945 – 1963

Colors: Ivory, Jade-ite, Peach Lustre, crystal, amber, white, and white trimmed in gold

An Anchor Hocking 1947 chain store catalog of glassware lists this as "Jade-ite Heat Proof Tableware," which is the only bona fide name known. "Jane Ray" is the name collectors have dubbed this ribbed Jade-ite pattern, and in fact, it has almost become synonymous for Anchor-Hocking's Jade-ite. "Jane Ray" was listed in catalogs for nearly 20 years. Accessibility, as with blue "Bubble" and green Block, puts "Jane Ray" in front of many new collectors. If you like this pattern, start collecting now and buy the harder-to-find pieces when you have a chance to do so.

Today, soup, cereal, and vegetable bowls are selling 20% to 25% less than they were when we wrote this book two years ago. Those pieces along with the demitasse cup and saucer have been uncovered in unbelievable quantities through the Internet. Not only that, but the prevalence of jade glassware in the form of substantial reproduction marketing has caused collectors to spread their buying in other jade areas even though "Jane Ray" has not been remade in any form.

The 9" flanged soup actually sells in the $225.00 range, yet we have seen them priced for double and even triple that. They are rare, but dealers need to be aware that customers who watch prices will see an exorbitant price on wares and leave the booth thinking everything in there is priced "too high to buy." How do we know this? They come to our booth and tell us exactly that. "When I saw that, I knew I couldn't afford anything in that booth," they'll say.

Notice that "Jane Ray" has other colors than Jade-ite. There are demitasse cups and saucers in crystal, Peach Lustre, and amber. "Jane Ray" Jade-ite demitasse sets were the most difficult pieces to find until flanged soups were discovered.

		Ivory	Jade-ite	Vitrock
8 ▸	Bowl, 4⅞", dessert	20.00	8.00	9.00
15 ▸	Bowl, 5⅞", oatmeal		14.00	15.00
1 ▸	Bowl, 7⅝", soup plate		18.00	
12 ▸	Bowl, 8¼", vegetable		20.00	20.00
	Bowl, 9", flat soup		200.00	
6 ▸	Cup	16.00	5.00	6.00
13 ▸	*Cup, demitasse		28.00	10.00
9 ▸	Creamer		9.00	
2 ▸	Plate, 6¼"		50.00	
11 ▸	Plate, 7¾", salad		9.00	
3 ▸	Plate, 9⅛", dinner	24.00	9.00	15.00
10 ▸	Platter, 9" x 12"		18.00	
7 ▸	Saucer	6.00	1.00	2.00
14 ▸	**Saucer, demitasse		30.00	10.00
5 ▸	Sugar		8.00	
4 ▸	Sugar cover		18.00	

*Peach Lustre $8.00
**Peach Lustre $12.00

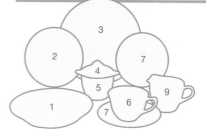

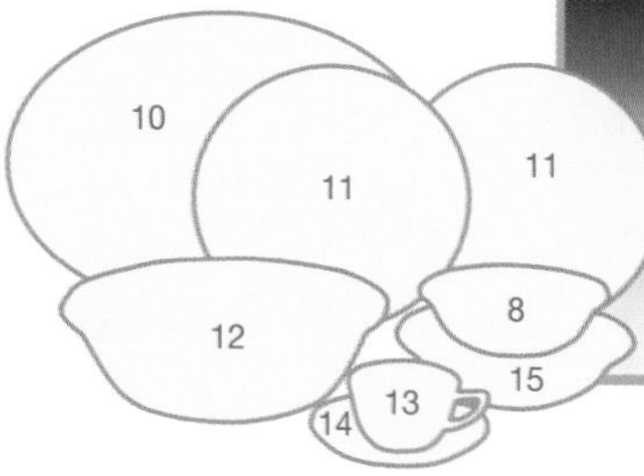

FIRE-KING MEADOW GREEN, ANCHOR HOCKING GLASS CORPORATION, 1967 – 1977

Color: white w/decal

Meadow Green could become more admired as some collectors begin buying the avocado colored wares of the late 60s and 70s. It was introduced by Anchor Hocking as a line of glassware and ovenware to synchronize with the color schemes of Avocado and Harvest Gold. As with Indiana's Daisy, this color was made purposely to complement kitchens of the day. Collectors are beginning to become aware of it, and we keep hearing that green and gold are returning as decorator colors. As with Blue Mosaic, cups, creamers, and sugars have solid colors. However, in this case, two distinctive hues of green can be found on the exteriors which do not have the floral decal. The lid for the sugar is white and also without a decal as is normal for Anchor-Hocking's lids.

Meadow Green is still reasonably priced for glassware 40 years in age. We have been informed that Meadow Green can be used in both ovens and microwaves. There are quite a few listings for this on Internet auctions and it sells inexpensively when it sells, but postage costs for this heavier pattern seem to keep bidding very low.

Casseroles came with non-decaled crystal or white lids. Crystal seems to be preferred by cooks since you can check on what's cooking without lifting the lid. However a premium of a couple of dollars is being sought for white lids since they are more difficult to find. Add that to the price listed below since prices are for items with clear lids.

11 ▸	Bowl, 4⅝", dessert	2.00		Casserole, 3 qt., w/cover	10.00
10 ▸	Bowl, 5", cereal	3.00	4 ▸	Creamer	3.00
9 ▸	Bowl, 6⅝", soup	5.00	7 ▸	Cup	2.50
	Bowl, 8¼", vegetable	10.00		Custard, 6 oz.	1.50
	Bowl, 1½ qt., mixing	6.00		Loaf pan, 5" x 9"	6.00
	Bowl, 2 qt., mixing	8.00	12 ▸	Mug, 9 oz.	2.00
	Bowl, 2½ qt., mixing	10.00	6 ▸	Plate, 7⅜", salad	2.00
	Cake dish, 8", square	5.00	3 ▸	Plate, 10", dinner	3.00
	Cake dish, 9", round	6.00	5 ▸	Platter, 12" x 9"	6.00
	Casserole, 12 oz., hndl.	3.00	8 ▸	Saucer	.50
	Casserole, 1 qt., w/cover	6.00	1 ▸	Sugar	5.00
	Casserole, 1½ qt., w/cover	7.00	2 ▸	Sugar lid	1.00
	Casserole, 1½ qt., oval, w/cover	7.00		Utility dish, 1½ qt.	5.00
	Casserole, 2 qt., w/cover	8.00		Utility dish, 2 qt.	6.00

FIRE-KING PEACH LUSTRE, "LAUREL," ANCHOR HOCKING GLASS CORPORATION, 1952 – 1963

Peach Lustre was proclaimed the "The New Sensation" in Anchor Hocking's 1952 catalog. This laurel leaf design was also made in another color (see Gray Laurel page 74). The laurel design was incorporated in the name of that pattern, but not so with Peach Lustre. Anchor Hocking used the Peach Lustre name to refer to color only in other patterns, so don't be surprised or confused by that cross reference. For example, "Jane Ray" demitasse sets can be found in Peach Lustre. Twelve years of production of Peach Lustre should have made a rather large collecting resource, and it would have, had the color held consistently.

Sadly, this color was not too long-lasting. Prices listed below are for pieces with excellent color with no wear whatsoever. The one major failing to collecting Peach Lustre is color decline. Dishwashers and harsh detergents were lethal on the glaze. Wear creates white streaks on the surface. Understand that worn or rubbed pieces will be hard to sell for any price. Seeing as there is so much still around, collectors can afford to be choosy about what they buy in Peach Lustre.

The 11" serving plate ceased to be produced on August 25, 1960. It is the most difficult piece to acquire, particularly with good color. It's a great size serving dish, and was evidently well utilized if the ones we see today are any indication.

Crystal stemware like that shown under "Bubble" was also engraved with a laurel cutting to go with all laurel patterns.

3 ▸	Bowl, 4⅞", dessert	3.00		6 ▸	Plate, 9⅛", dinner	6.00
	Bowl, 7⅝", soup plate	9.00			Plate, 11", serving	10.00
	Bowl, 8¼", vegetable	9.00		5 ▸	Saucer, 5¾"	1.00
1 ▸	Creamer, ftd.	3.00		2 ▸	Sugar, ftd.	3.00
4 ▸	Cup, 8 oz.	3.00				
	Plate, 7⅜", salad	7.00				

78

FIRE-KING PRIMROSE, ANCHOR HOCKING GLASS CORPORATION, 1960 – 1962

Color: white w/decal

Primrose was the first Anchor Hocking decaled pattern to couple dinnerware and ovenware in one design. Primrose was deliberately created with pieces intended for either task. This combined purpose seemed to make Fleurette and Honeysuckle obsolete and they were quickly discontinued with the introduction of Primrose.

Starting with Primrose, many of Anchor Hocking's patterns produced during this era were introduced as dinnerware lines, although they were embossed "ovenware" on the back to inform consumers that they were "heat-proof" and could be "prewarmed" in the oven. No ovenware was proposed for use on the stovetop, but most "ovenware" patterns can be used in the microwave with caution so collectors tell us.

Primrose was only shown in the 1960 – 1962 catalogs. Primrose's apparent shortages have been alleviated by Internet sales and auctions. All tumblers, along with the lidded ovenware items, are not as arduous to find in this pattern as was once believed. The 11 ounce white tumblers are the only Fire-King ones known besides those of the "Game Bird," but fears of shortages for them have been put to rest. However, the five ounce juice is harder to obtain and the crystal Primrose tumblers (two sizes) which were packed in boxed sets are not showing up very often. Many Primrose sets have been gathered without finding crystal tumblers of either size.

All Primrose oven covers are clear crystal Fire-King. White lids were not made until later patterns were introduced. All pieces of ovenware were guaranteed against oven breakage for two years. Dealers would exchange a new item for any broken pieces.

The deep loaf pan was sold as a baking pan by adding a crystal glass cover. Crystal glass lids are harder to find than their respective pans.

Primrose has some rarely seen pieces, but occasionally a few of them still surface. Check our *Anchor Hocking's Fire-King & More* book for listings on these pieces including gravy boats, shakers, vases, and even an egg plate.

	Item	Price		Item	Price		Item	Price
15 ▸	Bowl, 4⅝", dessert	3.00	9 ▸	Creamer	5.00	6 ▸	Saucer, 5¾"	1.00
	Bowl, 6⅝", soup plate	6.00	12 ▸	Cup, 5 oz., snack	2.00	7 ▸	Sugar	4.00
10 ▸	Bowl, 8¼", vegetable	11.00	5 ▸	Cup, 8 oz.	2.00	8 ▸	Sugar cover	5.00
	Cake pan, 8", round	10.00	14 ▸	Custard, 6 oz., low or dessert	3.00	11 ▸	Tray, 11" x 6", rectangular, snack	4.00
	Cake pan, 8", square	10.00		Pan, 5" x 9", baking, w/cover	15.00			
	Casserole, pt., knob cover	7.00		Pan, 5" x 9", deep loaf	12.00		Tumbler, 5 oz., juice (crystal)	50.00
	Casserole, ½ qt., oval, au gratin cover	10.00		Pan, 6½" x 10½", utility baking	10.00	2 ▸	Tumbler, 5 oz. (white)	18.00
				Pan, 8" x 12½", utility baking	35.00	16 ▸	Tumbler, 10 oz., water (crystal)	50.00
	Casserole, 1 qt., knob cover	10.00	3 ▸	Plate, 7⅜", salad	4.00	1 ▸	Tumbler, 11 oz. (white)	15.00
4 ▸	Casserole, 1½ qt., knob cover	12.00	13 ▸	Plate, 9⅛", dinner	5.00			
	Casserole, 2 qt., knob cover	12.00	17 ▸	Platter, 9" x 12"	12.00			

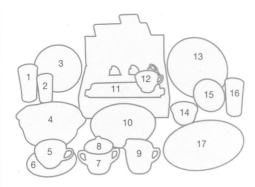

FIRE-KING RESTAURANT WARE, ANCHOR HOCKING GLASS CORPORATION, 1948–1967

Colors: Jade-ite and Milk White

Anchor Hocking's long running Restaurant Ware line is one of the most sought Jade-ite patterns, possibly surpassing "Jane Ray" in admirers. If things continue as they are, it will clearly overtake "Jane Ray's" ranking as #1 in the near future. Sadly, there are newly made pieces having been manufactured in China that are similar in shape to this pattern that were being retailed in department and decorator stores. Those imported items seem to have practically disappeared from those original markets, and are now being offered on secondary markets as genuine, original Jade-ite. Most original Hocking Restaurant Ware is marked Fire-King but the newly made is not marked in any way except for an occasional "Made in China" label which quickly disappears when purchased. The newer items are not as heavy or thick and have a very slick finish on the surface. They also are a slightly different hue from the original.

Restaurant Ware is functional for microwave ovens according to collectors who use theirs daily. Remember to test any dish in the microwave for just a little time to see if it gets hot. It should not get too hot to touch.

You can see a catalog sheet to the right that will show you the differences in the three sizes of Restaurant Ware cups and the mug.

Incidentally, white Restaurant Ware (like Jade-ite, only white) is being found in short supply and is spawning some serious new collector interest both here and in Japan.

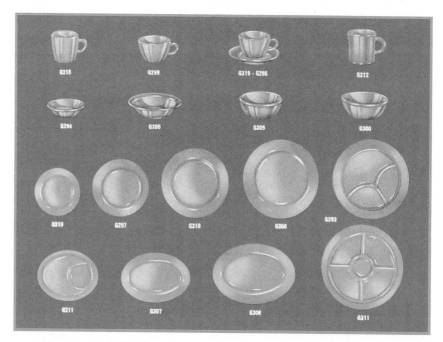

		Jadite White
15 ▸	Bowl, 4¾", fruit, G294	9.00
14 ▸	Bowl, 5", chili	9.00
	Bowl, 5", handled	400.00
	Bowl, 9¼", flat soup	60.00
16 ▸	Bowl, 8 oz., flanged rim, cereal, G305	20.00
13 ▸	Bowl, 10 oz., deep, G309	20.00
12 ▸	Bowl, 15 oz., deep, G300	20.00
	Cup, demitasse	30.00
5 ▸	Cup, 6 oz., straight, G215	12.00
8 ▸	Cup, 7 oz., extra heavy, G299	17.00
	Cup, 7 oz., narrow rim, G319	15.00
	Cup, 7 oz., tapered	25.00
3 ▸	*Gravy boat	300.00
1 ▸	Mug, coffee, 7 oz., G212	30.00
	Mug, 8 oz.	12.00

		Jadite White
	Mug, 6 oz., slim	25.00
	Pitcher, ball jug	495.00
11 ▸	Plate, 5½", bread/butter, G315	12.00
10 ▸	Plate, 6¾", pie or salad, G297	10.00
	Plate, 8⅞", oval, non-partitioned	65.00
	Plate, 8⅞", oval, partitioned, G211	60.00
	Plate, 8", luncheon, G316	40.00
6 ▸	Plate, 9⅝", 3-compartment, G292, 2 styles	20.00
	Plate, 9⅝", 5-compartment, G311	30.00
7 ▸	Plate, 9", dinner, G306	20.00
4 ▸	Platter, 9½", oval, G307	38.00
2 ▸	Platter, 11½", oval, G308	38.00
9 ▸	Saucer, 6", G295	8.00
	Saucer, demitasse	30.00
	Saucer, 7½", for handled bowl	150.00

*White, $20.00

FIRE-KING SAPPHIRE BLUE OVEN GLASS, ANCHOR HOCKING GLASS
CORPORATION, 1942 – 1950s

Colors: Sapphire blue, crystal; some Ivory and Jade-ite

Sapphire was Anchor-Hocking's ovenware that was well-known for its durability. Fire-King had a two-year guarantee. All you had to do was take the broken pieces to your local dealer and your piece was replaced at no charge if it failed in use.

No less than two generations used Fire-King Sapphire blue as their ovenware. Our moms and grandmothers baked in Fire-King. Many a tasty pie or bread pudding came from those blue dishes.

When Fire-King is talked about today, it is automatically assumed to mean Jade-ite. It used to be that when Fire-King was mentioned, Sapphire blue oven glass was what immediately came to mind. Collecting practices continually shift.

Sapphire blue remains usable for standard ovens, but it tends to develop heat cracks from sudden temperature changes if used in the microwave. That is the voice of experience speaking. A fellow mentioned to us not long ago that he'd learned that hard lesson also — and was at the show looking to replace his wife's casserole dish that he'd cracked.

Collectors are inclined to favor casseroles with pie plate covers instead of knobbed covers. Cooks prefer the knobbed lids because they are easier to lift when hot than the pie plate style, but there appear to be fewer bottoms available for these.

Nursers (baby bottles) are found in eight and four ounce varieties with the four ounce being more plentiful due to some original cases being unearthed in warehouse years ago. Once in a while, nipple covers have surfaced. These covers are embossed "BINKY'S NIP CAP U.S.A." (and not Fire-King). These are found in crystal also, but it is the blue one that is in demand although prices have slipped with quite a few more having been exposed on the Internet.

The dry cup measure looks like a mug with eight ounce measurements up the side and no spout for pouring. Beware of spouted measuring cups with the spout removed as shown in our photo. Without measurements on the side, you are looking at a mug and not a dry measure. Regular mugs come in two styles: thick and thin. The thin is uncommon; but the mug is one piece that has risen in price the last few years.

The reason the juice saver pie plate is so highly priced (but not as high as it once was) comes from the fact that most were heavily used and are deeply grooved from years of cutting pies in them. To obtain the price below, this pie plate has to be mint. Jade-ite ones are rarely offered for sale, as that price indicates.

You will find plain Ivory and Jade-ite mugs that hold eight ounces, not seven as do unembossed normal ones. The Jade-ite mug with the embossed Fire-King pattern is uncommon. Today, that Jade-ite mug without embossing is almost as costly as embossed ones. The mug with embossing is known as "Philbe." Only Fire-King products have the "Philbe" design.

		Ivory	Sapphire				Ivory	Sapphire
	Baker, 1 pt., 4½" x 5"		8.00	13 ▸	Custard cup or baker, 6 oz.		6.00	5.00
	Baker, 1 pt., round	4.00	8.00		Loaf pan, 9⅛" x 5⅛", deep		15.00	20.00
	Baker, 1 qt., round	6.00	12.00		Mug, coffee, 7 oz., 2 styles		*110.00	35.00
	Baker, 1½ qt., round	6.00	16.00		Nipple cover			120.00
	Baker, 2 qt., round	8.50	16.00	4 ▸	Nurser, 4 oz.			15.00
	Baker, 6 oz., individual	5.00	5.00	5 ▸	Nurser, 8 oz.			28.00
17 ▸	Bowl, 4⅜", individual pie plate		22.00	1 ▸	Percolator top, 2⅛"			3.00
16 ▸	Bowl, 5⅜", cereal or deep dish pie plate	12.00	22.00	8 ▸	Pie plate, 8⅜", 1½" deep			9.00
3 ▸	Bowl, measuring, 16 oz.		25.00	9 ▸	Pie plate, 9⅝", 1½" deep			10.00
	Cake pan (deep), 8¾", no tabs		40.00	10 ▸	Pie plate, 9", 1½" deep		10.00	10.00
	Cake pan, 9"		15.00	11 ▸	Pie plate, 10⅜", juice saver		*225.00	90.00
23 ▸	Casserole, 1 pt., knob handle cover	30.00	12.00	20 ▸	Refrigerator jar & cover, 4½" x 5"		**40.00	15.00
	Casserole, 1 qt., knob handle cover	25.00	16.00	19 ▸	Refrigerator jar & cover, 5⅛" x 9⅛"		**75.00	30.00
22 ▸	Casserole, 1 qt., pie plate cover		16.00		Roaster, 8¾"			40.00
21 ▸	Casserole, 1½ qt., knob handle cover	20.00	20.00	27 ▸	Roaster, 10⅜"			55.00
	Casserole, 1½ qt., pie plate cover		20.00	2 ▸	Skillet, 7" x 4⅝", handle			1,000.00
	Casserole, 2 qt., knob handle cover	25.00	20.00	14 ▸	Table server, tab handles (hot plate)		18.00	16.00
26 ▸	Casserole, 2 qt., pie plate cover		22.00	18 ▸	Utility bowl, 6⅞", 1 qt.			20.00
	Casserole, individual, 10 oz., 4¾"		10.00		Utility bowl, 8⅜", 1½ qt.			25.00
6 ▸	Cup, 8 oz., measuring, 1 spout		25.00	28 ▸	Utility bowl, 10⅛"			28.00
	Cup, 8 oz., dry measure, no spout		995.00		Utility pan, 8⅛" x 12½", 2 qt.			150.00
7 ▸	Cup, 8 oz., measuring, 3 spout		22.00	15 ▸	Utility pan, 10½" x 2" deep		18.00	25.00
12 ▸	Custard cup or baker, 5 oz.	10.00	5.00					

*Jade-ite w/embossed design (not Ivory)
**Jade-ite (not Ivory)

FIRE-KING "SHELL," ANCHOR HOCKING GLASS CORPORATION, 1965 – 1976

Colors: white, white trimmed in gold, Jade-ite, and Lustre Shell

Anchor-Hocking's "Shell" pattern name came about from the Golden "Shell" pattern (milk white with a 22K gold trim) and Lustre "Shell" which was a re-introduction of the old Peach Lustre color. Jade-ite "Shell" was never really named that but was illustrated in one Anchor Hocking catalog as having "English Regency" styling. Consequently, some collectors, mystifying things further, are now referring to it as "Regency Shell." Realize that "Regency Shell" and "Jade-ite Shell" are two names for the same product.

The major consternation for new collectors is differentiating between "Shell" and "Swirl" patterns in Fire-King. "Shell" patterns have scalloped edges on flat pieces while the "Swirl" patterns (pages 85 – 87) do not. Creamers and sugars in "Shell" are footed while "Swirl" creamers and sugars are flat except for the later made white ones. Those are footed but shaped differently, as can be seen on the bottom of page 87.

Lustre "Shell" was first promoted in 1966 and continued in catalogs until 1976. This Lustre "Shell" was the same color used for Peach Lustre (Peach Laurel), introduced in 1952 and discontinued in 1963. As far as we know, there was a demand for Anchor Hocking to remake this color; however it suffered the same deterioration of its predecessor. Lustre "Shell" color is found only on the exterior of some pieces leaving us to believe that Hocking was extremely aware of the difficulty.

A demitasse cup and saucer were added to the Lustre "Shell" line in 1972. As with other Fire-King patterns, demitasse saucers are harder to find than cups.

You may find pieces of Golden "Shell" painted with designs or advertisements. A popular decoration is of the 1964 New York World's Fair, though other artists' (and non artists') works are encountered. Some are well done and suitable for hanging in the house; others might add some color to the garage or local landfill.

		Golden	Jade-ite	Lustre
	Bowl, 4¾", dessert	3.00	11.00	3.00
	Bowl, 6⅜", cereal	8.00	16.00	8.00
	Bowl, 7⅝", soup plate	9.00	30.00	10.00
	Bowl, 8½", vegetable	7.00	28.00	15.00
	Creamer, ftd.	3.00	20.00	8.00
1 ▸	Cup, 8 oz.	3.00	10.00	4.00
	Cup, 3¼ oz., demitasse	6.00		6.00
	Saucer, 4¾", demitasse	6.00		6.00
	Plate, 7¼", salad	3.00	15.00	3.00
3 ▸	Plate, 10", dinner	4.00	20.00	6.00
	Platter, 9½" x 13"	7.00	75.00	
2 ▸	Saucer, 5¾"	.50	4.00	2.00
	Sugar, ftd.	3.00	20.00	8.00
	Sugar cover	3.00	55.00	5.00
	Tidbit, 3-tier			25.00

FIRE-KING "SWIRL," ANCHOR HOCKING GLASS CORPORATION, 1950s

Colors: Azur-ite, Ivory, Ivory trimmed in gold or red, white or white trimmed in gold, Jade-ite, and Pink

Azur-ite, light blue "Swirl," was first advertised in 1950. It was followed by Sunrise (factory name of red-trimmed Ivory). Actually, if you find Sunrise pieces with original labels, they will read Ivory and not Sunrise. Color names regularly took priority over pattern names at Anchor Hocking. Ivory "Swirl" was recorded in 1953; Golden Anniversary was launched in 1955 by adding 22K gold trim to Ivory "Swirl." Later in the 1950s, Anchorwhite replaced Ivory and Ivory was discontinued. In the latter 1950s, a gold border was added to Anchorwhite, but labels on this say "22K." Pink "Swirl" was introduced in 1956 as Pink. A "Wrought Iron" (name promoted in Anchor-Hocking catalog) pitcher and tumblers (6, 11, 15, 19, and 22 ounce) were made to complement the Pink "Swirl."

The Ivory is a beige tint as opposed to the flatter white of Anchorwhite. They are sometimes confused when shopping by flashlight at early morning flea markets, but should create little problem in normal light. Both gold trimmed patterns were heavily marketed and are readily available should you be interested in either. Watch for worn gold edges, since most collectors avoid those pieces for collections. If you are buying these to use, pieces with worn gold edges definitely will be bargain priced and usually less expensive than newly made glassware.

		Anchorwhite Ivory	Azur-ite	Golden Anniversary	Jade-ite	Pink	Sunrise
1 ▸	Bowl, 4⅞", fruit or dessert	5.00	7.00	2.00		6.00	4.00
9 ▸	Bowl, 5⅞", cereal	20.00	16.00				15.00
	Bowl, 7", mixing		175.00				
2 ▸	Bowl, 7¼", vegetable					35.00	
8 ▸	Bowl, 7⅝", soup plate	8.00	14.00	6.00		18.00	14.00
14 ▸	Bowl, 8¼", vegetable	16.00	22.00	8.00		22.00	16.00
	Bowl, 9¼", flanged soup	100.00	150.00				
10 ▸	Creamer, flat	6.00	8.00			8.50	8.00
	Creamer, ftd.	2.00		2.00			
6 ▸	Cup, 8 oz.	6.00	6.00	2.00	30.00	6.00	5.00
18 ▸	Pitcher, 80 oz.					25.00	
3 ▸	Plate, 7⅜", salad	6.00	8.00	4.00		7.00	6.00
4 ▸	Plate, 9⅛", dinner	8.00	9.00	5.00	55.00	8.00	8.00
13 ▸	Plate, 11", serving					20.00	
5 ▸	Platter, 12" x 9"	16.00	18.00	9.00	300.00		15.00
7 ▸	Saucer, 5¾"	2.00	2.00	.50	18.00	2.00	2.00
12 ▸	Sugar lid, for flat sugar	5.00	10.00			7.00	8.00
11 ▸	Sugar, flat, tab handles	8.00	8.00			6.00	8.00
19 ▸	Sugar, ftd., open handles	2.00		2.00			
15 ▸	Tumbler, 5 oz., juice					6.00	
16 ▸	Tumbler, 9 oz., water					8.00	
17 ▸	Tumbler, 12 oz., iced tea					15.00	

FIRE-KING TURQUOISE BLUE, ANCHOR HOCKING GLASS CORPORATION, 1957 – 1958

Color: Turquoise Blue

Turquoise Blue was listed by Anchor Hocking as dinnerware, but pieces are embossed ovenware on the reverse side except the egg plate, which is not marked at all. Evidently, the ribbed design on the bottom did not allow for a Fire-King logo. Many of Anchor Hocking's late 50s and 60s dinnerware lines are marked ovenware. This advised the consumer that the item could be pre-warmed in the oven before using. Turquoise Blue has become more collectible than any blue colored ware of this time.

Convenience of finding basic pieces lured collectors down an avenue they thought would be simple, but rarely has the trip been straightforward. Just when prices were slowly sinking in the States, along came Japanese collectors buying it on the Internet. You really have to value a pattern to pay as much for postage as they do to have it shipped overseas.

Simplicity in finding cups, saucers, 9" dinner plates, creamers, and sugars is enticing for those starting to collect Turquoise Blue. Small berry bowls are the next basic piece to locate. Although the 9" plate with cup indent is not as profuse as the dinner plate, it does not command the price of the dinner since many collectors do not buy the snack sets...yet. Snack sets often have gold trim and a good dishwasher with lemon based soap will eliminate it if the gold bothers you.

We used Turquoise Blue as our everyday dishes during the years my sons were becoming teenagers. From that experience we can tell you that 10" serving plates are rarely found and the 6⅛" plate may even be harder to locate. Many collectors are searching for one of either size. The traditional 9" dinner with its upturned edge does not make a satisfactory sized plate to feed teenage boys, but they did like the 8" vegetable bowls for cereal and soup. After selling that set and buying another for our everyday dishes, our younger son has decided he'd now like us to find him a set. Of course, most of what we sold has doubled in price and plates and mugs have tripled. This is nostalgia in fond childhood memories in action.

The batter bowl is rarely seen except in Illinois where it must have been a promotional item; and Internet auctions have slowed their upward prices for now. There are two dissimilar mixing bowl sets that go with Turquoise Blue, a three-piece set of "Splash Proof" round bowls and a four-piece set of oval spouted bowls known as "Swedish Modern." Collectors generally refer to them as "tear drop" bowls, today. The one quart round mixing bowl and the three quart tear-shaped mixing bowls are the most difficult sizes to find possibly because they were used the most.

13 ▸	Ashtray, 3½"	8.00
14 ▸	Ashtray, 4⅝"	10.00
15 ▸	Ashtray, 5¾"	12.00
	Batter bowl, w/spout	295.00
20 ▸	Bowl, 4½", berry	10.00
19 ▸	Bowl, 5", cereal	15.00
4 ▸	Bowl, 6⅝", soup/salad	22.00
12 ▸	Bowl, 8", vegetable	20.00
5 ▸	Bowl, tear drop, mixing, 1 pt.	30.00
6 ▸	Bowl, tear drop, mixing, 1 qt.	35.00
7 ▸	Bowl, tear drop, mixing, 2 qt.	40.00
8 ▸	Bowl, tear drop, mixing, 3 qt.	70.00
25 ▸	Bowl, round, mixing, 1 qt.	20.00
26 ▸	Bowl, round, mixing, 2 qt.	25.00
27 ▸	Bowl, round, mixing, 3 qt.	28.00
16 ▸	Creamer	8.00
2 ▸	Cup	5.00
10 ▸	Egg plate, 9¾"	20.00
9 ▸	Mug, 8 oz.	30.00
21 ▸	Plate, 6⅛"	18.00
22 ▸	Plate, 7¼"	15.00

1 ▸	Plate, 9"	12.00
17 ▸	Plate, 9", w/cup indent	5.00
23 ▸	Plate, 10"	30.00
11 ▸	Relish, 3-part, 11⅛"	12.00
3 ▸	Saucer	1.50
18 ▸	Sugar	8.00

FIRE-KING WHEAT, ANCHOR HOCKING GLASS CORPORATION, 1962 – late 1960s

Anchor Hocking's Wheat production commenced in 1962, and signified the downfall of Primrose. This was one of their most bountiful lines in both dinnerware and ovenware. Like the 1940s Sapphire blue Fire-King before it, everyone has seen the Wheat pattern of the 1960s and there is no difficulty in recognizing those bright wheat sheaves.

Many glass and pottery companies also produced wheat patterns during this period. It was a popular motif and there are many variations found. You will find an assortment of crystal glasses with wheat cuttings that were made to go with all the wheat patterns available. Not everyone cares for Wheat, but there are enough that remember it to keep the collecting spark alive. Wheat is relatively inexpensive, so you can buy extra pieces if the occasion arises. Mugs, 5" chili bowls, and the one-handled French casserole are the only pieces that are difficult to locate. The other detriment is wear on the wheat decals which is not as bad as those of the earlier decaled patterns.

Ovenware lids generate dilemmas today because casserole sizes of yesteryear do not accept many modern size lids. Replacement lids for the older casseroles are usually priced up to half of the price of the entire dish. Since lids were often broken in use, they are valuable possessions now; so treat them gently.

Both oval and round 1½ quart casseroles and the 10½" baking pan were used with candle warmers. These candle warmer servers were brass finished with walnut handles plus the candle which set underneath the dish. Evidently, many were never used as they are being found with the original candles intact although not in Florida. The heat does strange things with candles here. Replacement candles can be found at most kitchenware/hardware stores should you need one. Several readers say that they still make use of these for keeping food warm for parties.

10 ▸	Bowl, 4⅝", dessert	2.50
	Bowl, 5", chili	28.00
9 ▸	Bowl, 6⅝", soup plate	6.00
2 ▸	Bowl, 8¼", vegetable	10.00
	Cake pan, 8", round	10.00
	Cake pan, 8", square	9.00
1 ▸	Casserole, 12 oz. handled	95.00
	Casserole, 1 pt., knob cover	8.00
	Casserole, 1 qt., knob cover	10.00
	Casserole, 1½ qt., knob cover	10.00
	Casserole, 1½ qt., oval, au gratin cover	12.00
	Casserole, 2 qt., knob cover	13.00
	Casserole, 2 qt., round, au gratin cover	13.00
5 ▸	Creamer	3.00
	Cup, 5 oz., snack	3.00
6 ▸	Cup, 8 oz.	3.00
	Custard, 6 oz., low or dessert	2.00
	Mug	50.00

	Pan, 5" x 9", baking, w/cover	15.00
	Pan, 5" x 9", deep loaf	12.00
	Pan, 6½" x 10½" x 1½", utility baking	12.00
	Pan, 8" x 12½" x 2", utility baking	22.00
11 ▸	Plate, 7⅜", salad	6.00
12 ▸	Plate, 10", dinner	4.00
8 ▸	Platter, 9" x 12"	13.00
7 ▸	Saucer, 5¾"	1.00
4 ▸	Sugar	3.00
3 ▸	Sugar cover	5.00
	Tray, 11" x 6", rectangular, snack	3.00
	Tumbler, 10 oz.	3.00

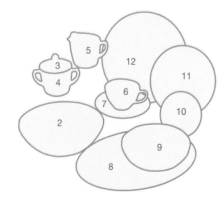

FLORAGOLD, "LOUISA," JEANNETTE GLASS COMPANY, 1950s

Colors: Iridescent, some Shell Pink, ice blue, and crystal

Floragold is sometimes referred to as "Louisa" by older collectors because it was patterned after an older carnival glass design. In fact, the carnival glass rose bowl from "Louisa" is gathered by Floragold collectors as a vase for their pattern. Ultimately the correct name, Floragold, was found and all but the earliest collectors label it correctly now.

Two years have passed since we wrote the story of the discovery of six Floragold wines. No one has come forth to tell us they have found water goblets or the decanter which were ostensibly with these wines when they were first purchased in Texas. We do know that the placement of one of the wines on the cover caused quite a stir in the collecting field. At last report, some of these wines sold on an Internet auction and through an Internet web site in the $1,300.00 range. Now, has anyone found those water goblets?

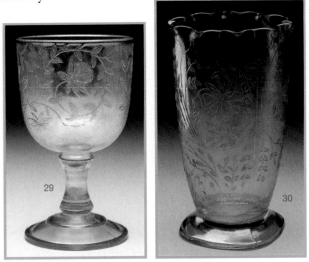

Ruffled bowls have finally begun to sell, albeit slowly and at prices very easy on the pocketbook. They are 50 years old now. Mint condition shaker tops are difficult to get. They were made of white or brown plastic, and over tightening them cracked the tops. They sell around $15.00 each, which makes the tops more precious than the shakers themselves. Remember that when you find shakers priced cheaply, but topless.

Cups outnumber all pieces found today because they were sold in sets of eight or 12 as part of eggnog sets. Either the pitcher or the large bowl accompanied these cups. That 5¼" saucer (no cup ring) is the same as the sherbet plate; there is no cup ringed saucer in Floragold. There are thousands of cups looking for saucers due to those past distribution ideas.

Large comports were made in ice blue, crystal, red-yellow, Shell Pink, and iridized in the late 1950s and into the early 1970s. All colored comports are selling in the $12.00 to $15.00 range except the iridized one which will fetch $25.00 – $30.00 with excellent applied color. These have a tendency to be unevenly sprayed and may have crystal showing. Multitudes of these have been auctioned on the Internet and prices have dropped dramatically from the $75.00 of a few years ago.

The vase was made from a 15 oz. iced tea by ruffling the top edge. One is pictured above.

		Iridescent				Iridescent
14 ▸	Ashtray/coaster, 4"	3.00		18 ▸	Cup	4.00
20 ▸	Bowl, 4½", square	4.00		1 ▸	Pitcher, 64 oz.	20.00
19 ▸	Bowl, 5½", round cereal	28.00			Plate or tray, 13½"	15.00
23 ▸	Bowl, 5½", ruffled fruit	5.00		3 ▸	Plate or tray, 13½", with indent	70.00
21 ▸	Bowl, 8½", square	12.00		27 ▸	Plate, 5¼", sherbet (saucer)	8.00
25 ▸	Bowl, 9½", deep salad	38.00		5 ▸	Plate, 8½", dinner	28.00
26 ▸	Bowl, 9½", ruffled	6.00		28 ▸	Plate, 11¾" (Iris shape)	495.00
24 ▸	Bowl, 12", ruffled large fruit	5.00			Platter, 11¼"	20.00
15 ▸	Butter dish and cover, ¼ lb., oblong	22.00		4 ▸	**Salt and pepper, plastic tops	60.00
16 ▸	Butter dish and cover, round, 6¼", sq. base	30.00		27 ▸	Saucer, 5¼" (no ring)	8.00
	Butter dish bottom	10.00		22 ▸	Sherbet, low, footed	12.00
	Butter dish top	20.00		29 ▸	Stem, 4", wine	1,250.00
	Butter dish and cover, round, 5½", sq. base	1,000.00		10 ▸	Sugar	5.00
13 ▸	Candlesticks, double branch, pr.	35.00		9 ▸	Sugar lid	10.00
6 ▸	Candy dish, 1 handle	9.00			Tidbit, wooden post (usually white)	45.00
11 ▸	Candy or cheese dish and cover, 6¾"	35.00		8 ▸	Tumbler, 10 oz., footed	10.00
17 ▸	*Candy, 5¼" long, 4 feet	7.50		7 ▸	Tumbler, 11 oz., footed	10.00
	Comport, large	35.00		2 ▸	†Tumbler, 15 oz., footed	90.00
	Comport, 5¼", plain top	1,100.00		30 ▸	Vase or celery	495.00
	Comport, 5¼", ruffled top	1,200.00				
12 ▸	Creamer	7.00				

*Shell Pink $20.00   **Perfect Tops   †Crystal $20.00

FOREST GREEN, ANCHOR HOCKING GLASS COMPANY, 1950 – 1967

Color: Forest Green

Forest Green was Anchor Hocking's exclusive term for their dark green pieces; however Forest Green has now become synonymous with any dark green. To be truly Forest Green, Anchor Hocking must have made it. They patented that name.

Forest Green was first used for the square Charm blank, but that glassware became better known as Charm; so we have removed all the Forest Green and Royal Ruby Charm pieces from the listing below. You will now find them priced only under Charm on page 71 to eliminate duplication and confusion.

After we eliminated Charm from our listing, Forest Green becomes pretty much an accessory pattern, albeit a bountiful one. Forest Green can provide all sorts of beverage items, vases, and serving pieces. The Forest Green oval vegetable is scalloped along the edges and has a swirled effect on the sides. These were premium items for a flour company in the South as were the Royal Ruby ones in the Midwest. At one time these were not easily found, but that time has passed with the dawn of the Internet.

Hocking's green "Bubble" was simply called Forest Green when it was introduced. According to Anchor Hocking catalogs, "Bubble" stemware was primarily called Early American line. The other stemware line sold along with Early American was called "Boopie" by an earlier author; but records from Hocking show the name to be Berwick. It has a swirling patterned foot.

Decorated tumblers such as "A Bicycle for Two" will bring a dollar or two more than plain tumblers. However, undecorated tumblers sell faster to collectors, but these remain inexpensive today.

Forest Green was widely distributed as premium items. Hocking must have furnished their products at an extremely attractive price since so many tumblers and vases are found today. In the Kentucky area, tumblers were used as containers for Sealtest brand dairy products, usually cottage cheese. Honey and tea bags were other commodities often found in Anchor Hocking tumblers. Massive quantities of 4" ball-shaped ivy vases testify to successful sales of Citronella candles packaged in those. We have previously pictured a boxed set of "Moskeeto-Lites." Those candles originally sold for $1.19. After using the candles, you had two free vases. There are many Forest Green and Royal Ruby vases in Florida where mosquitoes definitely increased sales.

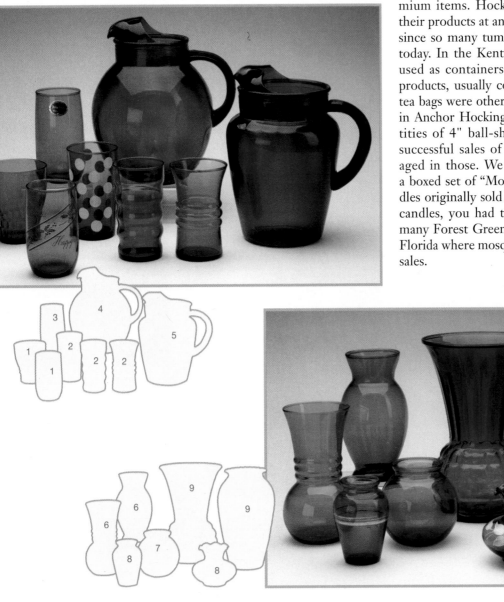

93

FOREST GREEN

14 ▸	Ashtray, 3½", square	3.00
15 ▸	Ashtray, 4⅝", square	4.00
16 ▸	Ashtray, 5¾", square	6.00
	Ashtray, 5¾", hexagonal	6.00
	Batter bowl w/spout	30.00
	Bowl, 4¾", ftd.	4.00
18 ▸	Bowl, 5¼" deep	8.00
	Bowl, 6", mixing	10.00
	Bowl, 7", mixing	14.00
	Bowl, 8", mixing	18.00
17 ▸	Bowl, 8½", oval vegetable	18.00
	Cocktail shaker, w/lid	50.00
13 ▸	Pitcher, 22 oz.	20.00
	Pitcher, 36 oz.	24.00
5 ▸	Pitcher, 80 oz. w/ice lip	28.00
4 ▸	Pitcher, 86 oz., round	28.00
	Plate, 6¾", salad	5.00
	Punch bowl	27.50
	Punch bowl stand	27.50
	Punch cup (round)	2.00
	Saucer, 5⅜"	1.00
19 ▸	Sherbet, flat	6.00
	*Stem, 3½ oz., cocktail	12.00

	*Stem, 4 oz., juice	14.00
	Stem, 4½ oz., cocktail	12.00
	Stem, 5½ oz., juice	12.00
	Stem, 6 oz., sherbet	8.00
	* Stem, 6 oz., sherbet	8.00
	*Stem, 9 oz., goblet	14.00
	Stem, 10¾ oz., goblet	13.00
	*Stem, 14 oz., iced tea	16.00
11 ▸	Tumbler, 5 oz., 3½", several styles	2.00
1 ▸	Tumbler, 7 oz., several styles	3.00
2 ▸	Tumbler, 9 oz., table, several styles	3.00
	Tumbler, 9 oz., fancy	4.00
	Tumbler, 9½ oz., tall	4.00
	Tumbler, 10 oz., 4½", ftd.	5.00
3 ▸	Tumbler, 11 oz., several styles	5.00
	Tumbler, 13 oz., iced tea	6.00
	Tumbler, 14 oz., 5"	6.00
	Tumbler, 15 oz., long boy	10.00
	Tumbler, 15 oz., tall iced tea	10.00
10 ▸	Tumbler, 32 oz, giant iced tea	25.00
8 ▸	Vase, 3½", 3¾"	4.00
7 ▸	Vase, 4", ivy ball	4.00
6 ▸	Vase, 6⅜"	5.00
9 ▸	Vase, 9", several styles	10.00
12 ▸	Water bottle, 32 oz.	60.00

*Berwick

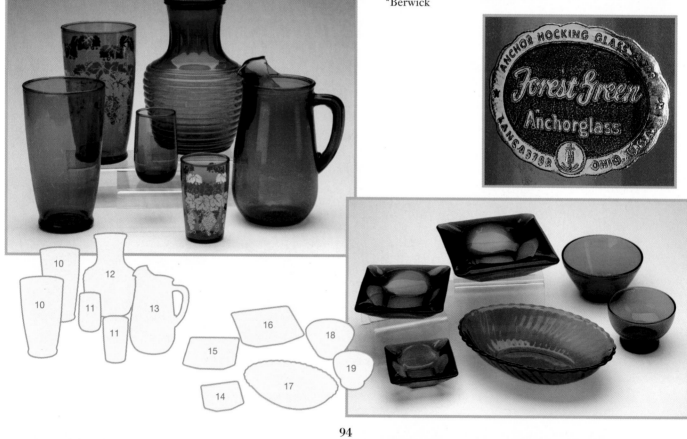

94

"GAY NINETIES," GAY FAD DECORATING COMPANY, 1950S ON HAZEL-ATLAS, FEDERAL AND ANCHOR-HOCKING GLASSWARE

Colors: Crystal satinized with hand-painted decorations

"Gay Nineties" is one of the more popular Gay Fad decorations. We became familiar with their work when we first began work on our *Anchor Hocking's Fire-King & More* book. Their factory site was right across the street from Anchor Hocking's factory in Lancaster, Ohio. Gay Fad decorations can be found on many glass companies glassware, but we recognize their work on both Anchor Hocking and Hazel-Atlas from working on books for each company.

Much of the "Gay Nineties" is found on Hazel-Atlas, but some pieces are Federal or Anchor Hocking with some tumblers possibly Libbey. Most of the pieces show dancing girls with their swirling dresses, but bartenders and piano players are also displayed. We may not have everything listed, so be sure to let us know about other items you find.

There are at least four different decanters; bourbon, gin, rye, and scotch. We have seen rum and white wine in other decorations, but not in "Gay Nineties."

6 ▸	Cocktail shaker, 32 oz.	35.00
3 ▸	Decanter w/stopper	17.50
1 ▸	Mug, 12 oz.	15.00
	Pilsner	15.00
4 ▸	Tumbler, 2 oz., whiskey	6.00
	Tumbler, 5 oz., juice	5.00
	Tumbler, 7 oz., old fashioned	6.00
	Tumbler, 9 oz., water	5.00
2 ▸	Tumbler, 12 oz., ice tea	10.00
5 ▸	Tumbler, 14 oz., double old fashion	10.00

GOLDEN GLORY, FEDERAL GLASS COMPANY, 1959 – 1966; 1978 – 1979

Color: White with 22K gold decorations

Golden Glory is a pattern that is reminiscent of Rodney Dangerfield in not getting much respect from collectors. A few Federal glass enthusiasts are apparently the only ones on the lookout for it. Be aware that 22K gold decorations wear off easily and most detergents will lighten or remove them. You might come across some items that were rarely used or are still boxed. Discovery of mint condition pieces always makes collectors happy and these later patterns lend more possibility for finding unopened boxes with labels attached.

A new find not listed in any Federal catalogs that we own is a mug that has been selling in the $15.00 range. The effective word there is selling — mainly to collectors of mugs. Speaking of catalogs, there are quite a few pages of Federal "Heat Proof" patterns pictured in our new *Florences' Ovenware from the 1920s to the Present*.

We have received several letters from readers reporting crystal tumblers and a water goblet with Golden Glory decorations. We have yet to see either of these, but be cognizant of their existence.

When first marketed in 1959, only 12 pieces of Golden Glory were introduced. Federal reintroduced it in 1978 and added three pieces in the catalog. These pieces included the larger 10" dinner plate, the smaller 6⅛" soup, and the 11¼" round platter. By the way, this later release did not include the oval platter, 8" soup, sugar, creamer, and tumblers which should make those items harder to find. However, according to a passionate collector, the hardest-to-find pieces are the 8½" vegetable bowl, tumblers, and the 7¾" salad plate; so we will take his word on that. We have been unable to acquire the round platter. We did see one, but you could barely see an outline of the pattern on the plate. Golden Glory was used and dishwashers were (and are) hard on gold decorations.

	Item	Price
1 ▸	Bowl, 4⅞", dessert	3.00
	Bowl, 6⅜", soup	6.00
6 ▸	Bowl, 8½", vegetable	7.00
9 ▸	Bowl, 8", rimmed soup	7.00
2 ▸	Creamer	3.00
7 ▸	Cup	2.00
13 ▸	Mug	15.00
12 ▸	Plate, 7¾", salad	2.00
5 ▸	Plate, 9⅛", dinner	3.00
	Plate, 10", dinner	4.00
	Platter, 11¼", round	12.00
4 ▸	Platter, 12", oval	10.00
8 ▸	Saucer	.50
10 ▸	Sugar	2.00
11 ▸	Sugar lid	5.00
	Tumbler, 9 oz., ftd.	10.00
3 ▸	Tumbler, 10 oz., 5"	8.00

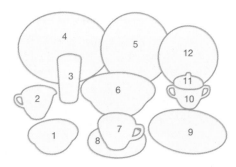

GOLDEN GRAPE DECORATION, #806 BARTLETT-COLLINS COMPANY, 1942 – mid-1950s

Colors: crystal w/silk screen and gold decoration, pink and some flashed colors

Golden Grape is a silk screened pattern achieved by applying finely ground glass particles to form a design. It was well distributed in the Midwest. We see some in Florida, but most found here is well used and usually missing the gold banded decoration. We were able to find more intact items as we shopped on our way to Texas and California last year.

Bartlett-Collins was located in Sapulpa, Oklahoma, and they saturated that area with all types and sizes of tumblers. We only have catalogs showing beverage items; so, there are surely pieces we do not have listed. Possibly tumblers were premiums which accumulated and many were stored without being used. We asked for readers to send us their finds in this pattern and one Texan sent us a fairly comprehensive list of items we were missing in our listing. Thank you!

We will not presume to list pricing for each of these pieces at this time but here they are: mixing bowls with diameters of 4¾", 5¾", 6¾", 8"; covered jar, 7½" w/o lid; three different ice tubs all 4¼" tall with diameters of 5¾", 6¼", 7¼"; sherbet 3½" diameter; candy dish with lid; shot glass, 2⅝"; pitchers, 26 oz., 6¼" high; 38 oz., 7" high; 80 oz. bulbous bottom, 8¼" high.

There is a discrepancy in the listing of measurements sent as all capacities in this book are to the top rim of the glass or tumbler. The capacities sent us are said to be to the gold line and not the top, but here are his heights to help identify them. They are: 3¼", 5 oz.; 3⅝", 5½ oz.; 3⅞", 5 oz.; 3⅞", 8 oz.; 4½", 9 oz.; 4⅝", 11 oz.; 4¾", 8 oz.; 5", 9½ oz.; 5¼", 11 oz.; 5¾", 18 oz.; 5⅞", 16 oz.; 6¼", 15 oz.; 6½, 14 oz.; 6½", 24 oz.

6 ▸	Bowl, 5", mixing	6.00	7 ▸	Shaker, pr.	15.00
	Bowl, 6", mixing	8.00	4 ▸	Stem, water goblet	10.00
	Bowl, 8", mixing	10.00		Sugar	5.00
	Bowl, 10", mixing	12.00		Tumbler, 5 oz., juice	3.00
3 ▸	Creamer	5.00	8 ▸	Tumbler, 9 oz., water	4.00
10 ▸	Ice tub	25.00		Tumbler, 9½ oz., tall	5.00
5 ▸	Pitcher, 32 oz.	15.00	2 ▸	Tumbler, 12 oz.	5.00
	Pitcher, 80 oz.	20.00		Tumbler, 13 oz.	7.00
			1 ▸	Tumbler, 18 oz., jumbo	9.00

GOTHIC, BIG TOP, PEANUT BUTTER GLASS, HAZEL-ATLAS COMPANY, c. 1950s

Colors: crystal, milk glass

The Big Top designation still haunts this pattern since Big Top peanut butter was sold in it for years. We have shown boxed sets in the past identified as Big Top Early American Pattern and Gothic. We now know that Hazel-Atlas produced this ware for Big Top peanut butter and that train loads of this glass were shipped to Lexington to accommodate that product.

We both grew up in Lexington, Kentucky, where a locally owned company (W.T. Young), manufactured Big Top peanut butter and used this glassware to distribute its product. We saw thousands of these containers over the years and never gave much thought to them. Procter and Gamble bought W.T. Young out and turned Big Top into what we know today as Jif.

Things change fast in the collecting world. In the last five years we have not only found a manufacturer and a name for this pattern, but we have produced a book on these collectibles called *Hazel-Atlas Glass Identification and Value Guide*.

The seven ounce juice tumbler is the item most collectors are missing; evidently avid peanut butter fans didn't buy the smaller size. Even so, the price on these juices has slowed and the large supply of sherbets and iced teas has also softened their prices. Collectors have informed us of their struggles to find the luncheon plate, cup, and saucer, however. Obviously, these three pieces were marketed in some other manner and are now in much shorter supply.

The footed tea with the original peanut butter inside was a garage sale find almost 30 years ago. It was exhibited in our Grannie Bear Antique shop for about 15 years. Many customers tried to buy it, but we weathered several serious offers. It wasn't Depression glass — just interesting, a "comment piece" on an area product. We had no idea then that we'd need it for a book later on.

		Crystal
5 ▸	Cup	5.00
1 ▸	Goblet, 5¼", 7 oz., juice	20.00
4 ▸	Plate, 8", luncheon	6.00
6 ▸	Saucer	1.00
3 ▸	Sherbet, 3⅝", 8 oz.	2.50
2 ▸	Tumbler, tea, 5¾", 10 oz.	5.00
7 ▸	Tumbler, 13 oz.	8.00

HARP, JEANNETTE GLASS COMPANY, 1954 – 1957

Colors: crystal, crystal with gold trim, and cake stands in Shell Pink, pink, iridescent white, red, and ice blue

Harp is one of those patterns that even noncollectors seem to notice. It could be the musical design or the abundant cake stands that attract attention, but there is some charisma present. Cake stands themselves have been so highly publicized in recent years for decor use that newly made varieties are emerging in department stores and mail-order catalogs. Harp cake stands are over 50 years old and are still available to any collector desiring one; so why not purchase this older one?

Harp cake stands are suggestive of late 1800s and early 1900s glassware. Most patterns after that time had cake plates instead of a stand.

There is really not enough Harp dishware to supply everyone a set who desires one. Cake stand supplies are holding up to the demand for now, but the availability of cups, saucers, and 7" plates is dwindling. The price has steadied, but if you run into cups and saucers, grab them. Harp was marketed for bridge parties with a cake stand, cups, saucers, and 7" plates. It's an ideal pattern for serving small groups even though bridge parties seem to be a thing of the past.

If gold trim bothers you, an art gum eraser and a little elbow grease will take care of that or you may use a lemon-based soap in your dishwasher. That trim is 22K gold which is a softer material and predisposed to erode with much use. However, we were taken to task by one lady who said we should never tell people that. She'd prefer worn original trim to none at all.

The following 13 types of Harp stands have been documented. Shell Pink, red, transparent pink, blue, and iridescent ones are the most coveted.

1. 2. Crystal with smooth or ruffled rims
3. 4. Either of above with gold trim
5. Iridescent with smooth rim
6. 7. White or Shell Pink (opaque) with beads on rim and foot
8. 9. Ice blue with beads on foot and smooth or ruffled rim

10. Pink transparent
11. Platinum decorated with smooth rim
12. Red
13. Fired-on red

		Crystal
4 ▸	*Ashtray/coaster	4.00
5 ▸	Coaster	3.00
1 ▸	Cup	25.00
3 ▸	**Cake stand, 9"	18.00
8 ▸	Plate, 7"	10.00
2 ▸	Saucer	7.00

		Crystal
7 ▸	†Tray, 2-handled, rectangular	28.00
6 ▸	Vase, 7½"	18.00

*Platinum decoration $8.00
**Ice blue, white, pink, or Shell Pink $45.00
†Shell Pink $60.00

99

HARVEST or "GOLDEN HARVEST," COLONY GLASSWARE

Colors: Iridescent, milk

According to our resources, Harvest was obtained most often through the redemption of S&H green stamps in the Midwestern states. You received a stamp for each $1.00 you spent at grocery or hardware stores and when a book of 300 or so was filled, you could redeem it for merchandise. Those were the days when stores offered you a chance to acquire other items you needed in everyday living.

It seems many S&H redemptions were for milk glass Harvest. Today, you get a little piece of plastic to scan for discounts only in that store. We would not have had a dining table and four chairs (commonly called a card table) when we married in 1964 had it not been for Top Value stamps given out in our area. When my aunt heard we only had two chairs, she gave us enough stamps to get two more. Kids, today, probably have no understanding of that procedure.

An advertisement for milk glass Harvest cautions you to never pour hot or cold liquid directly onto cold dishes, which is good advice for most glassware unless it says it's heat-proof or today, heat-resistant. This was sold in various packaged sets: punch bowl, three-piece console, luncheon, snack, and beverage.

Note: The sugar has no handles and is often misidentified as a sherbet.

		White			White
	Bowl, 8 qt., punch	20.00		Pitcher, 65 oz., 2 styles	25.00
8 ▸	Bowl, 10", ftd., console	18.00		Plate, 6", sherbet	6.00
	Butter, ¼ lb., w/cover	15.00	2 ▸	Plate, 8", salad	6.00
	Candy box w/cover (or ftd. wedding bowl)	25.00	11 ▸	Plate, 10", luncheon	6.00
	Cake stand, 12"	32.00		Platter, 14½"	14.00
	Candle, ftd. (sherbet design)	10.00		Salt & pepper, ftd.	12.50
	Canister, large	25.00	4 ▸	Saucer	.50
	Canister, medium	20.00		Sherbet, ftd.	5.00
	Canister, small	15.00	5 ▸	Sugar, ftd., no handle	5.00
1 ▸	Creamer, ftd.	5.00	9 ▸	Tray, tea & toast (snack) oval	4.50
3 ▸	Cup	3.00		Tray, 2 hdld. oval sug/cream liner	4.00
10 ▸	Cup, ftd. punch/snack	2.50		Tumbler, 5 oz., juice	4.00
	Goblet, ftd. water	5.00		Tumbler, 10 oz., water	6.00
	Pitcher, 40 oz.	16.00		Tumbler, 14 oz., cooler	6.00

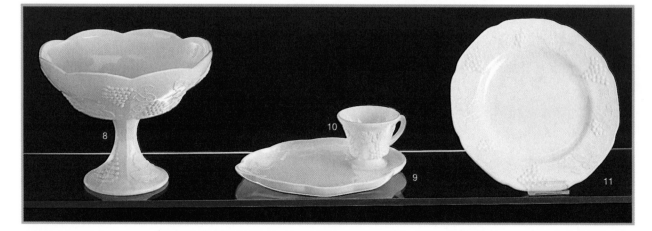

HEATHER, ETCHING #343, FOSTORIA GLASS COMPANY, 1949 – 1976

Color: crystal

Heather was first included in our *Elegant Glassware of the Depression Era* book due to wishes from collectors who loved it and asked us for a listing for it. Although Heather definitely is elegant glassware, its production dates fit this book and thus, it was transferred here when we first started this book in 1990.

Heather is being offered for sale at more Depression glass shows, a definite advantage for those now pursuing it. These people include those trying to fill in partial sets that have been passed down or purchased as a grouping. Prices have softened due to so much being offered through Internet sites, so there is no better time to stock up, than now. Heather is also a trendy girl's name, today; and we've met more than one collector who chose this pattern because it's the name of a family member.

All listings in Heather without a line number shown are etched on Century blank #2630. We have tried to give as accurate a listing for this pattern as possible from old catalogs, but we're sure there are additional pieces. Fostoria's catalog measurements often differ by as much as ½" notably on plates. Actual measurements of pieces we have owned are shown; otherwise, measurements are from catalogs; so, there may be discrepancies experienced. Any information offered from Heather patrons will be appreciated and included in future editions.

Heather, like all Fostoria patterns etched on #2630 blank, has drawbacks with scuffs and scrapes on the surfaces of flat pieces if they were used regularly. Often plates are prone to that predicament just from stacking them due to the ground bottoms scraping the top of the plate underneath. Protect them by what you serve on them (avoid food that needs a sharp knife) and by how you store them with paper plates stacked between.

	Item	Price		Item	Price		Item	Price
	Basket, 10¼" x 6½", wicker hndl.	65.00		Mayonnaise, 4 pc., div. w/2 ladles	35.00		Stem, #6037, 6⅛", 6 oz., parfait	15.00
	Bowl, 4½", hndl.	12.00		Mustard, w/spoon, cover	25.00		Stem, #6037, 6⅜", 9 oz., low goblet	16.00
	Bowl, 5", fruit	14.00		Oil, w/stopper, 5 oz.	26.00		Stem, #6037, 6", 4 oz., claret-wine	20.00
	Bowl, 6", cereal	18.00		Pickle, 8¾"	20.00		Stem, #6037, 6", 7 oz., saucer champagne	12.00
	Bowl, 6¼", snack, ftd.	15.00		Pitcher, 6⅛", 16 oz.	75.00		
	Bowl, 7⅛", 3 ftd., triangular	15.00		Pitcher, 7⅛", 48 oz.	175.00		Stem, #6037, 7⅞", 9 oz., goblet	15.00
	Bowl, 7¼", bonbon, 3 ftd.	18.00		Plate, 6", bread/butter	5.00	5 ▸	Sugar, 4", ftd.	12.00
	Bowl, 8", flared	25.00		Plate, 7½", crescent salad	30.00		Sugar, individual	12.00
	Bowl, 9", lily pond	25.00		Plate, 7½", salad	7.00		Tidbit, 8⅛", 3-ftd., upturned edge	20.00
	Bowl, 9½", hndl., serving	30.00		Plate, 8½", luncheon	10.00		Tidbit, 10¼", 2-tier, metal hndl.	35.00
4 ▸	Bowl, 9½", oval, serving	30.00		Plate, 8", party, w/indent for cup	18.00		Tray, 7⅛", for ind. sug/cr.	12.00
	Bowl, 10", oval, hndl.	33.00		Plate, 9½", small dinner	20.00		Tray, 9½", hndl., muffin	20.00
	Bowl, 10½", salad	40.00		Plate, 10", hndl., cake	20.00		Tray, 9⅛", hndl., utility	30.00
	Bowl, 10¾", ftd., flared	40.00		Plate, 10½", dinner, large center	32.00		Tray, 11½", center hndl.	25.00
	Bowl, 11", ftd., rolled edge	45.00		Plate, 10½", snack tray, small center	20.00		Tumbler, #6037, 4⅞", 5 oz., ftd., juice	12.00
	Bowl, 11¼", lily pond	40.00		Plate, 14", torte	50.00		
	Bowl, 12", flared	45.00		Plate, 16", torte	75.00		Tumbler, #6037, 6⅛", 12 oz., ftd., tea	15.00
2 ▸	Butter, w/cover, ¼ lb.	55.00	3 ▸	Platter, 12"	70.00		
11 ▸	Candlestick, 4½"	12.00		Preserve, w/cover, 6"	35.00		Vase, 5", #4121	40.00
	Candlestick, 7", double	20.00		Relish, 7⅜", 2-part	16.00		Vase, 6", bud	25.00
8 ▸	Candlestick, 7¾", triple	35.00		Relish, 11⅛", 3-part	22.00	9 ▸	Vase, 6", ftd., bud, #6021	30.00
	Candy, w/cover, 7"	35.00	1 ▸	Salt and pepper, 3⅛", pr.	35.00		Vase, 6", ftd., #4143	30.00
7 ▸	Comport, 2¾", cheese	15.00	10 ▸	Salver, 12¼", ftd. (like cake stand)	55.00		Vase, 7½", hndl.	60.00
	Comport, 4⅜"	20.00		Saucer	3.00		Vase, 8", flip, #2660	75.00
	Cracker plate, 10¾"	20.00		Stem, #6037, 4", 1 oz., cordial	35.00		Vase, 8", ftd., bud, #5092	60.00
6 ▸	Creamer, 4¼"	12.00		Stem, #6037, 4", 4½ oz., oyster cocktail	12.00		Vase, 8½", oval	60.00
	Creamer, individual	12.00				1 ▸	Vase, 10", ftd., #2470	100.00
	Cup, 6 oz., ftd.	12.00		Stem, #6037, 4¾", 7 oz., low sherbet	9.00		
	Ice bucket	65.00					
	Mayonnaise, 3 pc.	30.00		Stem, #6037, 5", 4 oz., cocktail	11.00		

HEATHER

HEIRLOOM, FOSTORIA GLASS COMPANY, 1959 – 1970

Colors: blue, green, pink and yellow opalescent, orange, and red

Heirloom is a Fostoria pattern that is consistently attributed to Duncan and Miller or Fenton. Nonetheless, those were not the only companies that made opalescent glassware. In fact, you are more likely to encounter opalescent Fostoria than Duncan since it was made 20 years later. Prices have adjusted downward as more and more sellers are setting their pricing sights a little more realistically for today's market. Internet exposure has also contributed quantities of Heirloom previously unknown. Grandma's treasures of 40 – 50 years are now entering the market and the timing of Heirloom's production is just right for that happening.

Heirloom opalescent colors are the main attraction, but there are devotees for red and orange (which Fostoria called Bittersweet). Not all pieces were made in each color; but pricing is so similar right now, we are listing only one price. White opalescent might slip 15 – 20%, but there are fewer pieces in that color combination. If necessary, we will expand the pricing in the future.

We should point out that the yellow with opalescent tri-candle is officially not a part of this line; but it is regularly collected to go with it; so we have included it here. It consists of an 8" peg vase, three floral/snack bowls, and a trindle candle arm which is always crystal. Pricing is obtained by adding the sum of the parts. We rarely see this labeled anything except Duncan.

1

		All colors
	Basket, 12"	45.00
3 ▸	Bonbon, 7" x 5½"	20.00
5 ▸	Bowl, 5⅜", square, florette	28.00
	Bowl, 6", hanky, 2½" high	25.00
	Bowl, 6", square	28.00
2 ▸	Bowl, 6½", crinkle	28.00
	Bowl, 7"	28.00
13 ▸	Bowl, 8½", star	35.00
	Bowl, 9", square	40.00
7 ▸	Bowl, 10"	45.00
	Bowl, 10", flower, float	45.00
6 ▸	Bowl, 10", oval	35.00
	Bowl, 11", crimped	50.00
16 ▸	Bowl, 11", shallow	45.00
	Bowl, 12", oval centerpiece	40.00
	Bowl, 15", oblong	65.00
4 ▸	Bowl, 16", oval, centerpiece	60.00
11 ▸	Candle, 3" x 5", flora/snack bowl	25.00
15 ▸	Candle, 3½"	20.00

		All colors
14 ▸	Candle, 3⅞", flora	25.00
	Candle, 6"	40.00
	Epergne, 6½" high x 5" wide	100.00
8 ▸	Epergne, 9½" high x 16" wide	150.00
9 ▸	Plate, 8"	25.00
	Plate, 11"	45.00
	Plate, 17"	77.50
12 ▸	Trindle candle arm (crystal)	25.00
	Vase, 4½", handled	75.00
1 ▸	Vase, 6"	18.00
	Vase, 8", peg	30.00
10 ▸	Vase, 9", pitcher	80.00
	Vase, 10", candle	60.00
	Vase, 11"	20.00
	Vase, 11", winged	110.00
	Vase, 18"	130.00
	Vase, 20"	130.00
	Vase, 24"	160.00

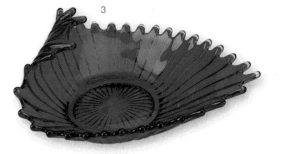

3

HERITAGE, FEDERAL GLASS COMPANY, 1940 – 1955

Colors: crystal, some pink, blue, green, and cobalt

Federal's Heritage is a smaller pattern appealing to a few collectors, but not as many as in the past. As we have searched the Internet, dozens of pieces are being auctioned, but few are selling. Have you noticed how cheap prices are, but how expensive the postage and handling costs are becoming? It seems sellers are trying to make up the selling price with additional shipping costs, so you are better off going to a Depression glass show where you can see and handle whatever you wish to buy before you pay for it.

Heritage was advertised in 1954 in several women's magazines and some pieces were cataloged by Federal as late as 1956. At present, prices for crystal creamers, sugars, and 8½" berry bowls have dropped a bit due to more being available than there are collectors needing them — even though these are the most frustrating pieces to find. Sugar bowls seem to turn up more often than the creamer and always have for several decades.

Reproduction berry bowls from the late 80s and early 90s are so roughly made that they are creating little hassle for collectors. McCrory's and similar stores marketed reproductions of Heritage bowls in amber, crystal, and green. Many bowls are marked "MC" in the center. We say "many" because not all reports from readers have mentioned this mark. Another letter stated that a bowl had an "N" mark, so possibly these were also made for someone else. In any case, the smaller berry bowls sold three for $1.00 and the larger for $1.59 each. The pattern on these pieces is crude and should not fool anyone. Sparsely designed hobs on the reproductions are easy to see when compared to the fully designed hobs of the original. The green reproduction is much darker and closer to the 1970s avocado green. Notice the Depression green of the original bowl in the photo. Federal never made Heritage in amber.

Authentic pink, blue, and green berry bowls remain in short supply. These are undeniably rare. It is a shame that only berry bowl sets were made in these colors. The cobalt blue bowl pictured is the only one of that color known.

Crystal Heritage sets can be gathered more easily than many other patterns given that there are so few pieces. There are only 10 separate objects to find. The limitation you have is how many place settings you wish to own. Thankfully, you normally have to find only one creamer and one 8½" berry bowl no matter how many place settings you collect. Some collectors are buying several of the larger, but cheaper, fruit bowls and ignoring the harder to find smaller berry bowl altogether.

		Crystal	Pink	Blue Green				Crystal	Pink	Blue Green
1 ▸	Bowl, 5", berry	6.00	80.00	90.00			Plate, 8", luncheon	6.00		
7 ▸	Bowl, 8½", large berry	22.00	225.00	325.00		5 ▸	Plate, 9¼", dinner	10.00		
4 ▸	Bowl, 10½", fruit	12.00				6 ▸	Plate, 12", sandwich	12.00		
8 ▸	Cup	6.00				9 ▸	Saucer	1.00		
3 ▸	Creamer, ftd.	15.00				2 ▸	Sugar, open, ftd.	15.00		

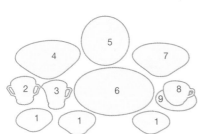

HOBNAIL, FENTON ART GLASS COMPANY

Color: white

Fenton's Hobnail is one pattern that we borrow for photography. Good friends have a large collection which they bring to Paducah for us to use. You cannot imagine how much space 125 – 150 pieces take up in the photography studio — and that is just one pattern. Seldom buying and selling Fenton does leave us a little in the dark on pricing; so that, too, is left to collectors and dealers who are willing to help.

Measurements were taken as we photographed this collection and not all these match catalog listings, but we have faith in our rulers. Fenton's Hobnail is garnering new fans all the time and right now, you can stumble on this for sale in flea markets and antique malls, often for less than its worth.

Do check for damage to the hobnails since those protrude and often get knocked off and are not noticed unless closely inspected.

54 ▸	Apothecary jar, 11", w/cover, #3689	135.00
	Ashtray, 3¼" x 4½", rectangular, #3693	10.00
	Ashtray, 3½", round, #3972	6.00
	Ashtray, 4", ball, #3648	35.00
	Ashtray, 4", octagon, #3876	10.00
	Ashtray, 5", round, #3973	10.00
70 ▸	Ashtray, 5", square, #3679	17.50
67 ▸	Ashtray, 5¼", octagon, #3877	10.00
	Ashtray, 6½", octagon, #3878	12.00
71 ▸	Ashtray, 6½", pipe w/center flower, #3773	55.00
	Ashtray, 6½", round, #3776	10.00
	Basket, 4" x 6", 4-ftd., oval, #3634	25.00
	Basket, 4½", #3834	17.50
	Basket, 5½" x 5½", double crimped, #3735	15.50
	Basket, 5¾", 1¾" base, #3336	22.00
	Basket, 6½" x 4½", oval, two-hndl., #838	25.00
59 ▸	Basket, 6½" x 7½", double crimped, #3736	27.50
	Basket, 7" x 7", deep, #3637	65.00
	Basket, 7½" x 7", #3837	27.50
	Basket, 8" x 7¾", 3" base, #3032	30.00
	Basket, 8", 2¼" diameter base, #3335	30.00
	Basket, 8½", double crimped, #3638	30.00
	Basket, 10", #3830	50.00
	Basket, 10½" x 11½", deep, #3734	55.00
20 ▸	Basket, 13" x 7", oval, #3839	65.00
	Bell, 5½", #3645	15.00
60 ▸	Bell, 6", #3667	25.00
	Bell, 6¾", #3067	18.00
	Bonbon, 5" x 2½", two-hndl., #3935	20.00
	Bonbon, 5" x 2", #3630	15.00
	Bonbon, 5" x 2¾", star, #3921	12.00
	Bonbon, 6" x 1⅝", double crimped, #3926	10.00
	Bonbon, 7" x 2½", two-hndl., #3937	15.00
	Bonbon, 8" x 2¼", #3716	18.00
	Bonbon, 8" x 5½", #3706	20.00
	Boot, 4", #3992	14.00
72 ▸	Bottle, vanity, 5⅜", w/stopper, #3865	50.00
	Bowl, 4", berry, square, #3928	18.00
	Bowl, 4", candle orifice, #3873	22.50

	Bowl, 5", cereal, 2" high, #3719	80.00
	Bowl, 5½" x 6¾", candy, ribbon top, #3730	90.00
	Bowl, 5½", rose, #3022	20.00
	Bowl, 6" x 6", octagonal, peanut, #3627	18.50
	Bowl, 6½", candle orifice, #3872	17.50
	Bowl, 7", double crimped, #3927	12.50
	Bowl, 7½", candle, ftd., 5" high, #3971	60.00
	Bowl, 8", 3-toed, #3635	22.00
	Bowl, 8", candle, double crimped, #3771	27.50
	Bowl, 8", double crimped, #3639	30.00
	Bowl, 8", oval, #3625	25.00
	Bowl, 8½", console, rippled top, #3724	70.00

	Bowl, 9", cupped, #3735	135.00
	Bowl, 9", double crimped, 5" high, #3924	22.50
19 ▸	Bowl, 9", oval, ftd., #3621	60.00
61 ▸	Bowl, 9", scalloped/flared, #3626	60.00
	Bowl, 9", square, #3929	65.00
43 ▸	Bowl, 9½", chip 'n dip candle, #3924	25.00
	Bowl, 10", ftd., double crimped, #3731	40.00
	Bowl, 10¼", shallow, #3622	55.00
	Bowl, 10½", #3623	85.00
	Bowl, 10½", double crimped, #3624	30.00
	Bowl, 10½", ftd., crimped, #3723	35.00
	Bowl, 11", 3 holes for hanging, #3705	145.00
64 ▸	Bowl, 12" x 5", banana, #3620	40.00
21 ▸	Bowl, 12" x 7", banana, #3720	45.00
35 ▸	Bowl, 12", double crimped, #3938	25.00
	Butter and cheese, 4¼", w/8" plate, cover, #3677	160.00
33 ▸	Butter, ¼ lb., oval, 7¾" x 3¾", #3777	35.00
36 ▸	Butter, ¼ lb., rectangular, 7½" x 2⅛", #3977	30.00
22 ▸	Cake plate, 12⅞" x 5", pie crust crimped edge, #3913	50.00
	Candleholder, 2" x 5", pr., #3670	28.00
	Candleholder, 2¾" x 4¼", ftd., pr., #3673	45.00
73 ▸	Candleholder, 3", flat, ruffled edge, pr., #3974	30.00
	Candleholder, 3½", cornucopia, pr., #3971	70.00
6 ▸	Candleholder, 3½", hndl., pr., #3870	50.00
	Candleholder, 3½", rounded, flared top, pr., #3974	30.00
	Candleholder, 3½", single, ruffled edge, pr., #3770	90.00
5 ▸	Candleholder, 5½", 2-light, pr., #3672	125.00
9 ▸	Candleholder, 6½", cornucopia, pr., #3874	57.50
	Candleholder, 6", pr., #3674	30.00
56 ▸	Candleholder, 7", #3745	40.00
	Candleholder, 8", crescent, pr., #3678	175.00
28 ▸	Candleholder, 10", pr., #3774	65.00
3 ▸	Candy box, 5⅛", ftd., oval, #3786	35.00
	Candy box, 5¼", shoe w/cover, #3700	35.00
	Candy box, 6", w/cover, 6" diameter, #3984	60.00
11 ▸	Candy box, 6", w/cover butterfly finial, #3600	45.00
	Candy box, 6¾", w/cover, #3886	35.00
12 ▸	Candy box, 8⅛", w/cover, ftd., #3784	45.00
	Candy dish, 6½" x 4¾", #3668	45.00
	Candy dish, 6½" x 6½", #3668	45.00
	Candy dish, 6½", heart, #3033	22.50
	Candy jar, 5¼", w/cover, #3883	32.00
	Candy jar, 6½", w/cover, 4½" wide, #3688	45.00
16 ▸	Candy jar, 7¼", ftd., #3980	35.00
15 ▸	Candy jar, 7½", w/cover, #3688	45.00
	Candy jar, 8½", ftd., w/pointed knob cover, #3885	38.50
	Candy jar, 8½", ftd., w/rounded knob cover, #3887	35.00
44 ▸	Celery, 12", #3739	100.00
	Chip 'n dip, 12¼" x 3¼" bowl w/division, #3922	250.00
	Comport, #3703	45.00
62 ▸	Cigarette box, 4¼", sq., #3685	35.00
58 ▸	Cigarette lighter 2¼", cube, #3692	25.00

HOBNAIL

	Comport, 3¾", double crimped, #3727	17.50
51 ▸	Comport, jelly, 5¼", #3725	15.00
	Comport, 5¼", double crimped, #3728	16.00
69 ▸	Comport, 5½", double crimped, #3920	86.00
	Comport, 6" x 5½", octagonal stem, #3628	18.00
77 ▸	Cookie jar, 11", w/lid, #3680	110.00
	Creamer, 2⅛", plain hndl. and edge, #3900	10.00
	Creamer, 3½", plain hndl., #3901	10.00
26 ▸	Creamer, 3½", scalloped edge, #3708	17.50
32 ▸	Creamer, 3", beaded hndl. and edge, #3665	20.00
	Creamer, 3", beaded hndl. and ruffled edge, #3702	25.00
48 ▸	Creamer, 3", star shaped edge, #3906	12.50
50 ▸	Creamer, 4", #3606	10.00
	Creamer, 4¾", scalloped edge, #3902	22.50
	Cruet, 7¾", #3863	50.00
	Cup, child's, #489	60.00
	Decanter, 12", hndl., w/stopper, #3761	250.00
75 ▸	Egg cup, 4", #3647	65.00
	Epergne candle, 2" high x 5" wide, petite, #3671	40.00
55 ▸	Epergne candle, 6" wide, for 7" candleholder, #3746	70.00
	Epergne set, 6½", 2-pc., 7" horn, #3704	75.00
	Epergne set, 6½", 4-pc., 6" tri-horns, #3801	50.00
	Epergne set, 9½", 4-pc., 8" tri-horns, #3701	50.00
	Epergne set, 9", 5-pc. (#3920 comport, frog, 5" tri-horns), #3800	200.00
	Fairy light, 4½", 2-pc., #3608	15.00
	Fairy light, 8½", 3-pc., #3804	85.00
	Goblet, 3⅞", 3 oz., wine, #3843	15.00
66 ▸	Goblet, 4½", 4 oz., wine, #3843	14.00
65 ▸	Goblet, 5⅝", 8 oz., water, #3845	12.50

41 ▸	Hat, 2⅝", burred, #3991	15.00
	Hat, 2⅝", plain, #3991	25.00
	Jam & jelly set, 2 4¾" jars, lid, ladle, double crimped chrome hndl. tray, #3915	45.00
1 ▸	Jam set, 4 pc., 4¾" jar, lid, ladle, and 6" crimped saucer, #3903	50.00
	Jar, 5", jam w/spoon and lid, #3601	35.00
	Jar, 7¼", honey, round, ftd., w/cover, #3886	65.00
7 ▸	Jardiniere, 4¼", #A-011	15.00
	Jardiniere, 4½", scalloped, #3994	12.00
	Jardiniere, 5½", scalloped, #3898	35.00
14 ▸	Jardiniere, 5⅝", #A-011	20.00
	Jardiniere, 6", scalloped, 6" diameter, #3898	35.00
	Jelly, 5½" x 4½", #3725	30.00
	Kettle, 2½", 3-toed, 3" diameter, #3990	14.00
18 ▸	Lamp, 8", hurricane, hndl. base, scalloped top, #3998	65.00
	Lamp, 9", courting, electric, crimped top, #3713	135.00
27 ▸	Lamp, 9", courting, oil, crimped top, #3792	135.00
	Lamp, 11", hurricane, crimped top, #3792	115.00
	Lamp, 19", student, crimped top, #3707	250.00
	Lamp, 21", student, double crimped top, #3807	225.00
	Lamp, 22", Gone with the Wind, #3808	250.00
	Lamp, 22½", student, w/prisms, #1174	235.00
	Lamp, 26", double crimped, pillar, #3907	210.00
2 ▸	Lavabo, 3-pc. (urn w/lid and basin), #3867	120.00
57 ▸	Margarine tub, 5¼", #3802	22.00
	Mayonnaise set, 3-pc., bowl, 6" ruffled saucer, ladle, #3803	30.00
	Mustard jar, 3½", w/spoon and lid, #3605	35.00
4 ▸	Mustard jar, 3½", w/spoon and lid, #3889	18.00
38 ▸	Mustard, 3⅝", kettle, #3979	20.00

40 ▶	Napkin ring, 2" diameter, #3904	35.00
	Nut dish, 2½" x 4¾", #3650	58.00
39 ▶	Nut dish, 2½" x 5", #3729	45.00
	Nut dish, 2¾" x 4", ftd., #3631	35.00
34 ▶	Nut dish, 5" x 3¼", oval, #3732	20.00
	Nut dish, 5" x 5½", ftd., #3629	17.00
	Nut dish, 7" x 3½", oval, #3633	14.00
	Oil, 4¾", w/stopper, #3869	15.00
68 ▶	Oil, 8", w/stopper, #3767	55.00
	Pickle, 8" x 4", oval, #3640	15.00
	Pitcher, 5¼", squat, 4" diameter top, #3965	40.00
	Pitcher, 7", #3365	32.00
23 ▶	Pitcher, 7¾", 80 oz., no ice lip (fat neck), #3967	130.00
	Pitcher, 8", 54 oz., no ice lip (fat neck), #3764	70.00
52 ▶	Pitcher, 9½", w/ice lip, 70 oz., #3664	60.00
	Pitcher, 11", #3360	65.00
	Planter, 4½", square, scalloped top, #3699	14.00
	Planter, 8½" long, scalloped top, #3690	20.00
10 ▶	Planter, 8", crescent, 4-ftd., #3798	30.00
	Planter, 9½" long, scalloped top, #3690	32.00
	Planter, 9" wall, #3836	57.50
	Planter, 10" long, rectangular box, #3799	30.00
	Planter, 10", crescent, 4-ftd., #3698	50.00
	Plate, 8½", round, pie crust crimped edge, #3912	28.00
29 ▶	Plate, 8¼", round, pie crust crimped edge, #3816	28.00
	Plate, 13½", crimped edge, #3714	55.00
	Plate, 16", torte, #3817	70.00
	Powder box, 6½", round w/lid, #3880	60.00
76 ▶	Puff box, 4½", round, #3885	75.00
80 ▶	Punch base, 3¾" x 8½", #3778	100.00

	Punch bowl, 10½" x 5¼", plain edge, #3827	260.00
53 ▶	Punch bowl, 11¼" x 6½", octagonal, #3820	465.00
79 ▶	Punch bowl, 15" x 7½", crimped edge, #3722	325.00
	Punch cup, 2½" x 3", octagonal, #3840	20.00
81 ▶	Punch cup, 2¼" x 2¾", #3847	15.00
	Punch ladle, #9520	55.00
	Punch ladle (crystal), #9527	30.00
	Relish, 5¼" x 7½", 3-part, #3607	35.00
	Relish, 7½", 3-sections, #3822	16.00
	Relish, 7½", non divided, #3822	50.00
	Relish, 7½", scalloped, 3-sections, #3822	16.00
	Relish, 8½", heart-shaped, #3733	25.00
42 ▶	Relish, 12⅜", 3-sections, #3740	35.00
24 ▶	Salt & pepper, 3", flat, pr., #3806	20.00
74 ▶	Salt & pepper, 3¾", pr., #3609	25.00
46 ▶	Salt & pepper, 4¼", pr., #3602	40.00
	Salt dip, 2⅜" x 2¼" x ⅜", shell shape, #9496	45.00
	Server, 10", two-tier, 12" bowl & 3-section top, #3709	50.00
	Shaker, 4¾", cinnamon sugar, #3797	135.00
	Sherbet, 4", #3825	15.00
	Slipper, 5", kitten head and paws, #3995	10.00
37 ▶	Spoon holder, 7¼" long, #3612	115.00
	Stein, 6¾", 14 oz., #3646	110.00
	Sugar, 2⅛", plain handle and edge, #3900	10.00
	Sugar, 3", beaded handle and edge, #3665	20.00
	Sugar, 3", beaded handle and ruffled edge, #3702	25.00
47 ▶	Sugar, 3", star-shaped edge, #3906	12.50
	Sugar, 3½", plain handle, #3901	10.00
30 ▶	Sugar, 3½", scalloped edge, #3708	17.50
	Sugar, 4¾", scalloped edge, #3902	22.50

HOBNAIL

45 ▸	Sugar, 5¾", w/lid, #3606	12.50
	Syrup pitcher, 5¼", 12 oz., #3660	35.00
	Syrup pitcher, 5¾", 12 oz., #3762	30.00
	Tidbit, two-tier, 13½" and 8½", #3794	55.00
25 ▸	Toothpick, 2¾", #3895	40.00
31 ▸	Toothpick, 3", #3795	12.00
	Tray, 7½" x 3¾", oil/mustard, #3715	15.00
49 ▸	Tray, 7¾", chrome handle, #3879	25.00
	Tray, 12½" x 7", vanity, #3775	100.00
	Tray, 13½" sandwich w/metal handle, #3791	55.00
	Tumbler, 3½", 5 oz., flat, #3945	12.00
	Tumbler, 4¾", 9 oz. flat, #3949	15.00
8 ▸	Tumbler, 5", 12 oz., iced tea, #3942	18.50
	Tumbler, 5", 12 oz., iced tea, barrel shape, #3947	37.50
	Tumbler, 5¾", iced tea, ftd., #3842	38.50
	Tumbler, 6", 16 oz., flat, #3946	50.00
	Urn, 11", covered, #3986	185.00
	Vanity bottle, 7⅛", 3-pc., #3986	235.00
	Vase, 2¼", violet, ribbon crimped, #3754	35.00
	Vase, 3", crimped, #3855	12.50
	Vase, 3¾", double crimped, #3850	10.00
	Vase, 4", 3¾" diameter, #3952	10.00
	Vase, 4", 4¾" diameter, #3775	50.00
	Vase, 4", fan, pie crust edge, #3953	12.50
63 ▸	Vase, 4½", double crimped, #3854	15.00
	Vase, 5", 3-toed, #3654	12.50
13 ▸	Vase, 5", double crimped, #3850	17.50
	Vase, 5", scalloped, #3655	17.50
	Vase, 5½", double crimped, #3656	30.00
	Vase, 5½", ivy ball, ruffled, ped. ft., #3726	20.00

	Vase, 5¾", ivy, ribbed, ped. ft., #3757	20.00
	Vase, 6", double crimped, #3856	20.00
	Vase, 6", double crimped, #3954	25.00
	Vase, 6", ftd., swung, handkerchief, #3651	40.00
	Vase, 6", hand, #3355	30.00
	Vase, 6¼", 3" diameter base, fan, #3957	22.00
	Vase, 6¼", 5" diameter, double crimped, #3954	25.00
	Vase, 6½", ftd., swung, handkerchief, #3651	50.00
17 ▸	Vase, 6½", swung, handkerchief, #3750	22.50
	Vase, 7½", handkerchief, #3657	22.50
	Vase, 8", 4" diameter base, fan, #3959	40.00
	Vase, 8", bud, ftd., swung, #3756	18.00
	Vase, 8", double crimped, 3½" diameter, #3859	55.00
	Vase, 8", double crimped, 6½" diameter, #3958	28.00
	Vase, 8", double crimped, 6¼" diameter, #3858	50.00
	Vase, 8½" fan, #3852	150.00
	Vase, 8½", Jack in the Pulpit, #3356	28.00
	Vase, 9", #3659	55.00
	Vase, 9", swung, #3755	50.00
	Vase, 10", swung, ftd., bud, #3950	15.00
	Vase, 10", swung, handkerchief, #3855	40.00
	Vase, 11", double crimped, #3752	40.00
	Vase, 12", 3-toed, #3658	175.00
82 ▸	Vase, 12", swung, ftd., 2½" diameter, #3758	25.00
78 ▸	Vase, 12", swung, ftd., 3¼" diameter, #3753	27.50
	*Vase, 14", swung, handkerchief, #3755	50.00
	*Vase, 14", swung, pitcher, 3¼" diameter, #3750	50.00
	Vase, 18", ftd., 3¼" diameter, #3753	47.50
	Vase, 24", swung, #3652	37.50

*size varies upward

110

HOLIDAY, "BUTTONS AND BOWS," JEANNETTE GLASS COMPANY, 1947 – mid 1950s

Colors: Pink, iridescent; some Shell Pink and crystal

Although Holiday has been regarded as Depression glass by collectors and even some authors, it was not introduced until 1947 and in no way fits standard Depression glass except for the color pink. Color is not the decisive factor of determining what is and what is not, Depression era.

Holiday, or "Buttons and Bows" as many collectors still call it, can be a vexing pattern to collect due to all the mould variations made by Jeannette. There are three dissimilar cups and saucers. One set has plain centers on the cup and in the saucer ring. These are easy to match. Two other cup designs have a rayed center. You cannot combine these since one cup's base size of 2" will only fit a 2⅛" cup ring and the 2⅜" cup base will only fit a 2½" saucer ring. Two distinct designs of 10 ounce tumblers occur. One is flat bottomed and the other has a small raised foot and is narrower at the bottom. Two designs of sherbets are available. One has a rayed foot while the other is plain. Two distinct sherbet plates have 2¾" centers, but one has a beaded effect in the center, while the other has a center ring with a diamond effect. Mould variations occur in nearly all patterns, but Holiday's are especially mystifying for new collectors. Cups and saucers do not interchange well, but the other items can be matched without detracting from your collection unless you are a purist. In that case, Holiday may not be your cup of tea.

Holiday was a fashionable pattern in the late 1940s, and well utilized, judging by the plethora of damaged pieces we have noticed in buying sets out of homes and estates over the years. Be sure to examine the underside of the edges. Pointed edges are prone to chips, nicks, and "chigger bites," an auction term that varies from place to place. A small chip to one person is a giant chip to someone else. Remember that damaged glass cannot be "practically mint." Prices listed here are for mint condition glassware.

The footed iced teas are difficult to find as you may note by the price. Many collectors are skipping buying these due to price. There is a crystal tumbler out there sporting an enlarged version of this design that might suffice should you be able to find enough of them. Holiday cake plates, candlesticks, and console bowls remain difficult items to latch onto, but prices have become more reasonable of late. Many of these have been chipped and chunked over the years. If you are flabbergasted by how such recently manufactured (relatively speaking) glassware could have so many hard-to-find pieces, we now know the iced teas went to the Philippines and some to Australia. One came free with a six pack of a famous chocolate candy bar sold in stores in the Philippines.

Some collectors, to augment their sets, buy iridescent pieces of Holiday. Only four iridized pieces were made; and only the sandwich tray is not pictured. Iridized juice tumblers and small pitchers are easily found and are actually easier on the pocketbook than pink.

		Pink	Crystal	Iridescent
17 ▸	Bowl, 5⅛", berry	12.50		
23 ▸	Bowl, 7¾", soup	60.00		
24 ▸	Bowl, 8½", large berry	30.00		
13 ▸	Bowl, 9½", oval vegetable	26.00		
21 ▸	*Bowl, 10¾", console	95.00		
20 ▸	Butter dish and cover	35.00		
	Butter dish bottom	5.00		
	Butter dish top	30.00		
15 ▸	Cake plate, 10½", 3-legged	110.00		
16 ▸	Candlesticks, 3", pr.	95.00		
10 ▸	Creamer, footed	8.00		
18 ▸	Cup, three sizes	5.00		
3 ▸	Pitcher, 4¾", 16 oz., milk	60.00	15.00	10.00
4 ▸	Pitcher, 6¾", 52 oz.	24.00		

		Pink	Crystal	Iridescent
9 ▸	Plate, 6", sherbet	4.00		
14 ▸	Plate, 9", dinner	14.00		
	Plate, 13¾", chop	95.00		
2 ▸	Platter, 11⅜", oval	16.00		10.00
5 ▸	Sandwich tray, 10½"	12.00		10.00
19 ▸	Saucer, 3 styles	2.00		
8 ▸	Sherbet, 2 styles	6.00		
11 ▸	Sugar	8.00		
12 ▸	Sugar cover	15.00		
7 ▸	Tumbler, 4", 10 oz., flat	15.00		
1 ▸	Tumbler, 4", footed, 5 oz.	45.00		6.00
6 ▸	Tumbler, 4¼", footed, 5¼ oz.		8.00	
22 ▸	Tumbler, 6", footed	120.00		

*Shell Pink $45.00

HOLLY, CUTTING #815, FOSTORIA GLASS COMPANY, 1942 – 1980

Color: crystal

Fostoria's Holly was sold for nearly 40 years, confirmation that many brides chose this pattern over Navarre and Meadow Rose. That choice for crystal has today's collectors searching for Holly to fill incomplete family sets or simply purchasing it because they, too, love the pattern. Holly cuttings can be gathered on many of Fostoria's mould blanks as you can see from the listing. Its cut band is distinctive and easily identified. Other glass companies made similar cuttings, so be aware of that.

If you are trying to find a full set, you have two sizes of tumblers and eight different stems from which to choose; and those are the more easily found Holly items. As with most elegant patterns from that time, stemware was purchased to high-light china patterns; so stems abound today. "Food just looks better on solid, colored dishes than it does on crystal," said an older, elegantly dressed lady recently when we asked if she had any pieces other than stemware in her Fostoria pattern. She informed us that she never wanted any glass serving dishes, just her china. Basic Holly dinnerware and serving items are scarce now because of this prejudice of buying only stemware to accompany "good china."

As with many Fostoria patterns, the dinner plates are only 9½" (listed as 9" in catalog) and some collectors spurn that small size for serving. There are no service plates, as in Cambridge wares, to substitute as a large dinner. The 11" sandwich would be too large for a dinner plate unless there are teenagers involved; and then, in our experience with boys, that size would be almost big enough.

Fostoria referred to the double candlestick as a duo. We asked one lady what she collected as she perused books at our table and she replied, "Interesting miniature pieces, which don't take up much room in my display cabinet." You can see the #2364 ashtray and cigarette holder pictured in Buttercup, but we have been unable to round these up in Holly. They would fit a col-lecting criterion of smaller objects. These little items are rarely found, but increasingly sought by a growing cadre of minia-ture item collectors.

	Ashtray, #2364, 2⅝", individual	15.00
	Bowl, #1769, finger	20.00
	Bowl, #2364, 5", fruit	8.00
	Bowl, #2364, 8", rimmed soup	20.00
	Bowl, #2364, 9", salad	22.00
	Bowl, #2364, baked apple	12.00
	Bowl, #6023, 9", ftd.	50.00
19 ▸	Bowl, #2364, 12", flared	25.00
13 ▸	Bowl, #2364, 12", lily pond	25.00
	Bowl, #2364, 13", fruit	30.00
	Candlestick, #2324, 4"	12.00
7 ▸	Candlestick, #6023, 5½", duo	20.00
	Celery, #2364, 11"	15.00
	Cheese comport, #2364, ftd.	12.00
	Cigarette holder, #2364, 2" high	20.00
	Comport, #6030, 5"	20.00
	Comport, #2364, 8"	22.00
18 ▸	Cream, #2350½, 3¼"	8.00
2 ▸	Cream, #2666, ind.	12.00
20 ▸	Cup, #2350½	6.00
	Ladle, mayonnaise	10.00
22 ▸	Mayonnaise, #2364, 5"	15.00
12 ▸	Pickle, #2364, 8", oval	15.00
	Pitcher, #2666, 32 oz.	65.00
	Pitcher, #6011, 53 oz., 8⅞", ftd. jug	175.00
	Plate, #2337, 6", dessert	3.00
23 ▸	Plate, #2364, 6¾", mayonnaise	6.00
11 ▸	Plate, #2337, 7½", salad	6.00
	Plate, #2337, 8½", luncheon	8.00
	Plate, #2337, 9½", dinner	22.00
	Plate, #2364, 11", sandwich	20.00
	Plate, #2364, 14", torte	35.00
	Plate, #2364, 16", torte	60.00
	Plate, #2364, cracker	20.00
15 ▸	Relish, #2364, 8¼", two-part	14.00
14 ▸	Relish, #2364, 10", three-part	16.00
21 ▸	Saucer, #2350	2.00
	Shaker, #2364, 2⅝", individual pr.	25.00
	Shaker, #2364, 3¼", pr.	20.00
6 ▸	Stem, #6030, 3⅞", 1 oz., cordial	30.00
8 ▸	Stem, #6030, 3¾", 4 oz., oyster cocktail	10.00
	Stem, #6030, 4⅜", 6 oz., low sherbet	7.00
10 ▸	Stem, #6030, 5¼", 3½ oz., cocktail	8.00
9 ▸	Stem, #6030, 5⅝", 6 oz., high sherbet	8.00
5 ▸	Stem, #6030, 6", 3½ oz., claret/wine	15.00
	Stem, #6030, 6⅜", 10 oz., low goblet	12.00
24 ▸	Stem, #6030, 7⅞", 10 oz., water goblet	14.00
17 ▸	Sugar, #2350½, 3⅛"	8.00
3 ▸	Sugar, 2666, ind.	12.00
	Tray, #2364, 11¼", center hndl.	25.00
4 ▸	Tray, #2666, individual sug/cr (no cutting)	10.00
1 ▸	Tumbler, #6030, 4⅝", 5 oz., juice, ftd.	10.00
16 ▸	Tumbler, #6030, 6", 12 oz., iced tea, ftd.	15.00
	Vase, #2619½, 6"	50.00
	Vase, #2619½, 7½"	70.00
	Vase, #2619½, 9½"	85.00

HORIZON, #2650 LINE, FOSTORIA GLASS COMPANY, 1951 – 1954

Colors: crystal, Cinnamon, and Spruce Green

Fostoria's wavy lined, Horizon production lasted only a few years, but its earthy colors had attracted few buyers until recently when some new collectors began to take notice of its attention-grabbing 50s look. It is one of those patterns that you really love or can't stand. There appears to be no middle ground.

The brown and green tones were dubbed Cinnamon and Spruce Green by Fostoria. We have had a struggle finding serving pieces. To own them, we had to pay more for them than we wanted; but in order to have them for photography, we had to grab them when they surfaced.

Commodities from the 50s are on the upswing, today, as some people revisit their pleasant childhood memories or simply embrace the unusual styles stemming from that era. Though we don't know off hand the particular designer for Horizon, much of the glassware from this time period was an inspiration of familiar names in the art world. If this vaguely ultramodern styling is your forté, you'd better collect it before the small supply disappears.

	All colors			All colors
Bowl, #5650, 2⅝" high, dessert/finger	7.00	6 ▸	Plate, 7", salad	6.00
Bowl, 4½", fruit	5.00		Plate, 10", dinner	14.00
Bowl, 5", cereal	8.00	7 ▸	Plate, 11", sandwich	12.00
Bowl, 8½", salad	12.00		Plate, 14", torte	16.00
10 ▸ Bowl, 10½", salad	15.00		Platter, 12", oval	16.00
Bowl, 11½", four-part, server	15.00		Relish, 12", three-part	18.00
5 ▸ Bowl, 12", two-handled, server	20.00	4 ▸	Saucer	1.00
Candy, 5", w/cover	30.00	9 ▸	Sugar, 3⅛"	8.00
8 ▸ Coaster	6.00		Tumbler, #5650, 3⅜", juice/cocktail	5.00
1 ▸ Cream, 3½"	8.00		Tumbler, #5650, 3⅜", sherbet/old fashioned	6.00
3 ▸ Cup, 8½ oz.	5.00	2 ▸	Tumbler, #5650, 5", water/scotch & soda	7.00
Mayonnaise, 3-pc. set	20.00		Tumbler, #5650, 6", iced tea/highball	8.00

IRIS, "IRIS AND HERRINGBONE," JEANNETTE GLASS COMPANY, 1928 – 1932; 1950s; 1970s

Colors: crystal, iridescent; some pink and green; recently bi-colored red/yellow and blue/green combinations, and white

Iris has been hard hit both by the economy and the reproduction scoundrels looking to make an easy buck. It has also been broadly collected and beloved. However, reproduction Iris has been overshadowing Iris for the previous few years. We are relentlessly asked what is being made now or what do I do about my collection? Our answer to that is to sit tight, that this too will pass, but may take a few years. In the meantime, truth is that prices are adjusting — unfortunately, not up. The last deception that we can confirm is the cocktail which joins the reproduction dinner plates, iced teas, flat tumblers, and coasters that have previously been unloaded into our market.

Do not panic. This has happened before to Cherry Blossom and other major patterns and they have recovered. All the new crystal is exceedingly clear. If you place old crystal Iris on a white background it will appear to have a gray or even slightly yellow tint. The new is very clear without a tinge of color of any sort and looks like more expensive crystal. The new flat tumblers have no herringbone on the bottom — just Iris. The coaster is more than half-full of glass when you look from the side.

Sellers on Internet auctions have intensified sales of these reproductions. If it is so cheap you can't believe the price — beware. Check Internet sellers to see if they sell other reproductions — an excellent clue. Jeannette is often used as "certification" in the wording of Internet auctions. Sometimes the ploy is that the items were bought at an estate sale or auction and they don't know how old they are. Reproduced items get on the Internet first as "old," and unsuspecting bidders pay high prices before word gets out in the collecting world. Most of these sellers know their products are new; so if bidding, ask about their return policy before you bid. Reputable sellers will offer refunds or returns.

Prices for iced teas, dinner plates, coasters, and flat water tumblers have been cut hard. Several large collections are having a tough time finding buyers right now because owners want pre-reproduction prices. If you have to sell, be aware that prices are down. Now may be the time to buy harder-to-find pieces from established, reputable dealers.

Satinized (frosted) plates and bowls usually had hand-colored or painted irises on them. It wears off easily and pieces do not sell well unless the original decoration is still bright. Those rarely seen 8" crystal luncheon plates may be scarce because many more of them were frosted than were not. In any case, the frosted ones are a tough sell at $25.00, but you can find them priced much higher. You may affix a label with any price on it you want, but obtaining that price is a whole new proposition. Get realistic if you are trying to sell your Iris pattern now.

Original crystal production for Iris began in 1928. Some was made in the late 1940s and 1950s; candy bottoms and vases emerged as late as the 1970s. All these were made by Jeannette. The crystal Iris decorated with red and gold that keeps turning up was called Corsage and styled by Century in 1946, information obtained from a card attached to a 1946 wedding gift.

Iridescent Iris fits lock, stock, and barrel within the time composition of this book. The eight ounce water goblet, 5¼" four ounce goblet, 4" sherbet, and the demitasse cup and saucer are the most difficult pieces to find in iridescent.

Iridescent candy bottoms are another product of the early 70s when Jeannette also made crystal bottoms flashed with two-tone colors of red/yellow or blue/green. These were sold as vases; and, over time, the colors have peeled off or been purposely stripped to make them, again, crystal candy bottoms. These later issues lack rays on the foot which were on all earlier candy bottoms. White or painted white vases sell around $12.00 – 15.00. These are not rare. The exceedingly rare vase is transparent pink and not pink painted over white.

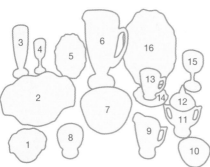

	Crystal	Iridescent	Green Pink
10 ▶ Bowl, 4½", berry, beaded edge	35.00	5.00	
1 ▶ Bowl, 5", ruffled, sauce	6.00	18.00	
Bowl, 5", cereal	75.00		
Bowl, 7½", soup	135.00	50.00	
7 ▶ Bowl, 8", berry, beaded edge	60.00	20.00	
20 ▶ Bowl, 9½", ruffled, salad	10.00	10.00	200.00
2 ▶ Bowl, 11½", ruffled, fruit	10.00	14.00	
Bowl, 11", fruit, straight edge	60.00		
Butter dish and cover	30.00	30.00	
Butter dish bottom	10.00	10.00	
Butter dish top	20.00	20.00	
19 ▶ Candlesticks, pr.	28.00	25.00	
Candy jar and cover	100.00		
†Coaster	40.00		
9 ▶ Creamer, ftd.	11.00	10.00	150.00
13 ▶ Cup	13.00	12.00	
23 ▶ *Demitasse cup	35.00	150.00	
24 ▶ *Demitasse saucer	110.00	250.00	
18 ▶ Fruit or nut set	100.00	150.00	
4 ▶ Goblet, 4", wine		20.00	
Goblet, 4½", 4 oz., cocktail	16.00		
Goblet, 4½", 3 oz., wine	12.00		
Goblet, 5½", 4 oz.	15.00	495.00	
21 ▶ Goblet, 5½", 8 oz.	18.00	295.00	
**Lampshade, 11½"	75.00		
6 ▶ Pitcher, 9½", ftd.	25.00	25.00	
5 ▶ Plate, 5½", sherbet	10.00	11.00	
Plate, 8", luncheon	65.00		
16 ▶ †Plate, 9", dinner	30.00	35.00	
17 ▶ Plate, 11¾", sandwich	22.00	32.00	
14 ▶ Saucer	6.00	6.00	
8 ▶ Sherbet, 2½", ftd.	20.00	10.00	
15 ▶ Sherbet, 4", ftd.	18.00	295.00	
11 ▶ Sugar	9.00	9.00	150.00
12 ▶ Sugar cover	10.00	10.00	
†Tumbler, 4", flat	65.00		
3 ▶ Tumbler, 6", ftd.	14.00	12.00	
22 ▶ †Tumbler, 6½", ftd.	18.00		
Vase, 9"	20.00	18.00	225.00

*Ruby, blue, amethyst priced as iridescent
**Colors: $85.00
†Has been reproduced

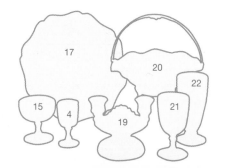

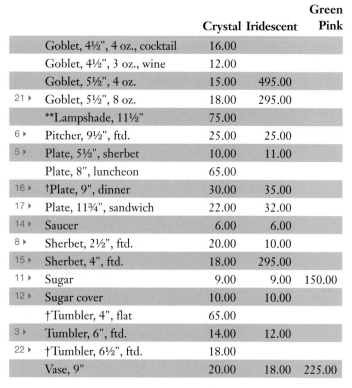

JAMESTOWN, FOSTORIA GLASS COMPANY, 1958 – 1982

Colors: amber, amethyst, blue, brown, crystal, green, pink, and red

    Our Jamestown listing came from several different Fostoria catalogs. The line numbers on each stem in those catalogs have two contradictory size and capacities listed. We don't know if there are two entirely different stems or the employee measuring for one of the catalogs did not do the job well. This is only one sticky situation about writing books on glassware that drives us to distraction if we do not own each piece. Which statistics do you use? We have recorded both stem listings for the "type A" personalities. We don't believe those half ounces and eighth inches are going to make much difference in the overall scheme of things. Accordingly, your measurements could differ slightly from those we have listed, so don't be too shocked. Our capacities are always measured with the item filled to the brim and heights perpendicular from the bottom to highest point of the object. No one has ever written to confirm what their stems measure; so we must be within the ballpark.

    Stems are readily available in Jamestown; serving pieces are not. Amber or brown Jamestown is sought by only a few collectors; bargains may exist in those colors if you are interested. Fostoria produced serving items for only a short time; that leaves both collectors and dealers scrounging for those. We have finally concluded that not every piece was made in each color. We have grouped colors into three pricing sections based upon sales information. Crystal is more in demand than amber or brown and priced higher than either. Occasionally some first-rate buys occur in amethyst Jamestown since it is sometimes confused with Moroccan Amethyst and priced as such.

    Ruby Jamestown has always sold well, but there is not a complete line of Ruby. Pink and blue Jamestown are selling better than Ruby at the present. Ruby stemware was made again in the 90s by Lancaster Colony who owns Fostoria's moulds. Newer stems sold for $16.00 each in outlet stores causing price adjustments on older Ruby Jamestown stemware. Sadly, there is little distinction between the old and newly made items. Both older stems and newer ones have three mould lines which we have heard touted as a point of distinction. Sorry to say, it is not.

JAMESTOWN

	Amber/Brown	Amethyst/Crystal/Green	Blue/Pink/Ruby
Bowl, 4½", dessert, #2719/421	6.00	12.00	16.00
Bowl, 10", salad, #2719//211	18.00	30.00	45.00
Bowl, 10", two hndl. serving, #2719/648	18.00	40.00	60.00
3 ▸ Butter w/cover, ¼ pound, #2719/300	20.00	35.00	55.00
Cake plate, 9½", hndl., #2719/306	15.00	30.00	40.00
Celery, 9¼", #2719/360	15.00	26.00	33.00
6 ▸ Cream, 3½", ftd., #2719/681	10.00	15.00	22.00
8 ▸ Jelly w/cover, 6⅛", #2719/447	25.00	45.00	60.00
Pickle, 8⅜", #2719/540	18.00	35.00	40.00
9 ▸ Pitcher, 7⁵⁄₁₆", 48 oz., ice jug, #2719/456	40.00	85.00	150.00
14 ▸ Plate, 8", #2719/550	8.00	12.00	18.00
Plate, 14", torte, #2719/567	22.00	35.00	55.00
11 ▸ Relish, 9⅛", 2-part, #2719/620	14.00	26.00	30.00
Salad set, 4-pc. (10" bowl, 14" plate w/wood fork & spoon), #2719/286	45.00	65.00	100.00
4 ▸ Salver, 7" high, 10" diameter, #2719/630	60.00	**120.00	150.00
Sauce dish w/cover, 4½", #2719/635	16.00	30.00	38.00
7 ▸ Shaker, 3½", w/chrome top, pr., #2719/653	20.00	25.00	40.00
13 ▸ Stem, 4⁵⁄₁₆", 4 oz., wine, #2719/26	8.00	16.00	18.00
15 ▸ *Stem, 4¼", 6½ oz., sherbet, #2719/7	6.00	8.00	12.00
*Stem, 4⅛", 7 oz., sherbet, #2719/7	6.00	8.00	12.00
2 ▸ *Stem, 5¾", 9½ oz., goblet, #2719/2	8.00	14.00	16.00
*Stem, 5⅞", 10 oz., goblet, #2719/2	8.00	14.00	16.00
5 ▸ Sugar, 3½", ftd., #2719/679	10.00	15.00	22.00
Tray, 9⅜", hndl. muffin, #2719/726	20.00	40.00	55.00
Tumbler, 4¼", 9 oz., #2719/73	8.00	16.00	25.00
10 ▸ Tumbler, 4¾", 5 oz., ftd., juice, #2719/88	8.00	16.00	22.00
12 ▸ Tumbler, 5⅛", 12 oz., #2719/64	8.00	16.00	22.00
1 ▸ Tumbler, 6", 11 oz., ftd. tea, #2719/63	9.00	16.00	21.00
Tumbler, 6", 12 oz., ftd. tea, #2719/63	9.00	16.00	21.00

*Made in recent years
**Green $250.00

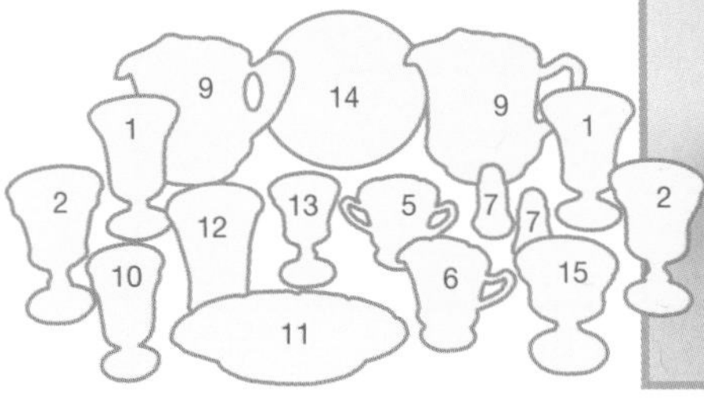

KING'S CROWN, THUMBPRINT, LINE NO. 4016, U.S. GLASS (TIFFIN) COMPANY,
late 1800s – 1960s; INDIANA GLASS COMPANY, 1970s

Colors: crystal, crystal with ruby or cranberry flash, crystal with gold or platinum

We have been assailed by collectors asking us to show pieces from all the different companies who made this pattern. Since at least 25 different companies made a form of King's Crown and look-alike wares during the past 100 or so years, we aren't ready to attempt that. It is doubtful a complete listing will ever be realized. Initially issued as Thumbprint Line No. 4016 by U. S. Glass in the late 1800s, this glassware was still being made by Tiffin in the early 1960s. The Tiffin catalog pages depicted are from 1955. Indiana bought the Tiffin moulds and subtly changed the design. Our listing is mainly related to the Tiffin and Indiana wares made after 1940.

You may find further items, but please realize that many of those are from an earlier time or a different company. The Tiffin plates seem to have starred designs in the center while the Indiana ones appear to be plain. In researching this mystifying pattern, we have discovered no simple rules. One of the stimulating things about King's Crown is that you never know what piece is available around the next corner. Collectors seem to like it all, no matter who made it. A note to anyone selling King's Crown is to watch where you place price stickers. Many a piece has gone unsold because a price sticker removed the color flashing. Please don't place the sticker on the color trim.

King's Crown has been one of the fastest selling patterns that we stock as long as we stay away from the multitude of stems that are available. Unfortunately, stems are what we keep running into and we have had to learn to control buying them no matter how reasonably priced. Buy any serving pieces you can find. There are more sugars, creamers, cups, finger bowls, and snack plates being located than are needed at present; so prices for them are on a downward trend.

Most collectors prefer the deeper red shade of flashing to the lighter shade called cranberry. The purple pieces are Tiffin's Mulberry. There are pieces flashed with gold, platinum, blue, green, yellow, cranberry, or ruby. Most flashed colors are selling for less than ruby, although gold is not far behind ruby. Demand makes ruby the desired color. You need to pay only what you are willing for crystal pieces without flashed-on colors, as there are few competitors buying it. Gold and platinum decorated products were also made at Indiana in the 70s.

Bear in mind that amber, avocado green, and iridized carnival colors are all Indiana's production of the late 1970s and 1980s. In 1976, they also made a smoky blue for the Bicentennial which they called Colonial Blue. It may be in shorter supply, but few collectors seem to care.

The price on the punch bowl set continues to rise, but slower than in the past. Demand for these is extraordinary. The 24" plate listed as the party server only measures 22½" to 23" on those we have measured.

Long drawn-out thumbprint designs are from the original Tiffin moulds. Some elongated thumbprint styles may have been made at Indiana before they changed the moulds; but if the pieces you have show rounded thumbprints, you definitely have King's Crown made by Indiana or another company — not Tiffin. Most Tiffin-made tumblers are flared at the top while Indiana's are straight. Hope to pay less than the prices listed for the more recently issued Indiana tumblers. You alone can decide what price you are willing to pay for these if you want them at all.

KING'S CROWN, THUMBPRINT

	Item	Price
	Ashtray, 5¼", square	35.00
15 ▸	Bowl, 4", finger	12.00
	Bowl, 5", mayonnaise	40.00
	Bowl, 5", divided mayonnaise	45.00
	Bowl, 5¾"	16.00
	Bowl, 6" diameter, 10½" high, ftd., wedding or candy	150.00
	Bowl, 8¾", 2-hndl., crimped bonbon	90.00
3 ▸	Bowl, 9¼", salad	75.00
	Bowl, 11½", 4½" high, crimped	125.00
	Bowl, 11¼", cone	75.00
	Bowl, 12½", center edge, 3" high	100.00
	Bowl, 12½", flower floater	70.00
	Bowl, crimped, ftd.	100.00
	Bowl, flared, ftd.	90.00
	Bowl, straight edge	70.00
19 ▸	Cake salver, 12½", ftd.	70.00
	Candleholder, sherbet type	20.00
	Candleholder, 2-lite, 5½"	95.00
17 ▸	Candy box, 6", flat, w/cover	55.00
	Cheese stand	30.00
11 ▸	Compote, 5¾", ftd. w/lid	20.00
1 ▸	Compote, 6", ruffled top	45.00
16 ▸	Compote, 6¼", ftd.	20.00
	Compote, 7¼", 9¾" diameter	55.00
	Compote, 7½", 12" diameter, ftd., crimped	125.00
5 ▸	Creamer (2 styles)	16.00
4 ▸	Cup	12.00
	Lazy Susan, 24", 8½" high, w/ball bearing spinner	395.00
	Mayonnaise, 3-pc. set	65.00
12 ▸	Pitcher	195.00
	Plate, 5", bread/butter	6.00
	Plate, 7⅜", mayonnaise liner	10.00
	Plate, 7⅜", salad	10.00
7 ▸	Plate, 9¾", snack w/indent	10.00
18 ▸	Plate, 10", dinner	35.00
	Plate, 14½", torte	90.00
	Plate, 24", party	150.00
	Plate, 24", party server (w/punch ft.)	285.00
	Punch bowl foot	125.00
	Punch bowl, 2 styles	700.00
6 ▸	Punch cup	12.00
	Punch set, 15-pc., w/foot	1,150.00
31 ▸	Punch set, 15-pc., w/plate	950.00
24 ▸	Relish, 14", 5-part	120.00
20 ▸	Saucer	4.00
23 ▸	Stem, 2 oz., wine	6.00
8 ▸	Stem, 2¼ oz., cocktail	10.00
	Stem, 4 oz., claret	12.00
	Stem, 4 oz., juice	6.00
14 ▸	Stem, 4 oz., oyster cocktail	6.00
9 ▸	Stem, 5½ oz., sundae or sherbet	5.00
13 ▸	Stem, 9 oz., water goblet	10.00
2 ▸	Sugar (2 styles)	16.00
	Tumbler, 4 oz., juice, ftd.	10.00
21 ▸	Tumbler, 4½ oz., juice	12.00
22 ▸	Tumbler, 8½ oz., water	10.00
10 ▸	Tumbler, 11 oz., iced tea (3 styles)	10.00
	Tumbler, 12 oz., iced tea, ftd.	15.00
	Vase, 9", bud	100.00
	Vase, 12¼", bud	120.00
	Wedding bowl, 6" diameter, 10½" high	90.00

United States Glass Company

TIFFIN, OHIO

KINGS CROWN

Also known as No. 4016 Thumbprint

Sugar

Cream

5" Bread and Butter Plate

Cup and Saucer

10" Dinner Plate

AVAILABLE PLAIN CRYSTAL, DECORATED CRANBERRY OR RUBY

KINGS CROWN

Goblet 9 oz.

Wine 2 oz.

Juice 4 oz.

Claret 4 oz.

Cocktail 2¼ oz.

Oyster Cocktail 4 oz.

Sundae 5½ oz.

Water Tumbler 8½ oz.

Juice Tumbler 4½ oz.

Footed Ice Tea 12 oz.

Ice Tea Tumbler 11 oz.

7⅜" Salad Plate

Finger Bowl 4" Diameter

KING'S CROWN, THUMBPRINT

KINGS CROWN

Center Edge Bowl 12½" Diameter 3" High

2-Lite Candle Holder 5½" High

Footed Fruit Compote 9¾" Diameter 7¼" High

Crimped Bowl 11½" Diameter 4½" High

Cone Bowl 11¼" Diameter 4¾" High

AVAILABLE PLAIN CRYSTAL, DECORATED CRANBERRY OR RUBY

LARIAT, BLANK, LINE NO. 1540, A.H. HEISEY & CO., 1940s – 1957

Colors: crystal; rare in black and amber

Lariat prices have remained in a slump, especially stems, which have apparently saturated the market in recent years. Those highly priced cordials found few buyers at previous levels, but after dropping drastically, they are beginning to be noticed as "bargains." Scarce pieces sell well since there are many collectors looking for seldom-found items. Conversely, the horsehead candy has softened in price since more have been found than there are collectors willing to pay the price. Common Lariat pieces are still available; you can determine scarce pieces by their prices in our listing.

Moonglo is the cutting most often seen on Lariat. Many non-Lariat collectors admire this cut; but surprisingly, few try to round it up. We have tried to beguile you with the number of pieces shown. Enjoy! The ads that we have shown in the past are becoming collectible in their own right. Watch for them in women's magazines of the 1940s and 1950s.

Lariat amber champagnes and black plates have been shown in earlier books but they are rarely found.

1

	Ashtray, 4"	15.00
	Basket, 7½", bonbon	85.00
	Basket, 8½", ftd.	150.00
	Basket, 10", ftd.	185.00
	Bowl, 2 hdld., cream soup	50.00
	Bowl, 7 quart, punch	130.00
25 ▸	Bowl, 4", nut, individual	28.00
	Bowl, 7", 2 pt., mayonnaise	20.00
17 ▸	Bowl, 7", nappy	15.00
	Bowl, 8", flat, nougat	20.00
	Bowl, 9½", camellia	22.00
	Bowl, 10", hdld., celery	30.00
	Bowl, 10½", 2 hdld., salad	32.00
	Bowl, 10½", salad	35.00
	Bowl, 11", 2 hdld., oblong, relish	28.00
	Bowl, 12", floral or fruit	36.00
	Bowl, 13", celery	40.00
	Bowl, 13", gardenia	30.00
	Bowl, 13", oval, floral	30.00
	Candlestick, 1-lite, individual	20.00
8 ▸	Candlestick, 2-lite	30.00
22 ▸	Candlestick, 3-lite	35.00
	Candy box, w/cover, caramel	75.00
	Candy, w/cover, 7"	90.00
	Candy, w/cover, 8", w/horse head finial (rare)	1,400.00
	Cheese, 5", ftd., w/cover	45.00
	Cheese dish, w/cover, 8"	50.00
	Cigarette box	45.00
	Coaster, 4"	8.00
	Cologne	75.00
19 ▸	Compote, 10", w/cover	100.00
6 ▸	Creamer	18.00
	Creamer & sugar, w/tray, individual	45.00
11 ▸	Cup	12.00
	Cup, punch	8.00
23 ▸	Ice tub	75.00
	Jar, w/cover, 12", urn	175.00
12 ▸	Lamp & globe, 7", black-out	120.00
21 ▸	Lamp & globe, 8", candle, hdld.	95.00
	Mayonnaise, 5" bowl, 7" plate w/ladle set	60.00

24 ▸	Oil bottle, 2 oz., hdld., w/#133 stopper	120.00
18 ▸	Oil bottle, 4 oz., hdld., w/#133 stopper	180.00
26 ▸	Oil bottle, 6 oz., oval	85.00
	Plate, 6", finger bowl liner	8.00
2 ▸	Plate, 7", salad	14.00
4 ▸	Plate, 8", salad	22.00
3 ▸	Plate, 10½", dinner	125.00
	Plate, 11", cookie	35.00
	Plate, 12", demi-torte, rolled edge	40.00
	Plate, 13", deviled egg, round	225.00
	Plate, 14", 2 hdld., sandwich	50.00
	Plate, 15", deviled egg, oval	290.00
	Plate, 21", buffet	70.00
	Platter, 15", oval	60.00
16 ▸	Salt & pepper, pr.	200.00
11 ▸	Saucer	3.00
14 ▸	Stem, 1 oz., cordial, double loop	175.00
15 ▸	Stem, 1 oz., cordial blown, single loop	120.00
	Stem, 2½ oz., wine, blown	20.00
	Stem, 3½ oz., cocktail, pressed	15.00
	Stem, 3½ oz., cocktail, blown	15.00
	Stem, 3½ oz., wine, pressed	20.00
	Stem, 4 oz., claret, blown	20.00
13 ▸	Stem, 4¼ oz., oyster cocktail or fruit	12.00
	Stem, 4½ oz., oyster cocktail, blown	12.00
	Stem, 5½ oz., sherbet/saucer champagne, blown	10.00
	Stem, 6 oz., low sherbet	7.00
10 ▸	Stem, 6 oz., sherbet/saucer champagne, pressed	10.00
	Stem, 9 oz., pressed	16.00
9 ▸	Stem, 10 oz., blown	16.00
5 ▸	Sugar	18.00
	Tray, rnd., center hdld., w/ball finial	165.00
7 ▸	Tray for sugar & creamer, 8", 2 hdld.	24.00
	Tumbler, 5 oz., ftd., juice	20.00
	Tumbler, 5 oz., ftd., juice, blown	20.00
	Tumbler, 12 oz., ftd., ice tea	25.00
	Tumbler, 12 oz., ftd., ice tea, blown	25.00
20 ▸	Urn jar & cover, 12"	150.00
1 ▸	Vase, 7", ftd., fan	25.00
	Vase, swung	135.00

LIDO, PLATE ETCHING #329, FOSTORIA GLASS COMPANY, 1937 – 1960

Colors: crystal and Azure

Fostoria's Lido is primarily collected in crystal. Azure would probably be the first choice, but it's rarely seen and is quite expensive when found. One collector confided that he bought Lido for at least 10 years and didn't believe the blue existed until he saw a photo in our book. He had over 150 pieces in crystal, but had never seen blue until he bought a tumbler from us. We occasionally price items for sale right after photography and hard to find items fly off our tables at shows before the book appears.

Azure was discontinued during World War II when ingredients for color were hard to get and evidently not much was produced. Blue brings double or more the prices for crystal on most items; but basic pieces sell for around 50% more than crystal since there are fewer collectors searching for it. Many collectors just hope to own one piece of blue.

Cathy first committed this design to memory because she thought it looked like fireworks exploding overhead; actually, it's an attention-grabbing interpretation of a stemmed plant.

All things taken into account, this is a prudently priced Fostoria pattern; but it was not as popular as some other patterns in its day; and consequently, less is offered for you to buy, today.

All items listed without a line number below are found on Baroque blank #2496. You may find other Lido items than those listed here.

		Crystal			Crystal
	Bowl, 4", one hndl., square	12.00		Plate, 10", hndl. cake	28.00
	Bowl, 4⅜", one hndl.	12.00	8 ▸	Plate, 10¼", dinner	35.00
	Bowl, 4⅝", one hndl., 3 cornered	12.00		Plate, 11", cracker	20.00
	Bowl, 5", one hndl., flared	12.00		Plate, 14", torte	40.00
	Bowl, 6¼", 3 ftd., cupped	18.00	3 ▸	Relish, 6", square, 2-part	15.00
6 ▸	Bowl, 7⅜" 3 ftd., bonbon	15.00	17 ▸	Relish, 10", 3-part	22.00
13 ▸	Bowl, 8½", 2 hndl.	30.00	2 ▸	Saucer	3.00
7 ▸	Bowl, 10½", 2 hndl., ftd.	30.00		Shaker, 2¾"	25.00
	Bowl, 12", flared	35.00		Stem, #6017, 3⅝", 4 oz., oyster cocktail	12.00
	Bowl, 12½", oval, #2545 Flame	40.00		Stem, #6017, 3⅞", ¾ oz., cordial	35.00
	Bowl, finger, #766	25.00		Stem, #6017, 4½", 6 oz., low sherbet	8.00
11 ▸	Candlestick, 4½", duo	25.00		Stem, #6017, 4⅞", 3½ oz., cocktail	12.00
	Candlestick, 4"	16.00		Stem, #6017, 5½", 3 oz., wine	18.00
	Candlestick, 5½"	18.00		Stem, #6017, 5½", 6 oz., high sherbet	10.00
	Candlestick, 6¾", duo, #2545 Flame	30.00		Stem, #6017, 5⅞", 4 oz., claret	18.00
	Candy w/cover, 6¼", 3-part	80.00		Stem, #6017, 7⅜", 9 oz., water	14.00
	Celery, 11"	20.00	14 ▸	Sugar	8.00
	Comport, 3¼", ftd. cheese	18.00		Sugar, individual	10.00
	Comport, 4¾"	16.00		Sweetmeat, 6", square, 2 hndl.	15.00
	Comport, 5½"	18.00		Tidbit, 8¼", 3-ftd., flat	18.00
	Comport, 5¾"	20.00		Tray, 6½" ind. sug/cr., #2496½	10.00
12 ▸	Creamer	9.00		Tumbler, #4132, 2⅛", 1½ oz., whiskey	25.00
	Creamer, individual	11.00		Tumbler, #4132, 3½", 4 oz., sham	12.00
1 ▸	Cup, ftd.	12.00		Tumbler, #4132, 3⅛", 7½ oz., old fashioned	14.00
16 ▸	Ice bucket	75.00		Tumbler, #4132, 3¾", 5 oz., sham	12.00
	Jelly w/cover, 7½"	45.00		Tumbler, #4132, 3¾", 9 oz., sham	14.00
	Mayonnaise, 3-pc. set, #2496½	30.00		Tumbler, #4132, 4⅛", 7 oz., sham	12.00
	Oil bottle w/stopper, 3½ oz.	65.00		Tumbler, #4132, 4⅞", 12 oz., sham	16.00
	Pickle, 8"	15.00		Tumbler, #4132, 5⅜", 14 oz., sham	18.00
	Pitcher, #6011, 8⅞", 53 oz., ftd.	165.00	15 ▸	Tumbler, #6017, 4¾", 5 oz., ftd. juice	12.00
	Plate, 6"	5.00	4 ▸	Tumbler, #6017, 5½", 9 oz., ftd. water	15.00
	Plate, 7", #2337	7.00	5 ▸	Tumbler, #6017, 6", 12 oz., ftd. iced tea	20.00
	Plate, 7½"	7.00		Tumbler, #6017, 6½", 14 oz., ftd.	25.00
9 ▸	Plate, 8½"	10.00		Vase, 5"	70.00
10 ▸	Plate, 9½", small dinner	28.00		Vase, 7"	100.00

LIDO

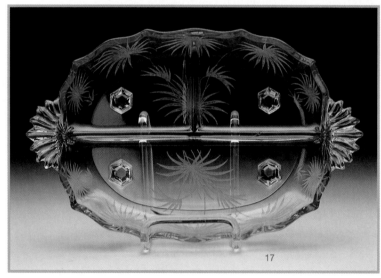

17

16

"LILY PONS," LINE #605, INDIANA GLASS COMPANY, c. 1930s – 1990s

Colors: amber, green; recently iridized, spray painted, and crystal

"Lily Pons" is the collectors' name for Indiana's #605 line which was initially made in the 30s, but has been manufactured intermittently ever since. Indiana has always made the most of using older moulds with newer colors. We have seen crystal plates, iridized vegetable bowls, and various sprayed colors of oval pickle dishes. The older Depression green color hasn't been remade and since Indiana ceased production, it probably is a safe color to consider for your Depression glass needs; but since most production was made later, we have included it in this 50s book.

We have had difficulty acquiring a sugar and creamer although we've previously owned several sets, but sold them before deciding to include this small line in our book. We've searched, but no one seemed to have them for sale now; so our picture is lacking their presence. Since the pieces look like flowers, they're always noticed and quickly disappear from our booth when displayed.

		Green	Other colors
	Bowl, 6½", ftd. bonbon	12.00	5.00
5 ▸	Bowl, 7", deep nappy	25.00	10.00
3 ▸	Bowl, 7", shallow preserve, 2 hdld.	20.00	8.00
1 ▸	Bowl, 8½", pickle	18.00	6.00
	Creamer	22.00	
2 ▸	Sherbet/fruit cocktail, flat	12.00	5.00
	Plate, 6", leaf dessert	10.00	5.00
4 ▸	Plate, 8", salad	12.00	6.00
	Sugar, open	22.00	25.00

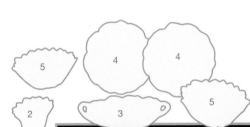

LODESTAR, PATTERN #1632, A.H. HEISEY & CO., c. 1950s

Color: Dawn

Heisey's Lodestar is the pattern shown, but it is only acknowledged as Lodestar in this Dawn color. Crystal pieces of this same design are christened Satellite and prices for crystal plummet spectacularly. Each piece has the star-like shape for its base. Dawn is costly as you can see by the prices listed below; but these are realistic selling prices, not hoped for prices.

13 ▸	Ashtray	75.00	6 ▸	Creamer	50.00
14 ▸	Bowl, 4½", sauce dish, #1626	40.00	11 ▸	Creamer, w/handle	60.00
2 ▸	Bowl, 5", mayonnaise	85.00	3 ▸	Jar, w/cover, 8", #1626	140.00
16 ▸	Bowl, 6¾", #1565	60.00	15 ▸	Pitcher, 1 qt., #1626	160.00
	Bowl, 8"	95.00		Plate, 8½"	65.00
12 ▸	Bowl, 11", crimped	100.00		Plate, 14"	90.00
	Bowl, 12", deep floral	100.00	9 ▸	Relish, 7½", 3-pt.	70.00
	Bowl, 14", shallow	130.00	10 ▸	Sugar	50.00
8 ▸	Candleblock, 2¾" tall, 1-lite star, #1543, pr. (Satellite)	275.00	1 ▸	Sugar, w/handles	70.00
18 ▸	Candlestick, 2" tall, 1-lite centerpiece, pr.	130.00	7 ▸	Tumbler, 6 oz., juice	40.00
	Candlestick, 5¾" tall, 2-lite, pr.	600.00		Vase, 8", #1626	200.00
5 ▸	Candy jar, w/cover, 5"	240.00	4 ▸	Vase, 8", crimped, #1626	210.00
17 ▸	Celery, 10"	65.00			

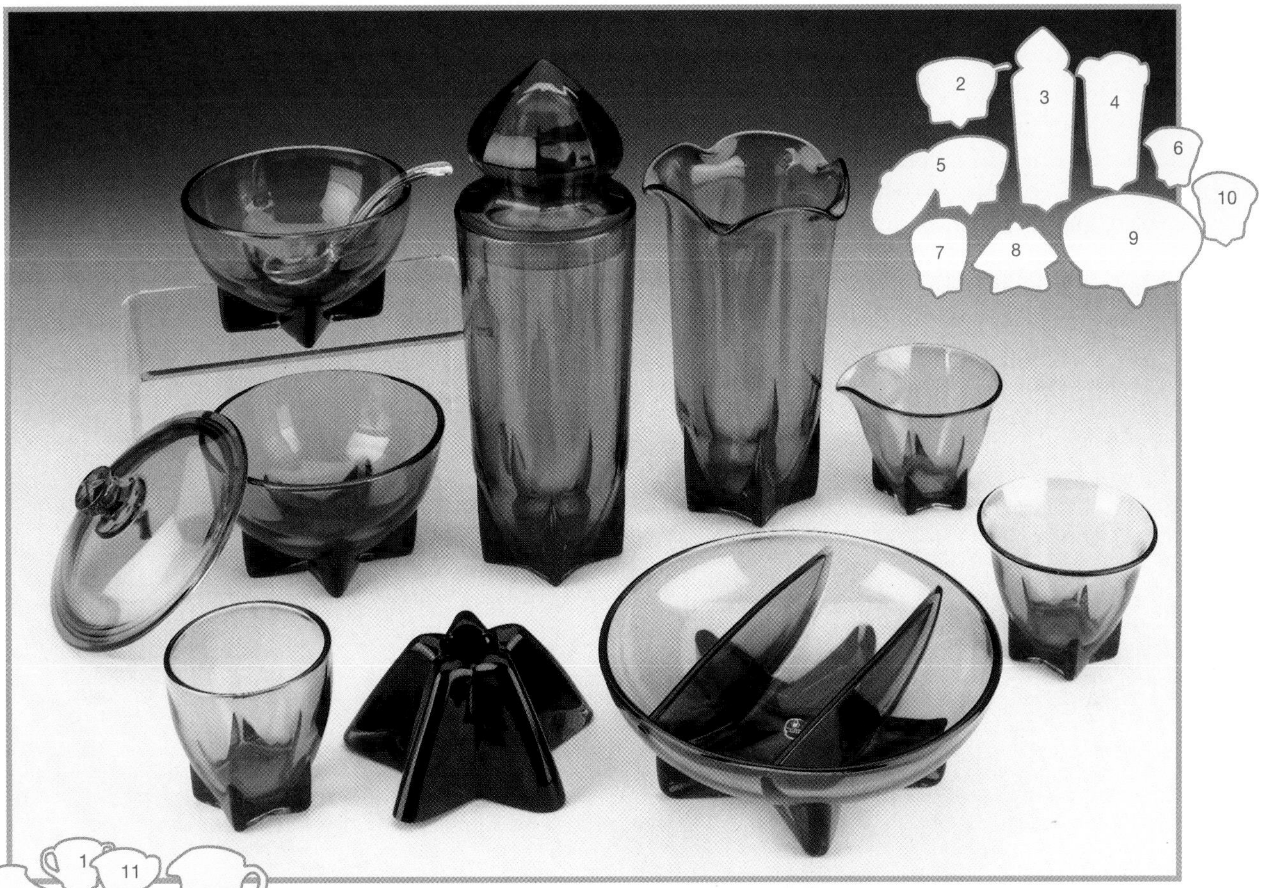
2
3
4
5
6
10
7
8
9

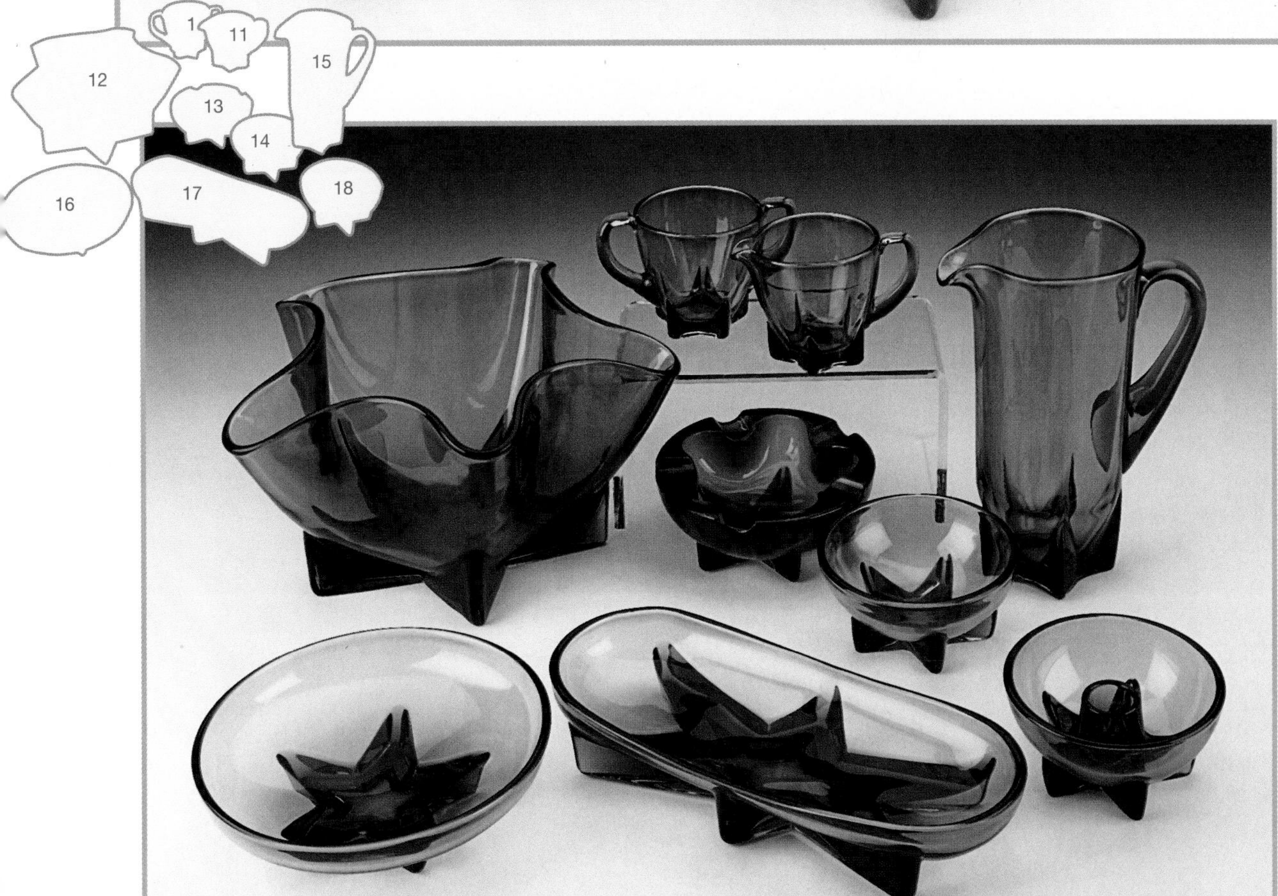
1
11
15
12
13
14
16
17
18

MANHATTAN, LINE #15078, U.S. GLASS COMPANY, c. 1902; ANCHOR HOCKING #0-5078, c. 1950; BARTLETT-COLLINS, c. 1970s

Colors: crystal, and with ruby or gold; avocado and amber, c. 1970s

Manhattan was an admired U.S. Glass pattern for years. Anchor Hocking produced a similar styled punch bowl in the 1950s. However, it had different dimensions from the older ware and was not a part of their well known Depression Manhattan pattern of a different style. According to Fred Bickenheuser, Hocking's punch bowl is 13½" in diameter with a 23" underliner plate and their punch cups have a more open handle than the older version. The older, more cupped, rose bowl shaped punch was only 12" across and the liner only measured 21½". We finally saw one of Hocking's punch sets for sale, but it was priced as gold and not glass.

In the 1970s, Bartlett-Collins produced some items in crystal, avocado, and amber to go with the color trends of that time; however, their large berry bowls had straight rims, rather than the scalloped ones pictured here. They called their version of the pattern St. Genevieve.

		Crystal				Crystal
10 ▸	Bowl, 4½", berry	3.00		1 ▸	Goblet, 6 oz., low sherbet	4.00
12 ▸	Bowl, 6", cereal	8.00		2 ▸	Goblet, 10 oz., water	8.00
	Bowl, 7", flat edge	9.00			Goblet, 12 oz., tea	10.00
11 ▸	Bowl, 8½", large berry	10.00			Plate, 6"	4.00
9 ▸	Celery, 9½"	12.00		3 ▸	Plate, 11", serving	10.00
	Compote, 9½"	10.00			Punch bowl	40.00
	Compote, 10½"	12.00			Punch cup	3.00
8 ▸	Creamer	5.00			Saucer	1.00
4 ▸	Cup	3.00		7 ▸	Sugar	5.00
5 ▸	Goblet, 4 oz., cocktail	6.00		6 ▸	Tumbler, 8 oz., flat water	12.00

MAYFLOWER, PLATE ETCHING #332, FOSTORIA GLASS COMPANY, 1938 – 1954

Color: crystal

Fostoria's etched Mayflower pattern has a bending, cornucopia of flowers as the fundamental motif. From time to time, this is mistaken for Fostoria's Corsage. On page 44 you can see the cone-shaped floral etching that is the Corsage design. You might have been able to blend these two patterns had Fostoria etched them on the same mould blank; but regrettably, they did not.

Mayflower is usually found etched on Fostoria's #2560 blank documented as Coronet. Look at the three curvy lines around the top of each Coronet mould blank. You can spot these easily on the candle, comport, two-handled bowl, creamer, and sugar. The rope appearing handles on the cup, sugar, and creamer are an exclusive trait of blank #2560.

The stemware and tumbler pictured are etched on line #6020, which is the only line on which Mayflower is known. Note its coiling rope appearing stem.

A few pieces of Mayflower are found on Fostoria's #2545 "Flame" blank. You can see "Flame" in the oval bowl and each of the single candlesticks shown beside it. Speaking of candlesticks, there are mounting numbers of collectors searching exclusively for them. Many are shown in our books, *Glass Candlesticks of the Depression Era* and *Volume 2*. We've met one candlestick collector who has over 4,000, but we forgot to ask if they were all singles or pairs.

Vases are infrequently found in Fostoria crystal patterns, so we try to find as many as we can to use in our photos. Thousands of miles of travel over several years were necessary to show these.

	Item	Price			Item	Price
	Bowl, finger, #869	35.00			Plate, 6¼", hndl., lemon, #2560	7.00
	Bowl, 5", hndl., whip cream, #2560	20.00			Plate, 7½", #2560	7.00
	Bowl, 5½", hndl., sweetmeat, #2560	18.00			Plate, 8½", #2560	12.00
	Bowl, 5¾" x 6¼", hndl., bonbon, #2560	18.00			Plate, 9½", #2560	30.00
	Bowl, 7¼", 3-ftd., bonbon, #2560	20.00			Plate, 10½", hndl. cake, #2560	25.00
	Bowl, 8½", hndl., #2560	40.00			Plate, 14", torte, #2560	40.00
	Bowl, 10", salad, #2560	40.00	9 ▸	Relish, 6½", hndl., 2-part, #2560	16.00
	Bowl, 10½", hndl., #2496	40.00	14 ▸	Relish, 10" x 7¾", 3-part, #2560	22.00
13 ▸	Bowl, 11", hndl., #2560	50.00		Salt & pepper, pr.	60.00
	Bowl, 11½", crimped, #2560	50.00		Saucer, #2560	3.00
	Bowl, 12", flared, #2560	45.00		Server, center handled, #2545	45.00
6 ▸	Bowl, 12½", oval, #2545 Flame	50.00		Stem, #6020, 3¾", 1 oz., cordial	35.00
	Bowl, 13", fruit, #2560	50.00		Stem, #6020, 3¾", 4 oz., oyster cocktail	12.00
	Candlestick, 4", #2560½	18.00		Stem, #6020, 4⅝", 6 oz., low sherbet	8.00
1 ▸	Candlestick, 4½", #2545 Flame	25.00		Stem, #6020, 4⅞", 3½ oz., cocktail	12.00
17 ▸	Candlestick, 4½", #2560	20.00		Stem, #6020, 5⅜", 3½ oz., wine	18.00
	Candlestick, 5", duo, #2496	25.00	4 ▸	Stem, #6020, 5½", 6 oz., saucer champagne	12.00
12 ▸	Candlestick, 5⅛", duo, #2560	25.00		Stem, #6020, 5¾", 4½ oz., claret	20.00
	Candlestick, 6¾", duo, #2545 Flame	50.00		Stem, #6020, 6⅛", 5½ oz., claret	20.00
8 ▸	Candlestick, 7½", #2545 Flame	55.00	3 ▸	Stem, #6020, 7¼", 9 oz., water	18.00
	Celery, 11", #2560	22.00	16 ▸	Sugar, #2560	10.00
15 ▸	Comport, 5½"	22.00		Sugar, individual, #2560	10.00
10 ▸	Creamer, #2560	10.00		Tray, 7½", individual cr./sug., #2560	12.00
	Creamer, individual, #2560	10.00		Tray, 10" x 8¼", hndl., muffin, #2560	24.00
	Cup, ftd., #2560	13.00		Tumbler, #6020, 4⅞", 5 oz., ftd. juice	12.00
11 ▸	Mayonnaise set, 3-pc., #2560	30.00		Tumbler, #6020, 5¾", 9 oz., ftd. water	14.00
	Olive, 6¾", #2560	16.00	2 ▸	Tumbler, #6020, 6⅜", 12 oz., ftd. ice tea	16.00
	Pickle, 8¾", #2560	20.00		Vase, 3¾", #2430	50.00
	Pitcher, 7½,", 60 oz., flat, #4140	225.00	5 ▸	Vase, 8", #2430	95.00
	Pitcher, 9¾", 48 oz., ftd., #5000	245.00		Vase, 10", ftd., #2545 Flame	110.00
	Plate, 6", #2560	4.00	7 ▸	Vase, 10", ftd., #5100	100.00

MEADOW ROSE, PLATE ETCHING #328, STEM BLANK #6016,
FOSTORIA GLASS COMPANY, 1936 – 1982

Colors: crystal and Azure

Meadow Rose was promoted as one of Fostoria's three all-time top sellers. Production lasted 47 years; so that longevity should speak volumes for its acceptance with the public. Meadow Rose is regularly confused with another of Fostoria's top three lines, Navarre. They are similar, but the center of the Meadow Rose medallion is open whereas the center of the medallion on Navarre is filled with pattern. See the catalog copy of Navarre on page 163 for comparison.

Matching stemware service for Meadow Rose was available through Fostoria until 1982. Prices for Meadow Rose have declined slowly due to an overabundance turning up. Stemware prices have suffered a faster decline with wine prices dropping

most. Even water goblets have edged slightly lower. As with other elegant patterns, today's collectors are choosing to buy the larger capacity water goblets to use for wine. Those original, smaller, three or four ounce wines do not seem to hold enough to fill their tastes. Meadow Rose collectors are still outnumbered by those searching for Navarre; but the gap is gradually closing with cheaper prices making a difference.

We have had problems finding Azure at reasonable prices to photograph. Were we collecting this pattern, we would be buying the blue or at least attempting to do so. Not surprisingly, blue was produced for only a few years since

materials needed to make that color were off limits for glass factories during World War II. Pieces found in Azure will fetch an additional 50% to 100% depending upon demand. If found on an Internet auction, it could go high or sometimes inexpensively depending upon who wants it or who is watching the auction site at that point in time. Thanks for all those who have sent lists of what they have in Azure which are now indicated by an asterisk in the listing.

If there is no mould blank number shown, then the item is #2496 or the Baroque blank that has the raised fleur-de-lis. All other mould blanks are listed with the item.

		Crystal				Crystal
	Bowl, 4", square, hndl.	12.00			Creamer, individual	12.00
	Bowl, 4½", #869, finger	30.00			Cup	15.00
	Bowl, 4⅝", tri-cornered	12.00			Ice bucket, 4⅜" high	90.00
	Bowl, 5", hndl., flared	20.00	7 ▸		Jelly w/cover, 7½"	65.00
	Bowl, 6", square, sweetmeat	20.00			Mayonnaise, #2375, 3-piece	33.00
14 ▸	Bowl, 7⅜", 3-ftd., bonbon	22.00			Mayonnaise, 2496½, 3-piece	33.00
	Bowl, 8½", hndl.	35.00			Pickle, 8"	25.00
	Bowl, 10", oval, floating garden	40.00			Pitcher, #2666, 32 oz.	195.00
	Bowl, 10½", hndl.	50.00			*Pitcher, #5000, 48 oz., ftd.	295.00
4 ▸	*Bowl, 12", flared	50.00	8 ▸		Plate, 6", bread/butter	6.00
	Bowl, 12", hndl., ftd.	50.00			*Plate, 7½", salad	11.00
	Bowl, #2545, 12½", oval, Flame	55.00	9 ▸		Plate, 8½", luncheon	16.00
	Candlestick, 4"	12.00			Plate, 9½", dinner	35.00
	Candlestick, 4½", double	25.00			Plate, 10", hndl., cake	30.00
	Candlestick, 5½"	28.00			Plate, 11", cracker	22.00
	Candlestick, 6", triple	40.00			Plate, 14", torte	40.00
	Candlestick, #2545, 6¾", double, Flame	35.00			Plate, 16", torte, #2364	75.00
	Candlestick, #2510, 7" wide, duo	85.00			Relish, 6", 2-part, square	22.00
	Candy, w/cover, 3-part	100.00	1 ▸		Relish, 10" x 7½", 3-part	25.00
	Celery, 11"	25.00			Relish, 13¼", 5-part, #2419	60.00
	Comport, 3¼", cheese	20.00	6 ▸		Salad dressing bottle, #2083, 6½"	295.00
	Comport, 4¾"	22.00			Salt & pepper, #2375, 3½", ftd., pr.	75.00
3 ▸	*Creamer, 4¾", ftd.	14.00	12 ▸		*Sauce dish liner, 8", oval	20.00

MEADOW ROSE

	Sauce dish, 6½" x 5¼"	75.00
13 ▸	*Sauce dish, div. mayo., 6½"	30.00
	Saucer	3.00
10 ▸	*Stem, #6016, ¾ oz., cordial, 3⅞"	40.00
5 ▸	*Stem, #6016, 3¼ oz., wine, 5½"	26.00
	*Stem, #6016, 3½ oz., cocktail, 5¼"	15.00
	*Stem, #6016, 4 oz., oyster cocktail, 3⅝"	15.00
	*Stem, #6016, 4½ oz., claret, 6"	28.00
	*Stem, #6016, 6 oz., low sherbet, 4⅜"	12.00
11 ▸	*Stem, #6016, 6 oz., saucer champagne, 5⅝"	15.00
	*Stem, #6016, 10 oz., water, 7⅝"	22.00
2 ▸	*Sugar, 4½", ftd.	14.00
	Sugar, individual	12.00
	Tidbit, 8¼", 3 ftd., turned-up edge	20.00
	Tray, #2375, 11", center hndl.	30.00
	Tray, 6½", 2496½, for ind. sugar/creamer	18.00

*Tumbler, #6016, 5 oz., ftd., juice, 4⅝"		15.00
*Tumbler, #6016, 10 oz., ftd., water, 5⅜"		15.00
*Tumbler, #6016, 13 oz., ftd., tea, 5⅞"		20.00
Vase, #4108, 5"		75.00
Vase, #4121, 5"		75.00
Vase, #4128, 5"		75.00
Vase, #2470, 10", ftd.		110.00

*Indicates items made in Azure which will bring
an additional 75% to 80%

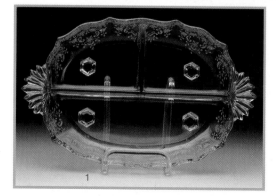

138

MODERNTONE PLATONITE, HAZEL-ATLAS GLASS COMPANY, 1940 – early 1950s

Colors: Platonite pastel, white, and white decorated

Blue and red decorated Platonite Moderntone seems to be the most well-liked in this world of diverse colors and designs. However, that world is rapidly extending as there are over 600 Moderntone items listed in the last three weeks on an Internet auction. There are 375 additional items listed in stores on that auction site. Admittedly only 75 – 80% of listings are actually Platonite, but that should indicate availability of this one pattern. Believe us, there are other patterns with equally long offerings of items for sale.

We have had inquires wanting to know where is the best place to find blue Deco lines or the red and blue Willow. Honestly, we don't know as ours has been acquired from all over the country a piece or two at a time. It has never been plentiful, but worth the wait to obtain it. One dealer told us she was swamped with wishes for additional pieces after she ran a few Willow items on an Internet auction last year. Unfortunately, there is little of either of these decorations surfacing today. All extra pieces we've bought, not needed for photography,

rarely last more than one show when we exhibit them for sale. The red Deco is found more frequently than the blue, but that is not to say it is commonly witnessed.

Platonite Moderntone, one of the more modestly priced patterns from this era, has become a starting point for many young couples just beginning to buy collectible glass. You can choose to mix colors or search only for your favorite. Pieces still turn up at garage and yard sales for a dollar or less. Many times a boxed lot can be bought for a few dollars. People know it is not Depression glass, but do not realize it is now valued. Not everyone is fond of this fired color ware; but if you are, buy it every chance you can. No one thought the supply of Jade-ite Fire-King would ever disappear; but there are scores of collectors now wondering why they did not buy more when the supply seemed unlimited.

At present, demand is negligible for plain white Platonite Moderntone; but that may well change. One lady told us she was mixing white pieces with her cobalt and was very well pleased with the result.

Pastel colors are the lighter shades of blue, green, pink, and yellow. To date, there is no noteworthy price diversity between those found with white interiors to those with colored interiors. We have found faster sales for colored interiors than the white. It's a matter of predilection. Buy what you like.

Two distinct shades of pink are found, but we have been guaranteed by Moderntone collectors that this variation in shade is of no importance to them; but it seems noteworthy to us.

Those four 9 ounce tumblers shown on the top of page 144 are fired-on Moderntone tumblers in pastel colors we had never

seen before and were unusual enough that we had to buy them. Maybe they look different because they are fired over crystal and not white Platonite. We wonder if you have any other pieces fired over crystal? The seller marked these Swanky Swigs, but these are larger, and the light blue one does not fit the known Swanky Swigs color scheme. Platonite Moderntone bowls come with or without rims. Bowls without rims are more difficult to find, and those with rims tend to have more inner rim problems, which is a repellent for collectors. Pastel pink 8" bowls with or without rims and yellow 12" platters are easier to find than other pastel colors.

Someone sent us a photo showing that yellow platters were a premium item at one time, which would account for the large quantities being found. Other colored platters are rarely seen. Moderntone children's dishes are shown on pages 146 – 148.

MODERNTONE PLATONITE

	Pastel Colors	White w/stripes	Deco/Red or Blue Willow
16 ▸ Bowl, 4¾", cream soup	5.00	10.00	20.00
10 ▸ Bowl, 5", berry, w/rim	4.00	7.00	15.00
19 ▸ Bowl, 5", berry, w/o rim	5.00		
21 ▸ Bowl, 5", deep cereal, w/white	6.00	9.00	
17 ▸ Bowl, 5", deep cereal, w/o white	8.00		
11 ▸ Bowl, 8", w/rim	*12.00	18.00	35.00
Bowl, 8", w/o rim	*20.00		
9 ▸ Bowl, 8¾", large berry			35.00
15 ▸ Creamer	4.00	9.00	20.00
12 ▸ Cup	3.50	8.00	20.00
5 ▸ Mug, 4", 8 oz.		10.00	
Plate, 6¾", sherbet	2.00	3.00	8.00
7 ▸ Plate, 7¾", salad	3.00	5.00	
2 ▸ Plate, 8⅞", dinner	4.00	10.00	20.00
8 ▸ Plate, 10½", sandwich	12.00	16.00	30.00
4 ▸ Platter, 11", oval			30.00
Platter, 12", oval	**12.00	20.00	40.00
6 ▸ Salt and pepper, pr.	14.00	15.00	
13 ▸ Saucer	1.00	2.00	4.00
3 ▸ Sherbet	4.00	6.00	16.00
14 ▸ Sugar	4.00	9.00	20.00
18 ▸ Tumbler, 9 oz.	7.00		
†Tumbler, cone, ftd.		5.00	

*Pink $9.00   **Yellow $9.00   †White only

140

MODERNTONE PLATONITE

Colors: dark fired colors of cobalt, turquoise, yellow, orange, Chartreuse, Burgundy, green, gray, rust, gold

Unlike pastel Moderntone colors, just spotting the darker, later colors of Platonite is the first problem; but obtaining any one particular color is a genuine chore. Many collectors are blending the darker colors so that they have more choices. Relative to the quantities of pastel, there are diminutive amounts of darker colors offered for sale. Buy those whenever you find them.

Prices below separate colors into two groups based on demand and availability. The first group consists of cobalt blue, turquoise green, lemon yellow, and orange. All these colors can eventually be collected in sets. They can be found with white or colored interiors, but white interiors are in the majority.

Building a set of any of the further colors, Chartreuse, Burgundy, green, gray, rust, or gold is unlikely. Should you embark upon this undertaking, you will find that none of these colors are found with white interiors. Collectors have inaccurately called the dark green, forest green, and the Burgundy, maroon. We have also heard the gold referred to as butterscotch. As with the two pinks, some collectors consider gold merely a deviation of Lemon (yellow) and not a separate color.

Four pieces listed in pastel colors have not been found in the darker colors. To our knowledge, cream soups, bowls with rims, sandwich plates, and shakers have not been seen. Green (dark) colored tumblers, one pictured, are the only ones we have encountered in the later colors. If you discover others, we'd appreciate you letting us know.

With the arrival of rainbow color collecting, collectors are blending all the colors available with great satisfaction and skill! We believe you'll have fun collecting this as well as using it.

		Cobalt Turquoise Lemon Orange	Burgundy Chartreuse Green/Gray Rust/Gold
16 ▸	Bowl, 4¾", cream soup	11.00	
10 ▸	Bowl, 5", berry, w/rim	12.00	
19 ▸	Bowl, 5", berry, w/o rim	8.00	12.00
21 ▸	Bowl, 5", deep cereal, w/white	12.00	
17 ▸	Bowl, 5", deep cereal, w/o white		15.00
9 ▸	Bowl, 8", w/rim	32.00	
20 ▸	Bowl, 8", w/o rim	32.00	38.00
15 ▸	Creamer	8.00	11.00
12 ▸	Cup	7.00	8.00
7 ▸	Plate, 6¾", sherbet	6.00	8.00
2 ▸	Plate, 8⅞", dinner	12.00	13.00
8 ▸	Plate, 10½", sandwich	20.00	25.00
	Platter, 12", oval	25.00	25.00
6 ▸	Salt and pepper, pr.	20.00	
13 ▸	Saucer	4.00	5.00
3 ▸	Sherbet	7.00	9.00
14 ▸	Sugar	8.00	11.00
18 ▸	Tumbler, 9 oz.	10.00	*30.00

*Green $16.00

MODERNTONE PLATONITE

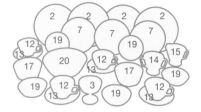

LITTLE HOSTESS PARTY DISHES HAZEL-ATLAS GLASS COMPANY, early 1950s

Moderntone children's sets have taken a plunge in prices for both the harder to find colored sets and the more commonly found ones. Price decline started with the discovery of over 300 sets in original boxes with turquoise teapots. Evidently children's sets were saved to pass down to grandchildren; and therefore quantities of these are appearing over the Internet in numbers never thought possible. If you have a set in storage, and see one like it sell for over $100 on an Internet auction, what is the first thing you do? You think nostalgia be hanged; buy the grandchildren a newer, cheaper set since they will probably break the old one anyway. Thus, the collecting market experiences a surplus and prices fall. Who cares if the one stored only sold for $65.00 — it was "found" money.

An all white set and a pink and black set in the original boxes can be seen in our *Hazel-Atlas Glass Identification and Value Guide* that explores Moderntone in more pictorial depth than we have room to do here. We show these sets, mixed, on the top of page 147. Notice the souvenir cup and saucer at center which was yet another way these small wares were distributed.

Teapots are the most difficult pieces to find, with lids being harder to locate than the bottoms. When buying teapot tops or bottoms individually, you should be aware that Burgundy shades vary greatly, and Turquoise ones slightly. The hues of color may not match unless you have both pieces in hand.

	Little Hostess Party Set pink/black/white (top 147)	
1 ▸	Cup, ¾", bright pink, white	15.00
2 ▸	Saucer, 3⅞", black, white	8.00
3 ▸	Plate, 5¼", black, bright pink, white	10.00
5 ▸	Creamer, 1¾", bright pink	20.00
4 ▸	Sugar, 1¾", bright pink	20.00
6 ▸	Teapot, 3½", bright pink	65.00
12 ▸	Teapot lid, black	100.00
	Set, 16-piece	300.00

	Little Hostess Party Set lemon/beige/pink/aqua (bottom 147)	
7 ▸	Cup, ¾", bright pink, aqua, lemon	15.00
8 ▸	Saucer, 3⅞", same	8.00
9 ▸	Plate, 5¼", same	12.00
5 ▸	Creamer, 1¾", pink	15.00
4 ▸	Sugar, 1¾", pink	15.00
10 ▸	Teapot, 3½", brown	80.00

	Little Hostess Party Set	
11 ▸	Teapot lid, lemon	80.00
	Set, 16-piece	325.00

	Little Hostess Party Set gray/rust/gold Turquoise (top 146)	
	Cup, ¾", gray, rust	10.00
	Cup, ¾", gold, turquoise	10.00
	Saucer, 3⅞", all four colors	5.00
	Plate, 5¼", same	5.00
	Creamer, 1¾", rust	10.00
	Sugar, 1¾", rust	10.00
	Teapot, 3½", turquoise	30.00
	Teapot lid, turquoise	40.00
	Set, 16-piece	185.00

	Little Hostess Party Set green/gray/chartreuse/ burgundy (bottom 146 left)	
	Cup, ¾", green, gray, chartreuse	10.00
	Cup, ¾", burgundy	10.00

Saucer, 3⅞", green, gray & burgundy, chartreuse		5.00
Plate, 5¼", burgundy		10.00
Plate, 5¼", green, gray, chartreuse		8.00
Creamer, 1¾", chartreuse		10.00
Sugar, 1¾", chartreuse		10.00
Teapot, 3½", burgundy		30.00
Teapot lid, burgundy		40.00
Set, 16-piece		185.00

	Little Hostess Party Set pastel pink/green/blue yellow (bottom 146 right)	
Cup, ¾", all four colors		5.00
Saucer, 3⅞", same		3.00
Plate, 5¼", same		5.00
Creamer, 1¾", pink		10.00
Sugar, 1¾", pink		10.00
Set, 14-piece		75.00

MODERNTONE LITTLE HOSTESS PARTY DISHES

MOON AND STAR, ADAMS & CO., c 1880; U.S. GLASS, 1890s; L. G. WRIGHT, 1930s – 1960s; FENTON GLASS CO. FOR L.G. WRIGHT; L.E. SMITH, 1940s AND MINIATURE CARNIVAL WARES FOR LEVAY DISTRIBUTING CO., 1970s; WEISHAR ENTERPRISES, ½ SIZE MINIATURES, 1990s, CURRENTLY JADITE

Colors: crystal; amber, amberina, amethyst, blue, blue satin, blue opalescent, brown, cranberry opalescent, green, green satin, mint, green opalescent, milk glass, ruby, ruby satin, pink, pink satin, vaseline, vaseline satin, vaseline opalescent, jadite

Collectors persuaded us to incorporate Moon and Star in our book. We can't refrain from adding that it was the proverbial "can of worms" due to all the different manufacturers, time periods involved, and the fact it is currently being made. Jadite colored Moon and Star appears so often that it is a thorn in the flower garden of Moon and Star. All Jadite pieces have been made in the last few years and none of it is the least bit old. However, jade is currently in; so we presume sales must be brisk.

A large red jardiniere and covered compote were purchased in an antique mall as we shopped our way back from a show last year. We photographed them and they sold immediately upon being put out for sale. There are three sizes of jardinieres; that one looks as large as a waste paper can.

Although new items and colors continue to be made, collectors do not seem disheartened. Many people are buying this design (formerly named Palace) as fast as it can be produced; so, we're stuck with at least touching bases with the L.G. Wright and L.E. Smith production lines which mostly fit the time parameters for this book. L.G. Wright Company's forté in glass was built around remaking older company wares, either by purchasing the original moulds or by remaking moulds of discontinued lines. Smith items are designed with an "S" in the listings and Wright's with a "W."

Their first foray into the Moon and Star pattern was some crystal items (goblets, dessert bowls, egg cups, miniature night lamps, etc.) in late 1930s and early 1940s. These wares were shinier and more polished than their antique ancestors, but sold well.

		Amber Crystal Green	Blue Ruby Vaseline	Other colors
	Ashtray, 4½" dia., 6-sided, S	10.00	12.50	11.00
	Ashtray, 5" dia., 6-sided, W	28.00	38.00	32.00
	Ashtray, 8" dia., 6-sided, S	15.00	20.00	25.00
	Ashtray, 8½" dia., 6-sided, W	20.00	30.00	25.00
16 ▸	Banana dish, folded sides, 9", S	25.00	38.00	30.00
	Banana dish, folded sides, 12", W	25.00	38.00	28.00
	Basket, 4", double twig hndl.	20.00	25.00	22.50
11 ▸	Bowl, 6" dia., ftd., crimped rim, W	10.00	18.00	
	Bowl, 7½" dia., S	15.00		
	Bowl, 8" dia., console, low ft., W			35.00
	Bowl, 8" dia., flared, scalloped, S	16.00	28.00	
	Butter dish & lid, 5¾" dia., W	40.00	55.00	45.00
17 ▸	Butter dish & lid, 7" dia., S	35.00	50.00	40.00
	Cake stand, 11", high, skirt rim, 2-pc., S	50.00	50.00	45.00
9 ▸	Cake stand, 11", low, no rim, S	45.00	70.00	60.00
	Cake stand, 12", low, W	55.00	80.00	65.00
	Candlestick, 4⅝", S	12.00	22.50	15.00
2 ▸	Candlestick, 6", S	18.00	30.00	25.00
13 ▸	Candlestick, 6", W	18.00	30.00	25.00
	Candy jar w/lid, 10", S	45.00	60.00	55.00
	Candy jar w/lid, 12", S	75.00	120.00	95.00
	Canister, 1 lb., S	8.00	12.00	12.00
	Canister, 2 lb., S	12.00	18.00	15.00
	Canister, 3½ lb., S	12.00	20.00	15.00
	Canister, 5 lb., S	15.00	25.00	18.00
15 ▸	Compote, 4" w/lid, ftd., W	30.00	45.00	40.00

		Amber Crystal Green	Blue Ruby Vaseline	Other colors
	Compote, 4½" w/lid, ftd., W			45.00
5 ▸	Compote, 6" w/lid, ftd., W	35.00	50.00	45.00
	Compote, 6½", crimped, S	15.00	25.00	20.00
	Compote, 8", flared, W	40.00	55.00	45.00
14 ▸	Compote, 8", ruffled, W	35.00	50.00	40.00
	Compote, 8", w/lid, S	55.00	90.00	65.00
	Compote, 8", w/lid, W	65.00	100.00	75.00
	Compote, 10", rolled edge, S	45.00	60.00	55.00
	Compote, 10", scalloped, S	40.00	55.00	50.00
	Compote, 10", scalloped, W	48.00	63.00	53.00
	Compote, 12", rolled edge, S	65.00	100.00	75.00
	Creamer, 3", individual, S	8.00	12.00	10.00
	Creamer, W	15.00	25.00	20.00
	Decanter, W	55.00	80.00	85.00
	Epergne, 8" high, S	25.00	45.00	35.00
7 ▸	Goblet, 9 oz., W	15.00	25.00	20.00
	Goblet, 11 oz., S	15.00	25.00	20.00
21 ▸	Jardiniere, 6"	100.00	200.00	150.00
	Jardiniere, 7"	125.00	225.00	175.00
20 ▸	Jardiniere, 8"	150.00	250.00	200.00
	Lamp, 10", miniature, w/shade, W	70.00	100.00	90.00
6 ▸	Lamp, 12", oil, flat, bulbous, S	68.00	100.00	80.00
	Lamp, 16" elec. metal base, S	110.00		
	Lamp, 24", table w/shade, S	175.00		295.00
	Nappy, 6", crimped, W	15.00	30.00	
	Pitcher, 32 oz., tall, W	65.00	100.00	90.00

MOON AND STAR

		Amber Crystal Green	Blue Ruby Vaseline	Other colors
	Relish, 8", 3 pt., S	20.00	30.00	25.00
	Relish, 8", oval, boat, W	25.00	35.00	30.00
	Relish, 8", rectangular, W	35.00	60.00	45.00
	Relish, 8", triangular, W	35.00	60.00	45.00
	Salt dip, S	12.50	25.00	20.00
	Salt dip, W	15.00	30.00	25.00
	Salt shaker, 4", W	15.00	25.00	20.00
19 ▶	Salt shaker, 4", straight, S	15.00	25.00	20.00
4 ▶	Sauce dish, 4½", round, ftd., W	15.00	25.00	20.00
	Sherbet, 4½", 6 oz., flared, W	15.00	25.00	20.00
12 ▶	Sherbet, 6 oz., S	15.00	25.00	20.00
	Soap dish, 6", oval, W	18.00	30.00	25.00
	Spoon holder, 5¼", W	25.00	45.00	35.00
	Sugar shaker, 4½", W	25.00	45.00	35.00
8 ▶	Sugar, 3", individual, S	8.00	12.00	10.00
	Sugar, w/lid, W	18.00	30.00	25.00
	Toothpick, 3", W	10.00	15.00	12.50
18 ▶	Toothpick, 3⅛", S	10.00	15.00	12.50
3 ▶	Tumbler, ftd., 5 oz., juice, W	15.00	25.00	20.00
1 ▶	Tumbler, ftd., 7 oz., water, W	20.00	30.00	25.00
	Tumbler, 11 oz., flat, S	15.00	25.00	20.00
	Tumbler, ftd., 11 oz.	18.00	30.00	25.00
	Urn, ftd., S	8.00	12.00	10.00
10 ▶	Vase, 6½", bud, S	15.00	25.00	20.00
	Wine, 2 oz., W	15.00	25.00	20.00
	Wine, 3 oz., S	10.00	15.00	12.50

20

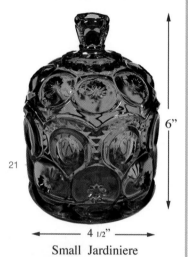

L.E. Smith "Moon and Stars"

21

6"

4 1/2"

Small Jardiniere

MOON GLOW, LINE #113, GREENBRIER, LINE #116, FEDERAL GLASS COMPANY, c. 1974

Color: rainbow iridescent hue

Moon Glow Line #113 and Greenbrier Line #116 with their pearl-like finishes were made just before Federal went out of business in the late 70s. There were only 11 different pieces manufactured counting the sugar bowl lid. We had minor obstacles locating pieces of this to photograph, but we did have a major problem discovering items with full iridescent sheen. Detergents and dishwashers devastated the surface of both of these late Federal patterns. The chop plate and vegetable bowl are the harder to find items along with the sugar lid. Moon Glow is quite attractive when all together and was advertised as oven-proof in 16-, 35-, or 45-piece sets.

Greenbrier (green-edged) was sold only in 16- and 45-piece sets. Green was described as "shimmering beauty." These two patterns are usually found in sets indicating they were not used as much as some other glassware of this time. If used, generally cups are missing. Both patterns are found mislabeled as carnival or even stretch glass. Prices fluctuate greatly at the moment, perhaps because most have no idea what it is or how to price it.

You can see catalog illustrations of both patterns in the Federal section of our *Florences' Ovenware from the 1920s to the Present* book.

7 ▸	Bowl, 4⅞", dessert	3.00
8 ▸	Bowl, 6⅜", soup/cereal	6.00
2 ▸	Bowl, 8½", vegetable	11.00
	Creamer	4.00
3 ▸	Cup	3.00
5 ▸	Plate, 7⅝", salad	3.00
6 ▸	Plate, 10", dinner	6.00
1 ▸	Plate, 11¼", chop	10.00
4 ▸	Saucer	1.00
	Sugar w/cover	9.00

Colors: crystal with opalescent hobnails and some green with opalescent hobnails; other experimental colors

Moonstone is an opalescent hobnail that really became popular with War World II brides. Anchor Hocking's catalogs imply it began production some time in 1941 and was made until 1946. Their war catalogs are not as explicit in listing dates as those before or after. This 1940s glassware continues to attract collectors. Moonstone was prominently displayed in all the five-and-dime stores during the middle of the war; and it's very likely that someone from your family had a piece or two. Notice the J.J. Newberry store display on page 153. This glassware was heavily promoted during the war, and evidently it worked as today's WWII grandkids, like us, remember it extremely well.

As was Fire-King ovenware, Moonstone was a household fixture in the homes of the 50s even though production had come to a close years before. Our grandmothers both used pieces of Moonstone as late as the 60s. Mine had a bottom to a puff box she kept bobby-pins in and Cathy's grandmother had a cloverleaf bowl.

Experimental pieces continue to show up in Moonstone, including a 9½" dinner plate. Had that plate been a regular production item, this set would now attract even more collectors who tend to avoid sets without dinner plates. A cookie jar was found several years ago and is pictured to the right. So far, there are no reports of others turning up. You can see 13 additional rare pieces and colors in our *Treasures of Very Rare Glassware* book.

Most of the pieces pictured on page 154 are compliments of Anchor Hocking's morgue and marked with "x." (Discontinued or experimental items were stored in a place appropriately called a morgue.)

Green Moonstone was distributed under the name Ocean Green and was made in sets containing goblets, cups, saucers, plates, creamer, and sugar. Notice the pieces shown are a slightly different style from the standard line in the catalog page.

The most worrisome regular production piece to find today is 5½" berry bowl listed as M2775 in the Hocking brochure. Notice that they are lacking in the Newberry store photo. Admittedly, goblets and cups and saucers are also excluded in that store window display; and they are easily found today. Crimped 5½" bowls are more available than their straight-side counterparts; but even they are not as abundant as once believed. The factory brochure shows six ruffled bowls to one of the straight edge. The sandwich plate measures 10¼", but we have seen very few of these recently except in Internet auctions.

Fenton Opalescent Hobnail pitchers and tumblers are good companion pieces to go with Anchor Hocking Moonstone sets since there are no pitchers, flat tumblers, or shakers found in Moonstone. We might add that if an opalescent Hobnail piece is not in our listing, it is likely a piece of Fenton Hobnail.

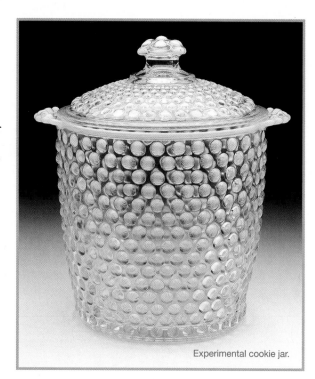

Experimental cookie jar.

	Opalescent Hobnail	
5 ▸	Bowl, 5½", berry	18.00
	Bowl, 5½", crimped, dessert	7.50
3 ▸	Bowl, 6½", crimped, handled	10.00
	Bowl, 7¾", flat	10.00
	Bowl, 7¾", divided relish	9.00
	Bowl, 9½", crimped	22.00
	Bowl, cloverleaf	11.00
	Candleholder, pr.	14.00
	Candy jar and cover, 6"	18.00
	Cigarette box and cover	15.00
	Creamer	10.00

	Opalescent Hobnail	
1 ▸	Cup	6.00
	Goblet, 10 oz.	18.00
	Heart bonbon, one handle	12.00
2 ▸	Plate, 6¼", sherbet	4.00
	Plate, 8⅜", luncheon	13.00
	Plate, 10¾", sandwich	24.00
	Puff box and cover, 4¾", round	20.00
2 ▸	Saucer (same as sherbet plate)	4.00
4 ▸	Sherbet, footed	7.50
	Sugar, footed	10.00
	Vase, 5½", bud	15.00

Opalescent "MOONSTONE" Glassware

"MOONSTONE" Glassware

	DOZ. TO CTN.	WT. OF CTN.
Tableware		
M2779— 3⅞" Cup	6	32#
M2729— 6¼" Saucer	6	32#
M2713— 6 oz. Sherbet	6	32#
M2729— 6¼" Sherbet Plate	6	32#
M2775— 5½" Dessert	6	32#
M2716—10 oz. Goblet	4	36#
M2740— 8⅜" Luncheon Plate	4	44#
Gift Ware		
M2769— 7¾" Divided Relish	2	27#
M2766— 6½" Crimped Handled Bowl	2	19#
M2755— 6¾" Clover Leaf Dish	2	22#
M2772— 6½" Heart Bonbon	2	20#
M2767— 7¾" Flat Bowl	2	23#
M2753— 3¼" Sugar	2	13#
M2754— 3¼" Creamer	2	12½#
M2722— 4¾" Puff Box & Cover	2	22#
M2799— 5" Cigarette Jar & Cover	2	25#
M2782— 5½" Vase	2	16#
M2792— 6" Candy Jar & Cover	1	20#
M2760—10¾" Sandwich Plate	1	21#
M2758— 9½" Crimped Bowl	1	21#
M2765— 5½" Crimped Dessert	6	33#
M2781— 4¼" Candleholder	2	10#
Suggested Sets - Bulk Packed		
M2700/1—7 Pce. Dessert Set (Bulk Packed in 2 Cartons)	12 Sets	54#
M2700/2—4 Pce. Buffet Set (Bulk Packed in 2 Cartons)	12 Sets	52#

Now Available at Low Prices

105 105

MOROCCAN AMETHYST, HAZEL WARE, DIVISION OF CONTINENTAL CAN, 1960s

Color: Amethyst

Moroccan Amethyst creates memories (not all fond) of our first house and baby days. When we moved into our first home we unpacked and proudly used a set of eight narrow-bottomed Moroccan teas we'd received as a wedding gift from Cathy's sorority sisters. We used them until Chad started walking. He would grab hold of things as he walked and if it happened to be the table cloth — twice — these tumblers would fall over and roll spinning contents along the tablecloth, table, walls, and floor. After the ruined antique table cloth, we sold them at our first garage sale for a dime each. When they were selling for $5.00, we couldn't believe it; so now we can relate to all those who have also sold items for pennies on the dollar. We could mention the 35 cent Nippon vase at that sale…. Youth has to learn.

In the past, colors have identified eras, usually in decades. This rich, purple color could be characterized with the 60s just as Harvest gold and Avocado green define the 70s. Numerous glassware companies had wares of this deep amethyst. Hazel Ware called all their products in this delightful shade of purple, Moroccan Amethyst, no matter what the shape or design; and these goods have found a loyal following with present day collectors. Not everyone likes amethyst; but those who do are quite passionate about it. Since real names have never been found, the various designs have acquired names based upon shapes as has been done in Capri. (Think about it. No collector wants to say he collects W4221. He wants a name to impart.) Square or rectangular based pieces are being called Colony as they are in Capri. Moroccan also has a Swirl just as in Capri. There are octagonal and pentagonal shape names which are self explanatory. There is a floral design in the bottom of the 4½" square ashtray; and the 4½" star candle and swirled shakers are missing from most collections.

Moroccan Amethyst items that are beginning to disappear from markets include the ice bucket, eight ounce old-fashioned tumbler, cocktail shaker, and the short, covered candy dish. That tall candy can be found without much tribulation. Candy lids are interchangeable. This was another case of cost-cutting in mould utilization. Vases are around, but are bought quickly when offered for sale.

A boxed set of iced tea tumblers was unearthed which also contained white coasters with 14 juts surrounding the edge. They also have the embossed apple blossom design in the center. These are 3¾" outside to outside, with an opening for the glass of 2⅝". We'd seen these ashtrays before in markets, but didn't imagine their playing a role in the Moroccan Amethyst collection. You can see this coaster and additional items in our *Hazel-Atlas Glass Identification and Value Guide*.

Crystal and white stemware are being found that match the Moroccan stems. You will find large swirled bowls in green, amber, and white, sometimes with matching small bowls suggesting these were marketed as salad sets or chip and dips with a metal stand attached to the large bowl with the smaller bowl held on top. These were a later production made to go with the 70s Avocado and Harvest gold colors and are usually reasonably priced. They were made from the same moulds as Moroccan; actual names for these colors are lacking. Crystal, amber, and green pieces made from these moulds may someday be desirable; but they attract little collector attention now.

MOROCCAN AMETHYST

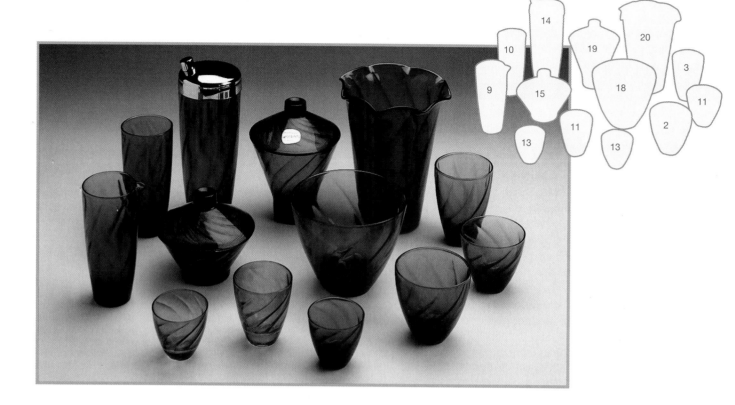

12 ▸	Ashtray, 3¼", triangular	5.50
	Ashtray, 3¼", round	5.50
22 ▸	Ashtray, 3½", square	8.00
40 ▸	Ashtray, 6", triangular	9.50
	Ashtray, 6⅞", triangular	9.50
	Ashtray, 8", square	13.00
33 ▸	Bowl, 4¾", fruit, octagonal	9.00
	Bowl, 4¾", swirled	8.50
7 ▸	Bowl, 5¾", deep, square	10.00
5 ▸	Bowl, 6", round	6.00
48 ▸	Bowl, 7", triangular	9.00
	Bowl, 7¾", oval	12.00
8 ▸	Bowl, 9¾", rectangular	10.00
1 ▸	Bowl, 9¾", rectangular, w/metal handle	18.00
	Bowl, 10", apple shape	40.00
23 ▸	Bowl, 10¾"	22.00
49 ▸	Candle, star shape, 4½"	40.00
15 ▸	Candy w/lid, short	20.00
19 ▸	Candy w/lid, tall	25.00
	Chip and dip, 10¾" & 5¾" bowls in metal holder	30.00
9 ▸	Cocktail w/stirrer, 6¼", 16 oz., w/lip	35.00
14 ▸	Cocktail shaker w/lid	35.00
16 ▸	Cup	5.00
32 ▸	Goblet, 4", 4½ oz., wine, crinkled bottom	9.00
38 ▸	Goblet, 4¼", 7½ oz., sherbet, crinkled bottom	7.00

	Goblet, 4⅜", 5½ oz., juice, crinkled bottom	8.00
45 ▸	Goblet, 5½", 9 oz., water, crinkled bottom	9.00
18 ▸	Ice bucket, 6"	35.00
34 ▸	Plate, 5¾", octagonal	4.50
	Plate, 7¼", salad	5.00
	Plate, 8", square	12.00
24 ▸	Plate, 8", square, snack	8.00
37 ▸	Plate, 9¾", dinner, octagonal	8.00
	Plate, 10", fan shaped, snack w/cup rest	9.00
	Plate, 12", round	12.00
4 ▸	Plate, 12", sandwich, w/metal /handle	15.00
6 ▸	Punch base	17.50
21 ▸	Punch bowl	20.00
50 ▸	Punch cup	2.00
	Salt & pepper shaker, pr.	50.00
17 ▸	Saucer	1.00
13 ▸	Tumbler, 2½", 4 oz., juice	6.00
11 ▸	Tumbler, 5 oz., juice	4.00
2 ▸	Tumbler, 3¼", 8 oz., old fashioned (2 styles)	10.00
3 ▸	Tumbler, 9 oz., water (2 styles)	6.00
47 ▸	Tumbler, 4¼", 11 oz., water, crinkled bottom	9.00
	Tumbler, 4⅝", 11 oz., water	9.00
46 ▸	Tumbler, 5", 12 oz., ice tea	10.00
10 ▸	Tumbler, 6½", 16 oz., iced tea	15.00
20 ▸	Vase, 8½", ruffled	25.00

NARCISSUS, CUT 965, A.H. HEISEY COMPANY, early 1940s – 1957

Color: crystal

Narcissus was a cutting applied to glassware by the A.H. Heisey Company, Newark, Ohio, from the early 1940s until its closing in 1957. Narcissus, cutting #965, was utilized on a number of Heisey blanks but more often on the Jamestown stemware line (#3408) and the Waverly general line blanks (#1519) than any others. This cutting was very popular because of its beauty, ease of identity, and the vast production, which offers a complete set of glassware to collect.

	Bell (made from goblet)	45.00
	Bottle, oil, #1519	175.00
	Bowl, floral, ftd., 11" (#1519	50.00
	Bowl, floral, 13", #1519	45.00
	Bowl, gardenia, 13, #1519	40.00
2 ▸	Candlestick, 2-lite, #134	35.00
	Candlestick, 3-lite, #1519	65.00
	Candy and cover, ftd., 5", #1519	140.00
	Celery tray, 12", #1519	35.00
8 ▸	Comport, low ftd., 6", #1519	35.00
	Comport, ftd. honey, 7", #1519	40.00
	Comport, ftd., nut, 7", #1519	70.00
	Creamer, ftd., #1519	30.00
11 ▸	Cup, #1519	24.00
	Mayonnaise, ftd. and underplate, #1519	55.00
10 ▸	Relish, oval, 3-part, 11", #1519	35.00
	Relish, round, 3-part, 8", #1519	35.00
	Plate, 7", #1519	12.00
5 ▸	Plate, luncheon, 8", #1519	16.00

	Plate, party, 14", #1519	35.00
1 ▸	Salt & pepper, #1519	75.00
12 ▸	Saucer, #1519	7.00
	Stem, goblet, 9 oz., #3408	28.00
9 ▸	Stem, sherbet/saucer-champaign, 6 oz., #3408	14.00
	Stem, claret, 4½ oz., #3408	32.00
4 ▸	Stem, cocktail, 3 oz., #3408	16.00
3 ▸	Stem, cordial, 1 oz., #3408	85.00
7 ▸	Stem, wine, 2 oz., #3408	24.00
	Sugar, #1519	30.00
6 ▸	Tumbler, ice tea, ftd., 12 oz., #3408	24.00
	Tumbler, juice, ftd., 5 oz., #3408	22.00
	Vase, round, ftd., 7", #1519	75.00

NATIONAL, JEANNETTE GLASS COMPANY, late 1940s – mid 1950s

Colors: blue, crystal, pink, and Shell Pink

A few recent National pattern sightings have consisted of sprayed-on colors on the 7⅛" footed tumblers rather than any heretofore unlisted items. The iced teas decorated in sprayed colors are pictured on 160 and the blue and white sugar and creamer on a tray are shown below. There is a bi-colored, blue/crystal candy with the top having a fascinating color-coordinated blue knob, so we are sure this is the original lid. You may also find a red decorated wheat design on bowls and possibly other pieces. Sprays of wheat were familiar embellishments on glassware from this era. We have seen one other piece decorated like this, and it would not surprise us to find a 15" plate so adorned.

National pitchers were regularly seen in restaurants around 10 years ago, although many are retired now due to breakage or those newly designed double spouted, plastic pitchers.

National is a Jeannette pattern recognized more by sight than by name. It is a heavy, bold pattern which some collectors find attractive. They are particularly charmed by the log-like handles on the cup, creamer, and sugar, which are reminiscent of early pattern glass — and our nation's log cabin roots. There are quite a few listings on Internet auctions, but few are selling at this moment. Maybe it has to do with an item worth $5.00 starting at $2.99 with $12.50 postage and handling tacked on. One collector says he buys all the shakers he can find to borrow the plastic tops for Floragold. Enterprising, we'd say.

Two pieces of National are recognized by collectors of Shell Pink. These are a frequently seen Shell Pink National candy bottom, and a "heavy bottomed" 9" vase which is rare. That vase is truly one of the harder to find items in Shell Pink and is not seen in crystal regularly. National crystal candy dishes are often found gold-trimmed.

As we introduce patterns to a book, we try to obtain as many colors and pieces as we can to list, a sometimes arduous task. Hopefully, the diversity shown here adds to your enjoyment of this pattern.

		Crystal
	Ashtray, small	3.00
	Ashtray, large	4.00
	Bowl, 4½", berry	4.00
	Bowl, 8½", large berry	12.00
	Bowl, 12", flat	15.00
	Candle, three ftd.	12.00
	*Candy, ftd., w/cover	15.00
	Celery, 9½"	15.00
	Cigarette box	12.50
12 ▸	Creamer	5.00
7 ▸	Cup	3.00
3 ▸	Jar, relish	12.50
15 ▸	Lazy Susan	35.00
	Pitcher, 20 oz., milk	15.00
	Pitcher, 64 oz.	22.00

		Crystal
2 ▸	Plate, 8", salad	5.00
11 ▸	Plate, 15", serving/punch liner	15.00
9 ▸	Punch bowl, 12"	25.00
10 ▸	Punch bowl stand	15.00
8 ▸	Punch cup	3.00
	Punch set, 15-pc.	80.00
	Relish, 13", 6-part	15.00
	Saucer	1.00
	Shakers, pr.	7.00
13 ▸	Sugar	5.00
14 ▸	Tray, 8", hndl., sug/cr	5.00
4 ▸	Tray, 12½", hndl.	12.00
6 ▸	Tumbler, 3¼", ftd.	8.00
7 ▸	Tumbler, 5¾", flat	8.00
1 ▸	**Tumbler, 7⅛", ftd.	12.50
5 ▸	†Vase, 9"	20.00

*Shell Pink bottom only, $10.00
**Flashed colors, $20.00
†Shell Pink, $165.00

159

NAVARRE, PLATE ETCHING #327, FOSTORIA GLASS COMPANY, 1937 – 1982

Colors: crystal; some blue, pink stems; rare in green and red w/gold etch

Fostoria's Navarre pattern was advertised as one of their three top selling etched patterns of all time. It was nationally promoted as found "at better stores everywhere." Chintz and Meadow Rose were the other two top sellers. Most Navarre was sold after 1940, although it was first introduced in 1937. Due to its period of manufacture, this is the only pattern duplicated in *Elegant Glassware of the Depression Era* and in *Collectible Glassware from the 40s, 50s, 60s....*

A variety of (now hard to find) pieces of Navarre were made near the end of Fostoria's production (late 70s and early 80s). These later made pieces were part of the rationale to include Navarre in this book. A greater part of these later pieces were signed "Fostoria" with acid etching on the base; a small number had only a sticker. Factory "seconds" that sold through the outlet stores were rarely signed. Quality signed pieces were run through the outlets only when those stores ran short of seconds. Shown on page 163 are a few of the later made pieces of Navarre in a catalog strip reprinted from a 1982 Fostoria catalog. The price on many of these items had really inflated to the point that some collectors were doing without or just buying one as an example instead of six, eight, or even 12. However, prices have been settling down to a more reasonable level and patrons are once again opening their pockets to own these pieces. Internet auctions have certainly helped expose these later stems and tumblers more than in the past. Sets including serving pieces, however, will be a tussle but can be completed with persistence and, right now, less expenditure.

A number of Navarre stems starting in 1973 were made with pink and blue bowls and are normally acid etched "Fostoria" on the foot. The Lenox Company bought the molds for this line from Fostoria and made and signed them Lenox. As a rule, the pink made by Lenox is a very washed-out pink and often shades toward a light purple rather than pink. These are difficult to match unless you stick to buying just Lenox or just Fostoria. Then again, you have to purchase what you can find. Besides, as glass supplies dwindle, collectors are being a great deal more tolerant of irregularities such as color hues than they once were.

NAVARRE

		Crystal	Blue	Pink
15 ▸	Bell, dinner	75.00	95.00	
	Bowl, #2496, 4", square, hndl.	15.00		
	Bowl, #2496, 4⅜", hndl.	15.00		
	Bowl, #869, 4½", finger	75.00		
	Bowl, #2496, 4⅝", tri-cornered	18.00		
	Bowl, #2496, 5", hndl., ftd.	15.00		
	Bowl, #2496, 6", square, sweetmeat	20.00		
	Bowl, #2496, 6¼", 3 ftd., nut	20.00		
	Bowl, #2496, 7⅜", ftd., bonbon	24.00		
	Bowl, #2496, 10", oval, floating garden	50.00		
	Bowl, #2496, 10½", hndl., ftd.	60.00		
8 ▸	Bowl, #2470½, 10½", ftd.	60.00		
	Bowl, #2496, 12", flared	60.00		
	Bowl, #2545, 12½", oval, Flame	75.00		
	Candlestick, #2496, 4"	15.00		
	Candlestick, #2496, 4½", double	30.00		
	Candlestick, #2472, 5", double	40.00		
	Candlestick, #2496, 5½"	35.00		
	Candlestick, #2496, 6", triple	30.00		
	Candlestick, #2545, 6¾", double, Flame	75.00		
3 ▸	Candlestick, #2482, 6¾", triple	40.00		
	Candy, w/cover, #2496, 3-part	110.00		
	Celery, #2440, 11½"	45.00		
	Comport, #2496, 3¼", cheese	20.00		
	Comport, #2400, 4½"	30.00		
	Comport, #2496, 4¾"	28.00		
	Cracker, #2496, 11" plate	25.00		
	Creamer, #2440, 4¼", ftd.	14.00		
	Creamer, #2496, individual	14.00		
	Cup, #2440	11.00		
	Ice bucket, #2496, 4⅜" high	110.00		
	Ice bucket, #2375, 6" high	130.00		
	Mayonnaise, #2375, 3-piece	45.00		
	Mayonnaise, #2496½, 3-piece	45.00		
	Pickle, #2496, 8"	25.00		
	Pickle, #2440, 6½"	27.50		
	Pitcher, #2666, 32 oz.	250.00		
	Pitcher, #5000, 48 oz., ftd.	325.00		
	Plate, #2440, 6", bread/butter	6.00		
	Plate, #2440, 7½", salad	10.00		
	Plate, #2440, 8½", luncheon	15.00		
	Plate, #2440, 9½", dinner	35.00		
	Plate, #2496, 10", hndl., cake	35.00		
	Plate, #2440, 10½", oval cake	50.00		

		Crystal	Blue	Pink
	Plate, #2496, 14", torte	35.00		
	Plate, #2364, 16", torte	110.00		
	Relish, #2496, 6", 2-part, square	22.00		
	Relish, #2496, 10" x 7½", 3-part	30.00		
	Relish, #2496, 10", 4-part	40.00		
4 ▸	Relish, #2419, 13¼", 5-part	65.00		
	Salt & pepper, #2364, 3¼", flat, pr.	65.00		
	Salt & pepper, #2375, 3½", ftd., pr.	95.00		
	Salad dressing bottle, #2083, 6½"	400.00		
	Sauce dish, #2496, div. mayo., 6½"	35.00		
	Sauce dish, #2496, 6½" x 5¼"	90.00		
	Sauce dish liner, #2496, 8", oval	20.00		
	Saucer, #2440	3.00		
	Stem, #6106, 1 oz., 4"	40.00		
	Stem, #6106, ¾ oz., cordial, 3⅞"	40.00		
	Stem, #6106, 3¼ oz., wine, 5½"	30.00		
	Stem, #6106, 3½ oz., cocktail, 6"	18.00		
1 ▸	Stem, #6106, 4 oz., oyster cocktail, 3⅝"	16.00		
11 ▸	Stem, #6106, 4½ oz., claret, 6"	40.00	45.00	
12 ▸	Stem, #6106, 4½ oz., large claret, 6½"	30.00	52.00	
14 ▸	Stem, #6106, 5 oz., continental champagne, 8⅛"	150.00	150.00	
	Stem, #6106, 6 oz., cocktail/sherry, 6³⁄₁₆"	75.00		
	Stem, #6106, 6 oz., low sherbet, 4⅜"	15.00		
2 ▸	Stem, #6106, 6 oz., saucer champagne, 5⅝"	15.00	30.00	
	Stem, #6106, 10 oz., water, 7⅝"	35.00	40.00	
10 ▸	Stem, #6106, 15 oz., brandy inhaler, 5½"	110.00		
9 ▸	Stem, #6106, 16 oz., magnum, 7¼"	100.00	150.00	
	Sugar, #2440, 3⅝", ftd.	14.00		
	Sugar, #2496, individual	14.00		
	Syrup, #2586, Sani-cut, 5½"	400.00		
	Tidbit, #2496, 8¼", 3-ftd., turned up edge	22.00		
	Tray, #2496½, for ind. sugar/creamer	25.00		
7 ▸	Tumbler, #6106, 5 oz., ftd., juice, 4⅝"	18.00		
5 ▸	Tumbler, #6106, 10 oz., ftd., water, 5⅜"	20.00		
13 ▸	Tumbler, #6106, 12 oz., flat, highball, 4⅞"	100.00		
17 ▸	Tumbler, #6106, 13 oz., flat, double old fashioned, 3⅝"	100.00		
6 ▸	Tumbler, #6106, 13 oz., ftd., tea, 5⅞"	25.00	55.00	
	Vase, #4108, 5"	95.00		
	Vase, #4121, 5"	90.00		
	Vase, #4128, 5"	80.00		
	Vase, #2470, 10", ftd.	110.00		

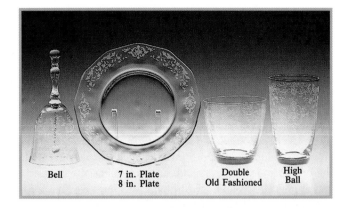

Bell   7 in. Plate   Double   High
      8 in. Plate   Old Fashioned   Ball

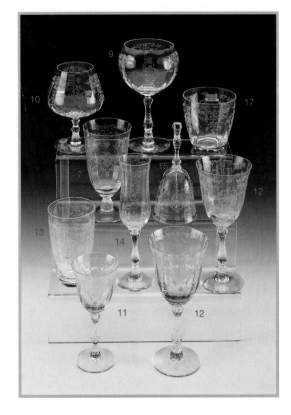

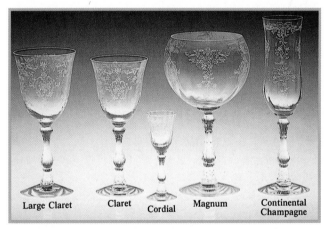

Wilma Blue   Wilma Crystal   Navarre Crystal

Goblet   Goblet   Goblet   Low Dessert/ Champagne   High Dessert/ Champagne

Large Claret   Claret   Cordial   Magnum   Continental Champagne

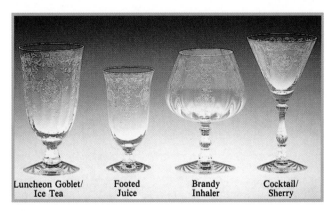

Luncheon Goblet/ Ice Tea   Footed Juice   Brandy Inhaler   Cocktail/ Sherry

NEW ERA, #4044, A.H. HEISEY CO., 1934 – 1941; 1944 – 1957 (stems, celery tray, and candlesticks)

Colors: crystal, frosted crystal, some cobalt with crystal stem and foot

New Era production began in 1934 and was first called Modern Line. By 1935, the catalog presented it as New Era. It was discontinued in 1941, but remade in 1944 and continued production until the factory closed in 1957.

This straight lined design was a reflection of the time it was conceived. Art Deco buffs often seek New Era because it embodies that Art Moderne movement. New Era stemware can be used with a variety of patterns, old or new. It is one of those patterns that emanate timeless appeal.

The double-branched candelabra with the New Era bobeches is very alluring and may be found higher priced than our listing. Our price is agreeable to Heisey collectors because they understand how frequently these candelabra are found. (Check out Internet auctions and note that over 50% of New Era listings are for these candles.) Collectors and dealers who do not specialize in Heisey have a vaulted estimation and appraise it greater. This mould was purchased from Heisey when the plant closed and reissued by Imperial for quite a few years. Seeing these candelabra more highly priced absolutely does not mean they are selling for those prices.

New Era serving pieces are unusually obscure. Dinner plates and other flatware without scratches in that plain, open center will keep you shopping for a long time unless you are very lucky. Some New Era is satinized as displayed on the larger plate in the photo. Years ago, when I was first learning about Heisey, I left eight dinners in an antique mall for $8.00 each because I didn't recognize them as New Era. Another dealer bought them and they sold for nearly $100.00 each at the National Heisey show a few weeks later. Those prices are long gone, but it was a valuable lesson learned. Only a few months later, I spotted some other New Era plates labeled as flower pot holders. Unfortunately, they were not dinners, but were bargain priced.

The decanters shown are rarely glimpsed; watch for them. That hunting scene is admired more by male collectors.

New Era stems and tumblers can be discovered having cobalt bowls with crystal stems. Several are pictured. All are rarely seen and desirable, but most collectors are happy to own only one of each stem rather than sets. Crystal stems are discovered etched with Venus, Sea Glade, Stardust, or Tahiti. Pilsners are adorned with a Tally Ho etch. Other New Era can be found with beautiful cuttings, some of which have no known names.

		Crystal				Crystal
12 ▸	Ashtray or indiv. nut	50.00	4 ▸	*Stem, 3 oz., wine		25.00
9 ▸	Bottle, rye, w/stopper	250.00		Stem, 3½ oz., high, cocktail		12.00
3 ▸	Bowl, 11", floral	45.00	20 ▸	Stem, 3½ oz., oyster cocktail		12.00
10 ▸	Candelabra, 2-lite w/2 #4044 bobeche & prisms	100.00	5 ▸	**Stem, 4 oz., claret		18.00
	Creamer	37.50	2 ▸	Stem, 6 oz., sherbet, low		12.50
18 ▸	Cup	10.00	1 ▸	Stem, 6 oz., champagne		13.00
15 ▸	Cup, after dinner	62.50	21 ▸	†Stem, 10 oz., goblet		16.00
	Pilsner, 8 oz.	27.50		Sugar		37.50
	Pilsner, 12 oz.	32.50		Tray, 13", celery		30.00
	Plate, 5½" x 4½", bread & butter	15.00		Tumbler, 5 oz., ftd., soda		10.00
14 ▸	Plate, 9"x 7", luncheon	25.00		Tumbler, 8 oz., ftd., soda		11.00
13 ▸	Plate, 10" x 8", dinner	45.00		Tumbler, 10 oz., low, ftd.		11.00
	Relish, 13", 3-part	25.00	11 ▸	††Tumbler, 12 oz., ftd., soda		18.00
19 ▸	Saucer	5.00	6 ▸	Tumbler, 14 oz., ftd., soda		20.00
16 ▸	Saucer, after dinner	12.50				
17 ▸	Stem, 1 oz., cordial	40.00				

*Cobalt bowl $175.00   **Cobalt bowl $165.00
†Cobalt bowl $150.00   ††Cobalt bowl $100.00

NEWPORT, "HAIRPIN," HAZEL-ATLAS GLASS COMPANY, 1940 – early 1950s

Colors: Platonite white and fired-on colors

Newport is one pattern split between this and our *Collector's Encyclopedia of Depression Glass* book. Platonite Newport was produced during the time frame of this book since Hazel-Atlas made it until the mid 1950s. On the other hand, transparent colors of cobalt blue, pink, and amethyst were made entirely before 1940. We have also released a book *Hazel-Atlas Glass Identification and Value Guide* which covers both periods of Newport production.

Platonite (opaque) white and white with fired-on colors were widespread Hazel-Atlas patterns throughout the 1940s and beyond. Newport is a pattern that definitely imparts itself to the notion of rainbow collecting. The colors are bright and profuse as you can see from our photographs; and blending those colors as pleases you will work well. The dark green and chartreuse are two colors often found intermingled, both by collectors today and retailers in the past.

As far as we know, the earlier colors manufactured all had white interiors or exteriors, depending on the piece. However, the turquoise blue bowl and dark green plate pictured have colors fired both front and back. One collector indicated to us that she bought the darker colors in both Newport and Moderntone and the colors matched well. Since Hazel-Atlas made both of these, that makes sense. Blending patterns as well as colors, is also a potential trend. Many are displaying table settings with a mixture of patterns serving guests from a single design of one color or employing multicolored ware.

We have shown nine tumblers in different colors for several books, and have finally been informed that a tenth color exists. We suspect there may be a couple of others to be seen.

White Platonite is found in two separate shades. One is opalescent white and probably dates from very early production; the other is a flat white similar to milk glass, which is the ware seen by the late 40s and early 50s when Hazel-Atlas got the colored versions on white really moving. Milk glass was popular then and so nearly every company contributed their patterns to the market. The Newport white shaker is often used by Petalware collectors for their pattern since there are no shakers in the MacBeth-Evans set. It is not unprecedented for novice collectors to be fooled into thinking these shakers really are Petalware if they do not know shakers were never made in that pattern.

		White	Fired-on colors
5 ▸	Bowl, 4¾", berry	3.00	7.50
	Bowl, 4¾", cream soup	5.00	10.00
	Bowl, 8¼, large berry	8.00	14.00
8 ▸	Cup	3.00	5.00
7 ▸	Creamer	4.00	7.50
	Plate, 6", sherbet	1.00	1.50
10 ▸	Plate, 8½", luncheon	2.50	5.00

		White	Fired-on colors
3 ▸	Plate, 11½", sandwich	6.00	15.00
	Platter, 11¾", oval	8.00	15.00
4 ▸	Salt and pepper, pr.	12.00	15.00
9 ▸	Saucer	.75	1.00
2 ▸	Sherbet	3.00	5.00
6 ▸	Sugar	4.00	7.50
1 ▸	Tumbler	5.00	10.00

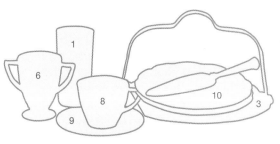

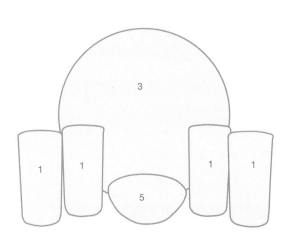

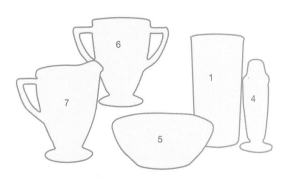

NO. 301, "BANANA FRUIT," "GARLAND," INDIANA GLASS COMPANY, late 1935 – 1970s

Color: crystal, crystal w/flashed colors, Wisteria, Orange, Rose, white

We added Indiana's No. 301 because it has been so often offered as Westmoreland's Della Robbia that there are quite a few collections gathered inadvertently. It is another of Indiana's lines that has a couple of dubbed names rather than using the number assigned it by the company. "Banana Fruit" is certainly descriptive and will help collectors differentiate it from Della Robbia for which it is often confused. There is no banana in the Della Robbia design. It has also been called "Garland."

Indiana made several pieces including the oval bowl, basket, and several styles of 10½" comports as late as the 70s. Those comports look more like footed bowls, but are listed in catalogs as comports.

The candlestick and oval bowl were presented in white during the Indiana 50s promotion of that color. We found a listing in an Indiana catalog that was undated but attributed (in pencil by someone) to 1935 while researching at the Fenton factory. We conjectured the catalog may have been early 30s by the other patterns included. The first emphasis of No. 301 production seems to have been in the 30s through the 40s. You will find various colors of decorative treatments from amber to purple on this ware.

*Crystal w/flashed colors

	Basket, 10¼" high, 3" deep	45.00
	Bowl, 5½", belled to 6"	12.00
	Bowl, 5½", crimped to 6"	12.00
	Bowl, 7", crimped to 7¾"	20.00
	Bowl, 7", belled to 7¾"	20.00
	Bowl, 7", cupped to 6"	16.00
5 ▸	Bowl, 8¼", rose	35.00
	Bowl, 12½", oval, 4-ftd.	20.00
	Bowl, 12½", cabarette, shallow	25.00
	Bowl, 12½", shallow	25.00
1 ▸	Cake plate, salver, 13¼", ftd.	30.00
4 ▸	Candle, 5½", double	20.00
	Comport, 9", straight top	25.00
	Comport, 10", fluted top	30.00
	Comport, 10½" diameter, 4¾" high	35.00
	Comport, 10½" diameter, ruffled top	40.00
	Comport, 12" diameter, 3½" high	35.00
2 ▸	Plate, 7⅜", luncheon	12.00
3 ▸	Plate, 9⅜", dinner	30.00
7 ▸	Salver, 12½", turned up edge	30.00
6 ▸	Salver, 13"	35.00

*Crystal or solid colors 50% less

NO. 1008, "OLEANDER," "WILLOW," "MAGNOLIA LEAF," INDIANA GLASS COMPANY, 1940s – 1970s

Colors: crystal, crystal w/sprayed colors, Terrace green, white

Indiana's No. 1008 has been called both "Oleander" and "Willow" by collectors. Indiana advertised it as "Willow," but it was advertised as "Oleander" by Montgomery Ward and "Magnolia Leaf" in a Butler Bros. wholesale catalog.

We started buying this pattern about six years ago when a dealer friend told us he had several customers in Texas searching for it. We bought a few pieces and took them to Texas where they "flew" off our table. After talking to the collectors, we started searching for it seriously. From that day on, we kept running into collectors asking for it at different shows.

After we started buying to include it the book, we were surprised at how well it was distributed. We spotted over 60 creamers

and sugars on one long trip to California and back. We found Fostoria to be the popular misrepresented company of origin on price labels. Prices ranged from $4.00 to $25.00 pair. Of course, no other pieces were spotted regularly, but pricing was best described as inconsistent. After adding it in the last book, we are seeing more pieces properly identified, but prices are still varied.

The frosted oval bowl and double candle with yellow flashing pictured are really Indiana's No. 1007 pattern, but were sold by Montgomery Ward as part of their "Oleander" line and, as such, are collected today as part of this pattern.

Our pricing comes from what we are receiving for the pieces we have sold in the last few years. The Terrace green and red decorated designs have become the most popular renditions to collect. We have also found that some collectors will buy every piece they see. One collector told us he had over 500 pieces, but will never sell any of it. He was regretful we put it in our book as he was buying it economically. Our hope is that it will uncover more unknown caches. The No. 17 egg nog cup in the legend, found on punch sets, also belongs with an Indiana Laurel footed pitcher, often thought to be Willow.

		*Crystal				*Crystal
13 ▶	Bowl, 12", ftd.	28.00	11 ▶	Comport, 2-hdld., rounded		20.00
12 ▶	Bowl, 12", oval (#1007)	30.00	8 ▶	Creamer		2.50
4 ▶	Bowl, 12½", ftd., flared	30.00	17 ▶	Egg nog cup, Laurel		10.00
	Bowl, 13", divided	30.00		Plate, 8"		30.00
3 ▶	Cake plate, 12", ftd., 2½" high	35.00	2 ▶	Plate, 12½", ftd.		25.00
1 ▶	Candle, 4½", single w/wings	20.00		Plate, 13½", flat, lazy Susan		35.00
6 ▶	Candle, 5", 2-hdld., square base	20.00	20 ▶	Plate, 16½", punch liner		30.00
15 ▶	Candle, 5½", double, 2-branches	20.00	19 ▶	Punch bowl, 10" x 5" high		40.00
16 ▶	Candle, 6", double (#1007)	20.00	5 ▶	Punch cup, ftd.		6.00
	Candy, 2-hdld., ftd., w/lid	40.00		Rose bowl, 7" x 3" high		40.00
18 ▶	Candy, round, flat, w/lid	30.00	9 ▶	Sugar		2.50
7 ▶	Comport, 2-hdld, cone shape	20.00	10 ▶	Tray, oval, 2-hdld., sugar/creamer		20.00
	Comport, 2-hdld, cone shape, 2-part	22.00	14 ▶	Vase, 10"		75.00

* Terrace Green add 50% or more

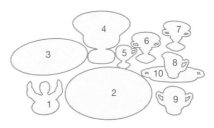

NO. 1008, "OLEANDER"

OAK CUTTING, WABASH CUTTING COMPANY (INDIANA), late 1940s – early 1950s

Color: crystal

One of the more perplexing aspects of researching glass occurs from unearthing the same cut pattern on numerous companies' blanks. Normally, a cutting is found on one line from one company. Oak Cutting breaks all the rules. It has been found on three different Fostoria mould blanks, two different from Heisey, and at least one from Viking. Not only are those companies represented, but at least two other glass companies' wares are spotted. One of those is thought to be Libbey, but that is unsubstantiated at present.

The Oak Cutting here is a radical example, but one we felt compelled to show to confirm why there is sometimes difficulty identifying a cutting using just the company blank. Because the blank is recognized as Heisey or Fostoria does not mean the cutting came from that factory.

Pictured are groups of Fostoria Glass Company items including nine different pieces of Century blank #2630, one piece of Baroque blank #2496, and a #2482 trindle candlestick. That is 11 pieces of Fostoria on three different blanks. Oak is cut on two different Heisey blanks including Lariat #1540 stems and Queen Ann #1509 mould blank. Viking Glass is represented by three different pieces including a butter dish and #5247 creamer and sugar. There are six unidentified pieces although we feel sure the two tumblers are Libbey due to their characteristic safety edged rim. We have priced items considering what uncut pieces fetch, added for the cutting, and factored what we had to pay to get this glass to illustrate this point.

FOSTORIA GLASS COMPANY

Century Blank #2630 Line

15 ▸	Bonbon, 7¼", 3-ftd.	25.00
20 ▸	Bowl, 9½", 2 hdld.	40.00
12 ▸	Creamer, individual	12.50
22 ▸	Mayonnaise	25.00
21 ▸	Mayonnaise liner	10.00
19 ▸	Relish, 11⅛", 3-part	30.00
13 ▸	Sugar, individual	12.50
16 ▸	Tidbit, 8⅛", 3-ftd.	22.00
14 ▸	Tray, 7⅛", individual sugar/creamer	15.00

Baroque Blank #2496

17 ▸	Bowl, 10", hdld.	45.00

Blank #2482

18 ▸	Trindle candlestick, 6¾" high	55.00

A. H. HEISEY GLASS COMPANY

Lariat Blank #1540

1 ▸	Stem, 9 oz., pressed water goblet	20.00
2 ▸	Stem, 5½ oz., pressed saucer champagne	18.00

Queen Ann Blank #1509

3 ▸	Relish, 10", triplex	35.00

VIKING GLASS COMPANY

11 ▸	Creamer, #5247	15.00
23 ▸	Sugar, #5247	15.00
9 ▸	Butter dish, ¼ pound	40.00

UNIDENTIFIED COMPANIES

10 ▸	Paperweight, rectangular	35.00
7 ▸	Pitcher, 16 oz.	20.00
8 ▸	Pitcher, 32 oz.	30.00
5 ▸	Salt dip w/spoon	20.00
6 ▸	Tumbler, juice (possibly Libbey)	10.00
4 ▸	Tumbler, water (possibly Libbey)	12.50

ORANGE BLOSSOM, LINE #619, INDIANA GLASS COMPANY, c. 1957

Color: milk white

Milk glass production by glass companies was a significant color trend during the 50s and early 60s. Most American glass companies were making as much and as many designs in milk colored glass as they could. Indiana made a few pieces of many of their earlier wares during this trend.

They had produced a pattern in the 1930s in a beige, custard color which collectors now designate as "Indiana Custard." As factories frequently did, the moulds from that prior production were revamped and then they re-issued Line #619 as Orange Blossom in milk glass. We have revealed this information in past Depression glass books, but we believe it's time it has its own place in this book about 50s wares. This pattern is quite small since it was presented only as a luncheon set. However, the Orange Blossom name was popular with bridal wares then, and thus, small or not, the pattern was noticed and gifted. Although we're beginning to be asked for it at shows, there's quite a bit more available at markets than wanted at the moment — excluding luncheon plates.

	Bowl, 5½", dessert	5.00
6 ▸	Creamer, ftd.	5.00
4 ▸	Cup	3.00
2 ▸	Plate, 5¾", sherbet	2.00
3 ▸	Plate, 8⅞", lunch	7.00
5 ▸	Saucer	.50
1 ▸	Sugar, ftd.	5.00

ORCHID, ETCHING #1507 on WAVERLY BLANK #1519 and QUEEN ANN BLANK #1509,

A.H. HEISEY & CO., 1940 – 1957

Color: crystal

Heisey's Orchid is normally found etched on two major mould blanks. Other lines were employed but Blank #1509, or Queen Ann, and Blank #1519, known as Waverly, were primarily used. In the past, collectors would not consider mixing lines, but some new followers do not seem to follow that conservative collecting approach and are just pleased for pieces that they do not have.

The pitcher and vases pictured are rarely found today unless you go to a show specializing in Heisey glassware. The Internet has brought masses of Heisey stemware out of every storage place known to mankind, and Orchid has been extremely well uncovered. Evidently, Orchid stems and footed tumblers were purchased by the thousands to be used with china sets. Because of all these exposed hoards, you can now buy stemware for 40 – 50% less than it cost four or five years ago. Even cordials are going begging unless you are willing to sell them for half their previous value. That is great if you are just starting to buy Orchid, but not so great if you want to sell yours. We expect this massive supply of stemware from the Internet to diminish in time, but not immediately. If you need Orchid stems, this is definitely the time to acquire them.

Today, most serving pieces and flatware items are being found in quantities to more than satisfy demand; so prices are slipping, but not as dramatically as for beverage items.

Orchid dinner plates without scuffs and scrapes are still difficult to acquire, but not as pricey. We looked at a "priceless dinner plate" (no price sticker) at a Western show and the dealer told us he could make us a deal on those "hardly used" plates. Evidently, hardly used in his estimation meant the owners only used dull knives instead of sharp ones to cut the meat. Hardly used should mean light scuffing and rubbing at best.

8 ▶	Ashtray, 3", #1435	20.00
	Basket, 8½", Lariat	1,200.00
	Bell, dinner, #5022 or #5025	150.00
	Bottle, 8 oz., French dressings	175.00
	Bowl, finger, #3309 or #5025	90.00
	Bowl, 4½", nappy, Queen Ann	37.50
54 ▶	Bowl, 5½", ftd., mint, Queen Ann	45.00
55 ▶	Bowl, 6", jelly, 2 hndl., ftd., Queen Ann	37.50
47 ▶	Bowl, 6", oval, lemon, w/cover, Queen Ann	270.00
31 ▶	Bowl, 6", oval, lemon, w/cover, Waverly	695.00
	Bowl, 6½", ftd., honey, cheese, Queen Ann	50.00
29 ▶	Bowl, 6½", ftd., jelly, Waverly	48.00
	Bowl, 6½", 2 pt., oval, dressings, Waverly	55.00
49 ▶	Bowl, 7", lily, Queen Ann	125.00
	Bowl, 7", salad	140.00
38 ▶	Bowl, 7", 3 pt., rnd., relish	55.00
	Bowl, 7", ftd., honey, cheese, Waverly	55.00
	Bowl, 7", ftd., jelly	45.00
	Bowl, 7", ftd., oval, nut, Waverly	90.00
52 ▶	Bowl, 7½", dolphin ftd., sauce	75.00
	Bowl, 8", mint, ftd., Queen Ann	65.00
	Bowl, 8", nappy, Queen Ann	70.00
53 ▶	Bowl, 8", 2 pt., oval, dressings, ladle	55.00
	Bowl, 8", pt., rnd., relish	62.50
	Bowl, 8½", flared, Queen Ann	67.50
	Bowl, 8½", floral, 2 hndl., ftd., Queen Ann	65.00
	Bowl, 9", 4 pt., rnd., relish	75.00

	Bowl, 9", ftd., fruit or salad	135.00
50 ▶	Bowl, 9", gardenia, Queen Ann	65.00
	Bowl, 9", salad, Waverly	195.00
	Bowl, 9½", crimped, floral, Queen Ann	75.00
	Bowl, 9½", epergne	525.00
51 ▶	Bowl, 10", crimped	55.00
	Bowl, 10", deep salad	150.00
	Bowl, 10", gardenia	75.00
24 ▶	Bowl, 10½", ftd., floral	115.00
	Bowl, 11", shallow, rolled edge	70.00
16 ▶	Bowl, 11", 3-ftd., floral, seahorse ft.	165.00
	Bowl, 11", 3-pt., oblong, relish	60.00
	Bowl, 11", 4-ftd., oval	125.00
	Bowl, 11", flared	135.00
	Bowl, 11", floral	70.00
	Bowl, 11", ftd., floral	115.00
	Bowl, 12", crimped, floral, Waverly	65.00
	Bowl, 13", floral	75.00
	Bowl, 13", crimped, floral, Waverly	95.00
	Bowl, 13", gardenia	70.00
	Butter, w/cover, ¼ lb., Cabochon	325.00
32 ▶	Butter, w/cover, 6", Waverly	150.00
	Candleholder, 6", deep epernette, Waverly	1,000.00
	Candlestick, 1-lite, Mercury	40.00
40 ▶	Candlestick, 1-lite, Queen Ann, w/prisms	150.00
	Candlestick, 2-lite, Flame	180.00
7 ▶	Candlestick, 5", 2-lite, Trident	40.00

21 ▸	Candlestick, 2-lite, Waverly	40.00
48 ▸	Candlestick, 3-lite, Cascade, #142	75.00
	Candlestick, 3-lite, Waverly	80.00
	Candy box, w/cover, 6", low ft.	160.00
22 ▸	Candy, w/cover, 5", high ft., Waverly	200.00
10 ▸	Candy, w/cover, 6", bow knot finial	165.00
	Cheese (comport) & cracker (11½") plate	135.00
	Cheese & cracker, 14", plate	155.00
	Chocolate, w/cover, 5", Waverly	220.00
	Cigarette box, w/cover, 4", Puritan	140.00
	Cigarette holder, #4035	85.00
30 ▸	Cigarette holder, w/cover, Waverly	195.00
9 ▸	Cocktail icer, w/liner, Universal, #3304	250.00
	Cocktail shaker, pt., #4225	240.00
14 ▸	Cocktail shaker, qt., #4036 or #4225	225.00
	Comport, 5½", blown	95.00
	Comport, 6", low ft., Waverly	65.00
	Comport, 6½", low ft., Waverly	70.00
	Comport, 7", ftd., oval	155.00
	Creamer, individual	30.00
26 ▸	Creamer, ftd.	25.00
33 ▸	Cup, Waverly or Queen Ann	30.00
	Decanter, oval, sherry, pt.	250.00
	Decanter, pt., ftd., #4036	700.00
	Decanter, pt., #4036½	375.00
	Ice bucket, ftd., Queen Ann	200.00
	Ice bucket, 2 hndl., Waverly	600.00
	Marmalade, w/cover	235.00
	Mayonnaise and liner, #1495, Fern	250.00
	Mayonnaise, 5½", 1 hndl.	55.00
	Mayonnaise, 5½", ftd.	85.00
	Mayonnaise, 5½", 1 hndl., div.	50.00
	Mayonnaise, 6½", 1 hndl.	65.00
	Mayonnaise, 6½", 1 hndl., div.	65.00
	Mustard, w/cover, Queen Ann	145.00
20 ▸	Oil, 3 oz., ftd.	175.00
11 ▸	Pitcher, 73 oz., #4164	400.00
15 ▸	Pitcher, 64 oz., ice tankard, #3484	450.00
17 ▸	Plate, 6"	9.00
	Plate, 7", mayonnaise	15.00
	Plate, 7", salad	15.00
19 ▸	Plate, 8", salad, Waverly	20.00
18 ▸	Plate, 10½", dinner, Waverly	130.00
39 ▸	Plate, 10½", #1509	120.00
	Plate, 11", demi-torte	45.00
	Plate, 11", sandwich	55.00
	Plate, 12", ftd., salver, Waverly	250.00
	Plate, 12", rnd., sandwich, hndl.	60.00
27 ▸	Plate, 14", ftd., cake or salver	195.00
	Plate, 14", torte, rolled edge	55.00
	Plate, 14", torte, Waverly	65.00
	Plate, 14", sandwich, Waverly	55.00
	Plate, 15", sandwich, Waverly	65.00

	Plate, 15½", Queen Ann	90.00
	Salt & pepper, pr.	65.00
46 ▸	Salt & pepper, ftd., pr., Waverly	80.00
34 ▸	Saucer, Waverly or Queen Ann	6.00
42 ▸	Stem, #5022 or #5025, 1 oz., cordial	100.00
	Stem, #5022 or #5025, 2 oz., sherry	115.00
44 ▸	Stem, #5022 or #5025, 3 oz., wine	60.00
3 ▸	Stem, #5022 or #5025, 4 oz., oyster cocktail	45.00
4 ▸	Stem, #5025, 4 oz., cocktail	20.00
	Stem, #5022 or #5025, 4½ oz., claret	90.00
41 ▸	Stem, #5022 or #5025, 6 oz., saucer champagne	22.00
35 ▸	Stem, #5022 or #5025, 6 oz., sherbet	18.00
36 ▸	Stem, #5022 or #5025, 10 oz., low water goblet	30.00
43 ▸	Stem, #5022 or #5025, 10 oz., water goblet	30.00
5 ▸	Stem, #5089, 10 oz., ftd., goblet	90.00
	Sugar, individual	30.00
28 ▸	Sugar, ftd.	25.00
	Tray, indiv., creamer/sugar, Queen Ann	90.00
	Tray, 12", celery	60.00
	Tray, 13", celery	60.00
45 ▸	Tumbler, #5022 or #5025, 5 oz., fruit, ftd.	35.00
37 ▸	Tumbler, #5022 or #5025, 12 oz., iced tea, ftd.	35.00
1 ▸	Tumbler, #2401, 10 oz.	100.00
56 ▸	Tumbler, 10 oz., flared	100.00
6 ▸	Tumbler, #3484, 12 oz.	75.00
2 ▸	Tumbler, #2402, 12½ oz.	125.00
	Vase, 4", ftd., violet, Waverly	110.00
	Vase, 6", crimped top	125.00
	Vase, 7", ftd., fan, Lariat	110.00
25 ▸	Vase, 7", ftd., fan, Waverly	150.00
	Vase, 7", crimped top, Lariat	120.00
23 ▸	Vase, 7", #1519, ftd.	225.00
	Vase, 8", ftd., bud	215.00
	Vase, 8", sq., ftd., bud	400.00
12 ▸	Vase, 9", #4192½, ftd.	500.00
	Vase, 10", sq., ftd., bud	295.00
	Vase, 12", ftd., bud	375.00
13 ▸	Vase, 14", #4198	1,100.00

OVIDE, HAZEL-ATLAS GLASS COMPANY, 1930 – 1950s

Colors: black, green, white Platonite, and white with trimmed or fired-on colors in 1950s

Ovide production began in the Depression era mostly in transparent colors; yet, production lasted well into the 1950s with opaque Platonite. Like Newport and Moderntone, there is quite a variety of colors or color combinations. Some collectors are buying this economically priced glassware to use as their daily dishes. According to these users, Ovide works well in both the microwave and the dishwasher. We haven't tested that aspect so proceed with caution and test for hot spots. It would seem that Hazel-Atlas had a better procedure for keeping their designs and colors on the surface of the glass than did some of the other glass companies. Of course, they did little with the decal decorations other companies used which were so prone to disappear with use.

Pattern names for color combinations (Sierra Sunrise and Informal) have been determined for some of the pastel-banded Platonite that was used in restaurants and competed with Anchor Hocking's Jade-ite and white Restaurant Ware lines. Few of the combination colors pictured here are found in large quantities today. Evidently, they were not as liberally dispersed.

Ovide pieces were made in the 50s in Moderntone colors of Burgundy, Chartreuse, green, and gray which will allow you to mix these patterns through color if you wish. That green is from an actual color label by Hazel-Atlas in spite of collectors calling it forest or dark green. This colored Ovide ware appears to have been Hazel-Atlas Glass Company's answer to the popular 50s Fiesta dinnerware.

Colors shown at the bottom of page 179 have been arduous for us to acquire. With so much pictured, it doesn't look to have been that difficult to accumulate, but it has taken nearly 20 years to amass what is there. We have never found a platter in any color other than the "butterscotch," but have been guaranteed by collectors that other colors do exist. Platters in all Hazel-Atlas's Platonite patterns seem to overwhelm in one color. All basic pieces should be found in all colors; but for now, we have only found serving pieces in "butterscotch." In most cases, you have a wide choice of Ovide from which to select without having to obtain a second mortgage to buy it.

Ovide is pictured in greater array in our new *Hazel-Atlas Glass Identification and Value Guide* which has 11 pages of colors and patterns included.

		White w/trims	Designs Decorated on White	Fired-on Colors
	Ashtray, square			4.00
8 ▶	Bowl, 4¾", berry	3.50	7.00	5.50
9 ▶	Bowl, 5½", cereal, deep		11.00	10.00
12 ▶	Bowl, 6", salad	8.00		
	Bowl, 8", large berry			18.00
3 ▶	Creamer	4.50	15.00	4.00
4 ▶	Cup	3.50	12.50	4.50
	Pitcher, 16 oz.		35.00	
	Plate, 6", sherbet	1.50	4.00	
7 ▶	Plate, 8", luncheon	2.50	14.00	4.00
1 ▶	Plate, 9", dinner	3.50		8.00
6 ▶	Platter, 11"	8.00	22.50	
	Refrigerator stacking set, 4-pc.		65.00	
	Salt and pepper, pr.	15.00		
5 ▶	Saucer	1.00	2.00	2.00
	Sherbet	4.00	10.00	
2 ▶	Sugar, open	4.50	15.00	4.00
10 ▶	Tumbler, flat	10.00	15.00	6.00
11 ▶	Tumbler, ftd., juice			6.00

PANELED GRAPE, PATTERN #1881, WESTMORELAND GLASS COMPANY, 1950 – 1970s

Colors: white and white w/decorations, and some mint green in 1979

Paneled Grape is one of four Westmoreland patterns that collectors readily recognize. Della Robbia and English Hobnail are familiar, but not everyone seems to know that Westmoreland made them. That WG marking on the bottom of Paneled Grape and Beaded Edge pieces probably helped associate these patterns with the maker.

Production of Pattern #1881 (Paneled Grape) began in 1950 and continued off and on for nearly 30 years. Westmoreland cataloged this pattern with both designations (#1881 and Paneled Grape) as you can see from a 1973 catalog shown on pages 184 – 186. We have eliminated six catalog pages (previously shown) to make room for additional patterns. You can refer to an earlier edition to see these omitted pages. Company pictures and descriptions are always helpful.

Paneled Grape isn't for everyone; but its followers are fervent in their affection for it. The biggest objection voiced by critics is its color. Some folks just don't like white glass.

Paneled Grape was profuse in pattern size and longevity and those vast productions are beginning to overpower supplies of items previously thought rare. As with other later patterns, it has remained in families and not been thrown or given away. It is being unearthed and listed on the Internet and prices are dropping due to the enormous quantities offered.

Paneled Grape was made in mint green in 1979, but collectors seem to want only a piece or two for an example. Some sellers are trying to promote it as Jadite green, but it is very lightly colored. Since it was a limited run near the end of the Westmoreland factory existence, collectors may be making a mistake ignoring this color.

A frequent question we are asked involves swung vases. Swung vases are actually swung while hot to lengthen their shape and therefore, their sizes vary depending upon who did the swinging and how hard it was swung. Few measure the same; that is why we list "size varies" on swung vases.

Punch sets and the triple candelabra are definitely not as hard to acquire as once thought. We have found and sold four complete punch sets, two partial sets, and five candelabra in the last few years. There was a time when a punch set was an "sight to see" at a glass show. Notice the Christmas decorated, metal-handle plate pictured. It sold at the first show we put it out for display.

PANELED GRAPE

White w/decorations

White w/decorations

22 ▶	Appetizer or canapé set, 3 pc. (9" three-part relish, round fruit cocktail, ladle)	40.00
	Basket, 5½", ruffled	25.00
	Basket, 6½", oval	25.00
	Basket, 8"	45.00
	Basket, 8", ruffled	65.00
	Bonbon, 8", ruffled, w/metal handle	50.00
	Bottle, 5 oz., toilet	30.00
	Bottle, oil or vinegar, w/stopper, 2 oz.	26.00
	Bowl, pedestal base, 5" (used w/12" – 12½" lipped, 10" rnd. bowls & epergne)	65.00
	Bowl, 4", crimped	15.00
	Bowl, 6", crimped, stemmed	30.00
	Bowl, 6", ruffled edge, stemmed	30.00
	Bowl, 6½" x 12½", 3⅛" high	125.00
19 ▶	Bowl, 6½", oval	23.00
	Bowl, 8", cupped	38.00
	Bowl, 8½", shallow	55.00
	Bowl, 9", ftd., 6" high, skirted base	50.00
	Bowl, 9", ftd., w/cover	80.00
	Bowl, 9", lipped	50.00
	Bowl, 9", lipped, ftd.	115.00
	Bowl, 9", square, w/cover	50.00
	Bowl, 9½", bell-shaped	45.00
	Bowl, 9½", ftd., bell-shaped	110.00
	Bowl, 10", oval	45.00
	Bowl, 10½", round	77.50
	Bowl, 11", oval, lipped, ftd.	125.00
	Bowl, 11½", oval, ruffled edge	30.00
	Bowl, 12", lipped	70.00
	Bowl, 12" ftd., banana	185.00
	Bowl, 12½", bell-shaped	135.00
	Bowl, 13", punch, bell or flared	150.00
	Bowl, 14", shallow, round	140.00
	Bowl, ftd., ripple top	85.00

White w/decorations

35 ▶	Butter w/cover, ¼ pound	25.00
	Cake salver, 10½"	62.00
29 ▶	Cake salver, 11", round ftd., w/skirt	60.00
	Canap or set, 3 pc. (12½" canap tray, 3½" cocktail, ladle)	150.00
8 ▶	Candelabra, 3-lite, ea.	95.00
28 ▶	Candle holder, 4", octagonal	10.00
14 ▶	Candle holder, 5", w/colonial hndl.	37.50
20 ▶	Candle holder, 8", 2-lite (4 of these form a circular center piece)	40.00
	Candy jar, 3-ftd., w/cover	32.50
	Candy jar, 6¼", w/cover	25.00
	Canister, 7"	175.00
	Canister, 9½"	210.00
	Canister, 11"	240.00
	Celery or spooner, 6"	40.00
	Cheese or old fashioned butter, 7", round, w/cover	30.00
13 ▶	Chocolate box, 6½", w/cover	25.00
32 ▶	Compote, 4½", crimped	30.00
7 ▶	Compote, 7", covered, ftd.	20.00
12 ▶	Compote, 9", ftd., crimped	50.00
	Condiment set, 5-pc. (oil and vinegar, salt and pepper on 9" oval tray)	135.00
1 ▶	Creamer, 6½ oz.	16.00
	Creamer, individual	11.00
9 ▶	Creamer, large (goes w/lacy edge sugar)	10.00
	Creamer, small	15.00
	Cup, coffee, flared	8.00
	Cup, punch, cupped	8.00
	Decanter, wine	90.00
	Dresser set, 4-pc. (two) 5 oz. toilet bottles, puff box, and 13½" oval tray	240.00
	Egg plate, 12"	85.00
31 ▶	Egg tray, 10", metal center handle	65.00
	Epergne vase, 8½", bell	60.00
	Epergne vase, pattern at top	250.00
30 ▶	Epergne set, 2-pc. (9" lipped bowl, 8½" epergne vase)	120.00
18 ▶	Epergne set, 2-pc. (11½" epergne flared bowl, 8½" epergne vase)	90.00

PANELED GRAPE

White w/decorations

		White w/decorations
	Epergne set, 2-pc. (12" epergne lipped bowl, 8½" epergne vase)	110.00
	Epergne set, 2-pc. (14" flared bowl, 8½" epergne vase)	235.00
	Epergne set, 3-pc. (12" epergne lipped bowl, 5" bowl base, 8½" epergne vase)	325.00
	Epergne set, 3-pc. (14" flared bowl, 5" bowl base, 8½" epergne vase)	350.00
	Flower pot	45.00
	Fruit cocktail, 3½" w/6" sauce plate, bell-shaped	22.50
	Fruit cocktail, 4½" w/6" sauce plate, round	25.00
	Ivy ball	45.00
	Jardiniere, 5", cupped and ftd.	28.00
	Jardiniere, 5", straight sided	25.00
	Jardiniere, 6½", cupped and ftd.	38.00
34 ▶	Jardiniere, 6½", straight sided	35.00
	Jelly, 4½", covered	27.50
	Ladle, small	10.00
	Ladle, punch	75.00
	Lighter in 2 oz. goblet	75.00
	Lighter in toothpick	75.00
	Marmalade, w/ladle	57.50
26 ▶	Mayonnaise set, 3-pc. (round fruit cocktail, 6" sauce plate, ladle)	25.00
	Mayonnaise, 4", ftd.	27.50
	Napkin ring	22.00
	Nappy, 4½", round	14.00
	Nappy, 5", bell shape	22.00
	Nappy, 5", round, w/handle	25.00
	Nappy, 7", round	30.00
	Nappy, 8½", round	32.00
	Nappy, 9", round, 2" high	42.00
	Nappy, 10", bell	45.00
	Oil bottle	20.00
	Parfait, 6"	25.00
	Pedestal, base to punch bowl, skirted	75.00
	Pickle, oval	21.00
	Pitcher, 16 oz.	38.00
33 ▶	Pitcher, 32 oz.	18.00
	Planter, 3" x 8½"	35.00
	Planter, 4½", square	40.00
2 ▶	Planter, 5" x 9"	20.00
	Planter, 6", small, wall	75.00
	Planter, 8", large, wall	135.00
	Plate, 6", bread	10.00
	Plate, 7" salad, w/depressed center	25.00
	Plate, 8½", breakfast	10.00
	Plate, 10½", dinner	25.00
	Plate, 14½"	55.00
	Plate, 18"	185.00
36 ▶	Platter, 9"	50.00
10 ▶	Puff box or jelly, w/cover	28.00

		White w/decorations
	Punch set, 15-pc. (13" bowl, 12 punch cups, pedestal and ladle)	310.00
	Punch set, 15-pc. (same as above w/11" bowl w/o scalloped bottom)	310.00
23 ▶	Relish, 9", 4-part	30.00
	Salt and pepper, 4¼", small, ftd., pr.	15.00
	*Salt and pepper, 4¼", small, ftd., pr.	18.00
4 ▶	Salt and pepper, 4½", large, flat, pr.	30.00
15 ▶	Sauce boat	35.00
16 ▶	Sauce boat tray, 9"	25.00
	Saucer	3.00
	Sherbet, 3¾", low foot	8.00
	Sherbet, 4¾", high foot	16.00
11 ▶	Soap dish	80.00
	Stem, 2 oz., cordial or wine goblet	8.00
	Stem, 3 oz.	25.00
	Stem, 5 oz., wine goblet	12.50
	Stem, 8 oz., water goblet	11.00
3 ▶	Sugar w/cover, lacy edge on sugar to serve as spoon holder	22.00
	Sugar, 6½"	12.00
	Sugar, small w/cover	18.00
	Tidbit or snack server, 2-tier (dinner and breakfast plates)	50.00
	Tidbit tray, metal handle on 8½" breakfast plate	15.00
37 ▶	Tidbit tray, metal handle on 10½" dinner plate	25.00
17 ▶	Toothpick	22.50
	Tray, 9", oval	50.00
	Tray, 13½", oval	90.00
	Tumbler, 5 oz., juice	18.00
	Tumbler, 6 oz., old fashioned cocktail	25.00
	Tumbler, 8 oz.	11.00
	Tumbler, 12 oz., iced tea	12.00
	Vase, 4", rose	20.00
	Vase, 4½, rose, ftd., cupped, stemmed	15.00
5 ▶	Vase, 6", bell shape	20.00
	Vase, 6½", or celery	35.00
	Vase, 8½", bell shape	28.00
24 ▶	Vase, 9", bell shape	20.00
6 ▶	Vase, 9", crimped & ruffled	25.00
25 ▶	Vase, 9½", bud	15.00
	Vase, 9½", straight	15.00
	Vase, 10" bud (size may vary)	20.00
	Vase, 11", rose (similar to bud vase but bulbous at bottom)	40.00
	Vase, 11½", bell shape	50.00
	Vase, 11½", straight	38.00
	Vase, 12", hand blown	195.00
	Vase, 14", swung (size varies)	18.00
	Vase, 15"	32.00
	Vase, 16", swung (size varies)	28.00
	Vase, 18", swung (size varies)	30.00

*Allover pattern

Collector's items from the vast "Paneled Grape" pattern

1881/9"
Bowl, Sq.

1881/9"
Compote, Crimped

1881
Compote, Crimped

1881/7"
Compote

1881
Candy Jar

1881
Decanter

1881
Celery/Vase

1881
Dish, 3 Ftd.

1881
Chocolate Box

1881
Candleholder

1881
Cocktail, Fruit

1881
Cheese

1881/9"
Bowl, Bell

1881/¼ #
Butter

1881
Cup/Saucer

1881
Candle

1881
Dish

1881/12"
Bowl, Lipped

1881
Bowl, Banana

1881
Bowl, Oval Lpd.

Excellent Gift Suggestions in a treasured pattern

1881/14½"
Plate

1881/10½"
Plate

1881/8½"
Plate

1881/6"
Plate

1881
Mayonnaise

1881/2 oz.
Oil

1881/4½"
Nappy

1881
Ice Tea

1881
Goblet

1881/1 Pt.
Jug

1881/1 Qt.
Jug

1881/6½"
Jardiniere

1881/5"
Jardiniere

1881
Pickle

1881
Mayo Set

1881
Puff Box/Jelly

1881
Flower Pot

1881
Planter, Oblong

1881
Planter, Window

1881
Planter, Sq.

1881
Ivy Ball

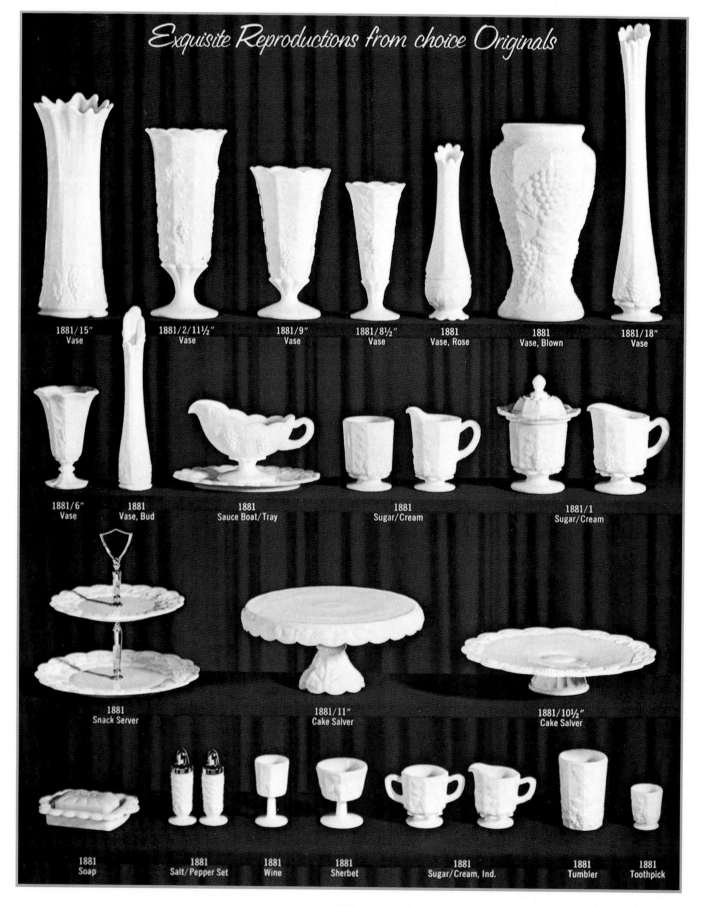

Exquisite Reproductions from choice Originals

1881/15"
Vase

1881/2/11½"
Vase

1881/9"
Vase

1881/8½"
Vase

1881
Vase, Rose

1881
Vase, Blown

1881/18"
Vase

1881/6"
Vase

1881
Vase, Bud

1881
Sauce Boat/Tray

1881
Sugar/Cream

1881/1
Sugar/Cream

1881
Snack Server

1881/11"
Cake Salver

1881/10½"
Cake Salver

1881
Soap

1881
Salt/Pepper Set

1881
Wine

1881
Sherbet

1881
Sugar/Cream, Ind.

1881
Tumbler

1881
Toothpick

PARK AVENUE, FEDERAL GLASS COMPANY, 1941 – early 1970s

Colors: yellow, crystal, crystal w/gold trim, and crystal w/flashed-on colors

There are seemingly few collectors searching for crystal Park Avenue, but yellow is a different matter. We continue to have difficulty finding yellow as you can see by only two tumblers in the photo below. We keep noticing sets of Federal's yellow Star in our travels, but not Park Avenue.

We divided the colors in the listing to better show that the demand for yellow has pushed those prices higher. We received several interesting letters saying we made buying it more difficult. We only try to reflect what the market is doing. Be warned. Few dealers carry these smaller patterns to Depression glass shows.

We did find a flashed colored berry set. Evidently, the original set had a large blue berry bowl and two small bowls in four different colors. These were the first we had heard of, but there would be more buyers of Park Avenue if there were more of these available. We did see a larger green bowl, so that bowl may have been made in the same four colors of the smaller bowls. Time will tell.

Crystal gold-trimmed pieces are difficult to discover with strong gold decorations remaining. Gold wore off easily since it was a very soft 22K. You will find the Federal Glass Company trademark (F within a shield) embossed on the bottom of most of the pieces. Let us reiterate that the F does not stand for Fire-King. No Park Avenue pitchers, as such, were made as far as catalog records indicate. Star pitchers shown on page 232 were regularly sold with tumblers from this set.

The small whisky tumbler (Federal's catalog used the British spelling of whisky without the "e"), as well as other sizes of tumblers in Park Avenue, may be found with jelly labels still affixed to them. We're told tons of the smaller ones were distributed at restaurants with grape jelly enclosed. "Delited" peach preserves were enclosed in the water tumbler according to the label on the one we located.

All pieces listed were made into the early 1960s except the whisky glass which was in production until the early 1970s.

		Yellow	Crystal
	Ashtray, 3½", square		4.00
	Ashtray, 4½", square		6.00
1 ▸	Bowl, 5", dessert	7.00	2.00
8 ▸	Bowl, 8½", vegetable	18.00	10.00
2 ▸	Candleholder, 5"		8.00
4 ▸	Tumbler, 2⅛", 1¼ oz., whisky		4.00
3 ▸	Tumbler, 3½", 4½ oz., juice	6.00	3.00
5 ▸	Tumbler, 3⅞", 9 oz.	8.00	3.00
7 ▸	Tumbler, 4¾", 10 oz.	10.00	4.00
6 ▸	Tumbler, 5⅛", 12 oz., iced tea	12.00	5.00

PETAL, LINE #2829, FEDERAL GLASS COMPANY 1954 – 1979

Colors: crystal, carnival iridescent, smoke, Aegean Blue, Sun Gold

Petal is a small, but progressively more popular line that was a contemporary of Federal's Heritage and is listed in their #54 catalog on the page after Heritage. Petal continued to be shown until a full line was listed in the #60 catalog, which helps demonstrate its status with the buying public even then. In 1974 a couple of new pieces were added in color. They included an 8" scalloped bonbon and a 4" bonbonnette. As late as 1979, six pieces, including three bowls and three plates, were still being cataloged. At that time, it was pictured alongside the Madrid Recollection line which caused such a furor when it first appeared on the market in 1976. It's possible that Indiana produced a few odd colored bowls from Federal's moulds since dark amber is being seen that does not appear to belong to Federal's repertoire of colors or catalog listings we own.

Many pieces have been assembled with accoutrements of metal and plastic from the basic listings including: 4¾" gold pedestal compote, 7¼" cherub pedestal snack tray, 3½" silver and crystal pedestal compote, 6⅜" gold marble pedestal compote, and jelly/nut in silver holder with spoon. Tidbits have been made in various combinations using two or three of the pieces listed. You may find tidbits with two plates, two bowls, or even one or two of each.

		Crystal	All colors
1 ▸	Bonbonnette, 4", scalloped		12.00
	Bonbon, 8¼", scalloped		15.00
2 ▸	Bowl, 5½"	5.00	6.00
3 ▸	Bowl, 8"	9.00	13.00
	Bowl, 10¼", squared sides	11.00	16.00
	Bowl, 10½	9.00	15.00
	Candle w/handle & hurricane shade, 5½"	10.00	
6 ▸	Plate, 6½	1.50	2.50
5 ▸	Plate, 9½"	3.50	7.00
4 ▸	Plate, 12"	6.00	12.00
	Snack tray w/metal handle	5.00	8.00
	Tidbit (various combinations, 2 or 3 pcs)	10.00 – 20.00	15.00 – 20.00

PINE CUTTING, NO. 835, FOSTORIA GLASS COMPANY, 1953 – 1972

Color: crystal w/cut

Pine Cutting was unveiled in the 1953 Fostoria catalog and matching stemware was listed in catalogs as late as 1972. The best news for authors in researching 1950s glassware is that there customarily are some factory catalogs in existence. Depression era paper goods (including some glassware catalogs) were often destroyed or even contributed to the paper drives of World War II. Collectors often speculate how many comics or baseball cards went into those drives.

Pine is beginning to be noticed by collectors who like the modernistic lines of the Contour mould blank (#2666) on which most of this pattern is cut. The candles seem to be popular and also were well distributed; anyone wishing a pair can own them without much difficulty. The stemware is found on Blank #6052½ often referred to as Continental. Not everyone recognizes this pattern or stem line, so you may find a bargain if you look carefully while shopping.

	Bonbon , 6⅞"	12.50	11 ▸	Relish, 7⅜", 2-part	14.00
	Bowl, finger	10.00		Relish, 10¾", 3-part	15.00
	Bowl, 8¼", oval	18.00		Salver, 12¼", ftd.	55.00
	Bowl, 10½", salad	25.00		Saucer	2.00
8 ▸	Butter & cover, ¼ lb.	30.00		Shaker, 3¼", pr.	25.00
6 ▸	Candle, 6", flora	17.50	3 ▸	Stem, 3⅛", 1¼ oz., cordial	18.00
7 ▸	Creamer, 3½"	10.00		Stem, 3⅞", 3¾ oz., cocktail	6.50
5 ▸	Creamer, individual	10.00		Stem, 3⅞", 4½ oz., oyster cocktail	12.50
	Cup	10.00		Stem, 4⅜", 4¼ oz., claret-wine	17.50
9 ▸	Mayonnaise bowl	15.00	12 ▸	Stem, 4⅜", 6½ oz., sherbet	6.50
10 ▸	Mayonnaise plate	5.00		Stem, 5⅞", 9¾ oz., water	10.00
	Pitcher, quart	75.00	1 ▸	Sugar, 2⅝"	10.00
	Plate, 7"	6.00	2 ▸	Sugar, individual	10.00
4 ▸	Plate, 8"	10.00		Tray, sugar and creamer	15.00
	Plate, 10", snack	12.00		Tumbler, 4⅞", 5½ oz., juice, ftd.	12.00
	Plate, 14", serving	20.00		Tumbler, 9⅛", 13 oz., ice tea, ftd.	9.50

"PINK ELEPHANTS," HAZEL-ATLAS, FEDERAL, LIBBEY GLASS, BARTLETT-COLLINS
COMPANIES, ET. AL., late 1940s

Color: pink design on crystal

"Pink Elephants" was a trendy theme with barware in the 50s and many glassware companies jumped on that topic with enthusiasm. Most recognized are the Hazel-Atlas products, but Federal as well as Libbey made similar designs. Federal's animated design on a frosted background particularly stands out in an assortment of wares. We have tried to picture a variety of items found in a couple of years of searching for wares for our *Hazel-Atlas Glass Identification and Value Guide*. We kept running into other "Pink Elephants" rather than those we were hunting; so that made an easy decision for a new pattern in this book. "Pink Pigs" can be similarly collected and are priced comparatively.

There are many more examples of "Pink Elephants" than the samples we have included; so, you will find others should you wish to pursue them. For the avid pachyderm lover, there are items other than glass to acquire including paper and metal products from napkins to trays. Hopefully, all "Pink Elephants" you gather will be real and not those imagined from imbibing too vigorously from the barware.

HAZEL-ATLAS GLASS COMPANY

5 ▸	Cocktail shaker, 32 oz.	50.00
	Ice tub, 5½", 44 oz.	55.00
6 ▸	Mug, concentric rings	28.00
	Pilsner, 10 oz.	80.00
	Tumbler, 2 oz., whiskey	12.00
7 ▸	Tumbler, 4 oz., heavy bottom, bar	15.00
4 ▸	Tumbler, 5 oz., juice	12.00
	Tumbler, 8 oz., old fashioned	18.00
	Tumbler, 9 oz., water	10.00
8 ▸	Tumbler, 12 oz., tea	14.00

LIBBEY GLASS COMPANY

16 ▸	Carafe	12.00
2 ▸	Tumbler, 9 oz., water	8.00
12 ▸	Tumbler, 12 oz., carousel (7" & 6")	12.00

BARTLETT-COLLINS GLASS COMPANY

11 ▸	Tumbler, 3½ oz., cocktail, flared rim	8.00

FEDERAL GLASS COMPANY

3 ▸	Decanter, w/glass stopper	150.00
17 ▸	Pilsner, 10 oz.	35.00
20 ▸	Tumbler, 2 oz., shot	12.00
19 ▸	Tumbler, 4 oz., bar	10.00
22 ▸	Tumbler, 8 oz., old fashioned	12.00
14 ▸	Tumbler, 10 oz.	11.00
13 ▸	Tumbler, 12 oz.	12.00
21 ▸	Tumbler, 13 oz., tea	15.00

MISCELLANEOUS

15 ▸	Tumbler, 2 oz., shot, say when	12.50
18 ▸	Tumbler, 10 oz., Jolly	12.50
10 ▸	Tumbler, 10 oz., red banner	12.00
1 ▸	Tumbler, 12 oz. split rail fence	15.00

PIONEER, LINE #2806 et al., FEDERAL GLASS COMPANY, c. 1940

Colors: crystal, some pink and sprayed treatments

Pioneer was a fundamental Federal line which initially had a short run in pink. After that, crystal was all that was made; a few larger pieces continued to be manufactured up until Federal went out of business in the late 70s with the biggest production throughout the 50s.

Some of the pieces came with intaglio fruit centers while others were left unadorned. At least one item (pictured in center) was made having two intaglio Scottie dogs which enchants collectors of those doggie trimmed wares. We have recently seen the smaller bowl with a "Mr. Peanut" embossing, not once or twice, but rather frequently; and we suspect possibly Indiana made them by changing Federal's moulds. When glass businesses fold, the molds are sold at liquidation and they, subsequently may be used as found, or changed a bit by another company. At least we know, the dark colored carnival pieces being found were an Indiana production.

The 12" plate in the background was given the sprayed goofus treatment which was a decoration more in line with earlier 1900s glass productions. It was probably adorned outside the factory as was the metal handled bowl. Most glass factories did not add metal accoutrements to their wares. Often bowls or plates were sold to another manufacturer who "did their own thing" with the glass.

This is a sturdy, heavier design, harking back to star cut wares made around the turn of the century; and we would imagine the Pioneer name it was given was Federal's appreciation of that. It's a much prettier pattern than our photograph here shows.

		*Crystal	Pink sprayed colors
7 ▸	Bowl, 5⅜", shallow nappy	8.00	12.00
2 ▸	Bowl, 7"	10.00	18.00
1 ▸	Bowl, 7¼", crimped	12.00	15.00
5 ▸	Bowl, 10½"	12.50	18.00
6 ▸	Bowl, 11", crimped	11.00	20.00
3 ▸	Plate, 8"	10.00	12.00
4 ▸	Plate, 12"	15.00	18.00

*Add 30 percent for intaglio fruit design and double price for Scottie.

192

PLANTATION, BLANK #1567, A.H. HEISEY & CO.

Colors: crystal; rare in amber

Heisey's Plantation used to be our bestselling pattern from this company. Today, we have fewer customers asking for it and they can buy it on Internet auctions cheaper than we can from those wanting to sell it to us. When trying to be honest with people who want to sell collections at the present, it is understandably difficult for them to credit a dealers' offer of 40 – 45% of what they paid for it. However, to stay in business, which is becoming a major problem for glass dealers, offers like that are becoming common place if a dealer even wants the collection. We just bought a large set of a terrific Fostoria pattern and may be stuck with a large part of it because we tried to make an exceedingly fair offer to someone really needing the money. No, that's not good business, but hopefully good humanity.

The pineapple is a historical symbol of welcome. You find it on bed posts, over doors, in crochet handwork and yes, in glassware patterns. Plantation's pineapples are not being plucked by new buyers, but now might be a time to stock some for the future. Not only are Plantation collectors charmed with it, but people who have no idea what the pattern is are smitten with its appearance. We have had resistance in the past for buying pieces with the Ivy etch; but we've recently had people inquire if we have any Plantation Ivy pieces. Maybe they just wanted to see what it was.

The pineapple hurricane lamp base measures 4½" wide and 5" tall. It was produced for less than five years, and some of those were made with a hole in the base for use as an electric lamp which candle collectors seem to ignore. A smaller pineapple candleblock was made through Heisey's production end in 1957 and only measures 3". Years and careless handling have made original #5080 shades with their plain rim and occasional etchings harder to locate than the pineapple base. The cigarette box shown is hard to come by; that pineapple knob gives away its identity to collectors.

Finding stems and tumblers in Plantation used to be a problem unlike many other Heisey patterns where stemware abounds. However, this is not now the problem it was five years ago. All flat tumblers are rare and that has not changed; do not pass them should you spot one.

Watch for the coupe plate showing a lady with a pineapple on her head. It's rare and few collectors have one.

PLANTATION

		Crystal
28 ▸	Ashtray, 3½"	35.00
	Bowl, 9 qt., Dr. Johnson, punch	600.00
	Bowl, 5", nappy	60.00
	Bowl, 5½", nappy	55.00
42 ▸	Bowl, 6½", 2 hndl., jelly	50.00
	Bowl, 6½", flared, jelly	80.00
	Bowl, 6½", ftd., honey, cupped	75.00
11 ▸	Bowl, 8", 4-pt., rnd., relish	80.00
	Bowl, 8½", 2-pt., dressing	70.00
21 ▸	Bowl, 9", salad	180.00
	Bowl, 9½", crimped, fruit or flower	90.00
	Bowl, 9½", gardenia	90.00
14 ▸	Bowl, 11", 3-part, relish	55.00
6 ▸	Bowl, 11½", ftd., gardenia	190.00
27 ▸	Bowl, 12", fruit or flower	100.00
	Bowl, 13", celery	65.00
36 ▸	Bowl, 13", 2-part, celery	60.00
	Bowl, 13", 5-part, oval relish	100.00
16 ▸	Bowl, 13", gardenia	90.00
15 ▸	Butter, ¼ lb., oblong, w/cover	110.00
	Butter, 5", rnd. (or cov. candy)	130.00
	Candelabrum, w/two #1503 bobech	180.00
31 ▸	Candle block, hurricane type w/globe	225.00
38 ▸	Candle block, 1-lite	110.00
	Candleholder, 5", ftd., epergne	120.00
	Candlestick, 1-lite	100.00
18 ▸	Candlestick, 2-lite	75.00
20 ▸	Candlestick, 3-lite	125.00
	Candy box, w/cover, 7" length, flat bottom	275.00
8 ▸	Candy, w/cover, 5", tall, ftd.	210.00
35 ▸	Card box, w/cover	250.00
	Cheese, w/cover, 5", ftd.	100.00
	Coaster, 4"	45.00

		Crystal
	Comport, 5"	60.00
	Comport, 5", w/cover, deep	120.00
12 ▸	Creamer, ftd.	40.00
39 ▸	Cup	40.00
	Cup, punch	25.00
3 ▸	Marmalade, w/cover	170.00
	Mayonnaise, 4½", rolled ft.	85.00
	Mayonnaise, 5¼", w/liner	80.00
29 ▸	Mayonnaise, twin, 5¼"	55.00
5 ▸	Oil bottle, 3 oz., w/#125 stopper	120.00
	Pitcher, ½ gallon, ice lip, blown	450.00
2 ▸	Plate, buffet w/ inserts, 18"	1,000.00
7 ▸	Plate, coupe (rare)	500.00
	Plate, 7", salad	25.00
30 ▸	Plate, 8", salad	35.00
	Plate, 10½", demi-torte	70.00
	Plate, 13", ftd., cake salver	225.00
33 ▸	Plate, 14", sandwich	75.00
	Plate, 18", buffet	165.00
	Plate, 18", punch bowl liner	145.00
37 ▸	Salt & pepper, pr.	100.00
40 ▸	Saucer	8.00
1 ▸	Sherbet, 3½ oz., pressed	80.00
	Stem, 1 oz., cordial	125.00
26 ▸	Stem, 3 oz., wine, blown	65.00
10 ▸	Stem, 3½ oz., cocktail, pressed	50.00
	Stem, 4 oz., fruit or oyster cocktail	35.00
	Stem, 4½ oz., claret, blown	70.00
	Stem, 4½ oz., claret, pressed	80.00
25 ▸	Stem, 4½ oz., oyster cocktail, blown	40.00
	Stem, 6½ oz., sherbet/saucer champagne, blown	35.00
9 ▸	Stem, 10 oz., pressed goblet	40.00
	Stem, 10 oz., blown goblet	40.00
13 ▸	Sugar, ftd.	40.00
	Syrup bottle, w/drip, cut top	120.00
4 ▸	Tray, 8½", condiment, sugar & creamer	125.00
41 ▸	Tumbler, 5 oz., ftd., juice, pressed	60.00
	Tumbler, 5 oz., ftd., juice, blown	40.00
22 ▸	Tumbler, 8 oz., water, pressed	125.00
23 ▸	Tumbler, 10 oz., pressed	125.00
32 ▸	Tumbler, 12 oz., ftd., iced tea, pressed	80.00
17 ▸	Tumbler, 12 oz., ftd., iced tea, blown	65.00
24 ▸	Vase, 5", ftd., flared	100.00
19 ▸	Vase, 9", ftd., flared	425.00

PRELUDE, NEW MARTINSVILLE & VIKING GLASS COMPANY, mid 1930s – 1950s

Color: crystal

Prelude was introduced at New Martinsville Glass Company in the mid-1930s and was a popular design as you can see from its longevity. When Viking Glass Company took over the New Martinsville Glass factory in 1943, they continued Prelude production but with the edge of pieces being more rounded to facilitate faster production.

We have eliminated catalog pages included in past editions; if you wish to see those for information, be sure to look in previous editions. Shakers only have flowers in their design; thus, they are often overlooked as Prelude. There are many different of stems and tumblers that can be found. Matching the style you want can become a problem since some stems and tumblers are found with a "ball" and others are missing it. It is always frustrating to see a water or wine only to note it is that other style. Remember, however, blending styles is a current happening.

Prelude includes some interesting pieces such as a wine carafe, cocktail shaker, and swans with the design etched on them, but there are not enough collectors to drive the prices "out of sight" for now. Should you desire to start a pattern with a multitude of pieces that won't send you to the bank to borrow money, Prelude might be the right choice.

Bonbon, 6", hndl.		9.00
Bonbon, 6", 3-ftd.		22.00
Bowl, 7", cupped		25.00
Bowl, 8", crimped		35.00
Bowl, 8", 3-part, shrimp		55.00
Bowl, 9", 3-ftd., crimped		40.00
16 ▶ Bowl, 9½", crimped, ftd.		40.00
Bowl, 10", crimped		45.00
14 ▶ Bowl, 10", 3-ftd.		40.00
Bowl, 10", shallow		35.00
Bowl, 10½", nut, center hndl.		40.00
Bowl, 11", 3 ftd.		55.00
Bowl, 12½", crimped		50.00
Bowl, 13", oval		42.00
Bowl, 13", shallow		20.00
Bowl, 15", 3-ftd.		72.50
2 ▶ Butter dish, 6½", oval, w/cover		37.50
Butter dish, 8½", oval, w/cover		35.00
Cake salver, 11", 5½" high		35.00
Cake salver, 11", w/metal base		35.00
Candlestick, 4"		15.00
Candlestick, 4½"		15.00
18 ▶ Candlestick, 5", double, #5214		15.00
Candlestick, 5½"		15.00
5 ▶ Candlestick, 6", double, #952		20.00
Candy box, 6", w/cover, closed knob		60.00
Candy box, 6½", w/cover, open knob		65.00

15 ▶ Candy box, 7", w/cover, 3-ftd.		65.00
Celery, 10½"		30.00
9 ▶ Cocktail shaker, w/metal lid		195.00
Compote, cheese		15.00
Compote, 5½" diameter, 3" high		25.00
Compote, 6"		22.00
12 ▶ Compote, 7", crimped		35.00
Compote, 7½", flared		35.00
22 ▶ Creamer		12.50
Creamer, 4-ftd.		15.00
Creamer, individual		12.50
Cup		25.00
Ensemble set, 13", bowl w/candleholder		145.00
Ensemble set, 13", bowl w/flower epergne		175.00
Lazy Susan, 18", 3-pc. set		175.00
Mayonnaise, 3-pc.		22.00
Mayonnaise, divided, 4-pc.		40.00
Nappy w/pc, 6", for candle		40.00
Oil bottle, 4 oz.		40.00
4 ▶ Pitcher, 48 oz., straight		50.00
Pitcher, 78 oz.		265.00
Plate, 6", bread & butter		6.00
Plate, 6½", hndl.		12.50
Plate, 6½", lemon, 3-ftd.		14.00
Plate, 7"		8.00
Plate, 7", lemon, 3-ftd.		15.00
Plate, 8", salad		10.00

Plate, 9"		20.00
Plate, 10", dinner		40.00
Plate, 10", 3-ftd.		25.00
8 ▶ Plate, 11"		20.00
Plate, 11", 3-ftd., cake		40.00
Plate, 11", cracker		22.50
Plate, 13", hndl.		20.00
Plate, 14", flat or turned-up edge		45.00
Plate, 16"		75.00
Plate, 16", 3-ftd.		75.00
Plate, 18"		85.00
Platter, 14½"		65.00
Relish, 6", 2-part		15.00
Relish, 6", 2-part, hndl.		18.00
Relish, 7", 2-part, hndl.		20.00
Relish, 7", 3-part, hndl.		15.00
3 ▶ Relish, 10", 3-part, hndl.		32.00
Relish, 13", 5-part		35.00
Salt and pepper, 3½" pr., 2 styles		40.00
Saucer		5.00
Stem, 1 oz., cordial		35.00
Stem, 1 oz., cordial, ball stem		40.00
Stem, 3 oz., wine		8.00
20 ▶ Stem, 3 oz., wine, ball stem		8.00
Stem, 3½ oz., cocktail		8.00
Stem, 4 oz., cocktail, ball stem		8.00
Stem, 6 oz., low sherbet		12.00
10 ▶ Stem, 6 oz., sherbet, ball stem		12.00
Stem, 6 oz., tall sherbet		15.00

19 ▸ Stem, 9 oz., water	25.00
23 ▸ Sugar	12.50
Sugar, 4-ftd.	15.00
6 ▸ Sugar, individual	12.50
Swan, 6"	32.50
Tidbit, 2 tier, chrome hndl.	40.00
24 ▸ Tray, 11", center hndl.	22.00
11 ▸ Tray, 11", oval tab handles	20.00

Tray, ind. cr./sug.	10.00
Treasure jar, 8", w/cover	120.00
Tumbler, 5 oz., ftd. juice	15.00
Tumbler, 5 oz., juice, ball stem	17.50
1 ▸ Tumbler, 9 oz., flat	18.00
7 ▸ Tumbler, 10 oz., water, ball stem	20.00
13 ▸ Tumbler, 12 oz., ftd., tea	22.00
Tumbler, 13 oz., tea, ball stem	25.00

Vase, 8"	40.00
Vase, 10", bud	30.00
Vase, 10", crimped	35.00
Vase, 11", crimped	40.00
Vase, 11", ftd.	75.00
Wine carafe	50.00

"PRETZEL," NO. 622, INDIANA GLASS COMPANY, late 1930s – 1980s

Colors: crystal, teal, and avocado with more recent issues in amber and blue

"Pretzel" is the collectors' name for Indiana's No. 622 pattern. We have never heard anyone say that they collect No. 622. "Pretzel" was apropos of the design and just fuses into memory. A display of "Pretzel" was presented at one of the Depression glass shows and people kept passing our table commenting how marvelous they thought it looked with so much displayed "together like that." Every now and then it's worth going to Depression glass shows just to see the table settings that are exhibited so artistically.

Has anyone spotted a teal saucer to accompany the cup? After years of searching, we finally gathered the pitcher and all three sizes of tumblers. Sorry to say, the water tumbler didn't find its way to the photo session; but you can see the pitcher, juice, and iced tea. Intaglio fruit centered and frosted crystal items are selling for 25 – 50% more than plain centered pieces.

We have been told of a calendar plate with a side design of "Pretzel." If you have one, please send more details.

		Crystal				Crystal
2 ▸	Bowl, 4½", fruit cup	4.00		15 ▸	Plate, 6", tab hndl.	2.50
	Bowl, 5½", advertising	4.00		14 ▸	Plate, 7¼", square, indent	9.00
1 ▸	Bowl, 7½", soup	10.00		12 ▸	Plate, 7¼", square, indent, 3-part	9.00
	Bowl, 9⅜", berry	12.00		9 ▸	Plate, 8⅜", salad	6.00
	Celery, 10¼", tray	1.50		11 ▸	Plate, 9⅜", dinner	12.00
16 ▸				10 ▸	Plate, 11½", sandwich	11.00
7 ▸	Creamer	5.00		4 ▸	**Saucer	1.00
3 ▸	*Cup	5.00		6 ▸	Sugar	5.00
5 ▸	Olive, 7", leaf-shaped	3.00		17 ▸	Tumbler, 5 oz., 3½"	40.00
13 ▸	Pickle, 8½", two hndl.	3.00			Tumbler, 9 oz., 4½"	35.00
19 ▸	Pitcher, 39 oz.	495.00		18 ▸	Tumbler, 12 oz., 5½"	60.00
8 ▸	Plate, 6"	2.00				

* Teal $125.00
** Teal $40.00

PYREX "BLUE WILLOW," CORNING GLASS WORKS, 1950s

Color: crystal with blue decoration

Corning's Pyrex was the main competition for Anchor Hocking's Fire-King Ovenware and "Blue Willow" was one of their patterns which collectors are beginning to gather. The major drawback is the blue design wore off with use. You can see the lack of blue on some of the pieces illustrated. Prices are for items with excellent blue design. There may be additional pieces than those in our listing; let me know what you find.

	Bowl, 4½", dessert	10.00
	Bowl, 6", cereal	12.00
7▸	Bowl, 10", soup	18.00
	Casserole, w/cover, 1 pt.	18.00
	Casserole, w/cover, 1 qt.	22.00
1▸	Casserole, w/cover, 2 qt.	25.00
4▸	Gravy boat	35.00
5▸	Gravy boat platter	15.00
2▸	Plate, 8"	10.00
6▸	Plate, 10"	20.00
3▸	Plate, 12"	25.00
8▸	Platter, 13"	45.00

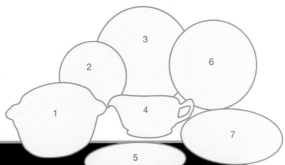

PYREX TALLY HO, CORNING GLASS WORKS, 1960s

Color: white w/decoration

Although labeled pieces of this pattern are Pyrex Tally Ho, there is an embossing of Made in England with a crown on the base of most pieces. Were it not for the Pyrex shapes and Pyrex labels on items being found, we would have ignored this pattern due to the embossing. With the Kentucky Horse Park seven miles from an antique mall where we have a booth, we started buying this pattern to sell there. It seems horse aficionados like horse decorated items too.

No.	Item	Price
14 ▸	Bowl, 4½", dessert	9.00
11 ▸	Bowl, 6", cereal	10.00
	Bowl, 8", vegetable	20.00
12 ▸	Bowl, 9", soup	15.00
15 ▸	Casserole, w/cover, 1 pt.	18.00
	Casserole, w/cover, 1 qt.	20.00
13 ▸	Casserole, w/cover, 1½ qt.	25.00
8 ▸	Creamer	10.00
4 ▸	Cup	8.00
10 ▸	Gravy boat	25.00
	Gravy boat platter	15.00
1 ▸	Mixing bowl, 7"	15.00
2 ▸	Mixing bowl, 8"	18.00
3 ▸	Mixing bowl, 9"	20.00
6 ▸	Plate, 8"	8.00
9 ▸	Plate, 10"	12.00
7 ▸	Plate, 12"	20.00
	Platter, 13"	35.00
5 ▸	Saucer	2.00
	Sugar	10.00

RADIANCE #2700, FOSTORIA GLASS COMPANY, 1956 – 1957

Colors: crystal, aqua, peach, and white milk glass

Few collectors have noticed Fostoria's Radiance which was only listed in catalogs for two years, making this one of the rarer Fostoria patterns from the 1950s. This heavier, linear design which was so "in" during the Deco era wasn't very well accepted by people in the fifties. So, for now, you can purchase designer Radiance almost cheaper than buying newly made glassware. We bought most of the pieces shown in one antique mall and have seen several sets sitting in other malls just waiting for a new owner.

By the way, this is a Sakier designed pattern which usually stimulates some collector interest just by that magic name.

		Crystal			Crystal
2 ▸	Bowl, 5½", cereal	8.00		Relish, 12⅝", 3-part	12.00
12 ▸	Bowl, 11", oval, serving	18.00		Sauce bowl	18.00
9 ▸	Bowl, 12", salad	20.00		Sauce plate	6.00
7 ▸	Celery	12.00	11 ▸	Saucer	1.00
	Creamer	7.00		Shaker, 2½", pr.	15.00
10 ▸	Cup	5.00	6 ▸	Sherbet, 3", 6 oz.	7.00
1 ▸	Plate, 7", salad	6.00		Sugar	7.00
5 ▸	Plate, 10", dinner	12.00	8 ▸	Tumbler, 4½", 5 oz., ftd. juice	6.00
	Plate, 14", buffet	20.00	4 ▸	Tumbler, 5¾", 10 oz., ftd., beverage	10.00
3 ▸	Platter, 15"	20.00			

RAINBOW, ANCHOR HOCKING GLASS CORPORATION, 1938 – early 1950s

Rainbow tableware was first unveiled in Anchor Hocking's 1939 catalog, but Tangerine (red) ball jugs were introduced the previous year. Along with Tangerine (2157) were Blue (2158), Green (2159), and Yellow (2160). For classification purposes, these are called Primary Rainbow colors and pictured on 203. The lighter colored Pastel Rainbow colors were designated Pink (159), Green (160), Yellow (161), and Blue (162).

We included Rainbow in the second edition of *Anchor Hocking's Fire-King and More* book as part of the "more" of the book. Some collectors were beginning to buy this fired-on ware and it had become such a hot collectible that another book on Fire-King showed only this non Fire-King Rainbow line on its cover. Because of those happenings many now believe Rainbow is Fire-King. The "thousand words" those photos spoke was a tad misleading, since people often accept pictures without reading. However, it is a colorful and pleasing collectible glassware from the 40s and was almost certainly Anchor Hocking's answer to the multicolored Fiesta influence of the time which many were embracing.

Rainbow has always been around the fringes of collecting, but no name had been unearthed for this ware so that collectors could embrace exposing it in our book. Bidding wars were the norm on the Internet auctions and we sold a table full of it at a Fire-King Expo in Tulsa. Since then, prices went wild on the harder to find items, especially pitchers (except Tangerine), platters, and vegetable and cereal bowls. Now, once again, prices have settled down, but the harder to find items are still in demand and are not turning up in quantities of some of the 50s and 60s patterns. Too, condition on these wares is a factor. What is left often has color spot damage.

We have separated the pricing into Pastel and Primary headings; but to bring the prices listed these pieces have to be mint (no missing paint spots). There are stems listed, which have a colored foot, but a crystal stem and bowl. These goblets were shown under Standard Glass Company listing in Anchor Hocking's 1940 catalog. They have cutting #112, called Criss-Cross & Punty, consisting of circular cuts and tic-tac-toe grids. We made a New York couple ecstatic when they completed their long search for stems in our booth.

		*Pastel	Primary
	Bowl, 5¼", utilty, deep		14.00
17 ▶	Bowl, 6", fruit	20.00	20.00

		*Pastel	Primary
22 ▶	Bowl, 9½", vegetable		50.00
13 ▶	Creamer, ftd.	15.00	10.00
15 ▶	Cup	7.00	7.00
1 ▶	**Jug, 42 oz., ball	70.00	85.00
	Jug, 42 oz., Manhattan	65.00	55.00
2 ▶	Jug, 54 oz.		60.00
	Jug, 64 oz.		65.00
3 ▶	†Jug, 80 oz., ball	85.00	125.00
	Jug, 80 oz., ball, Pillar Optic		85.00
	Plate, 6¼", sherbet	6.00	12.00
11 ▶	Plate, 7¼", salad	10.00	15.00
14 ▶	Plate, 9¼", dinner	15.00	18.00
8 ▶	Platter, 11"		70.00
16 ▶	Saucer	3.00	3.00
	Shakers, pr.		25.00
18 ▶	Sherbet, ftd.	12.00	10.00
25 ▶	Stem, 4 oz., cocktail	15.00	25.00
4 ▶	Stem, 7 oz., high sherbet	15.00	25.00
5 ▶	Stem, 10 oz., 7⅜"	15.00	25.00
12 ▶	Sugar, ftd.	15.00	10.00

*Add 25% for green   **Tangerine $30.00
†Tangerine $20.00

	*Pastel	Primary
7 ▸ Tumbler, 5 oz., fruit juice		10.00
Tumbler, 9 oz., bath, straight		10.00
10 ▸ Tumbler, 9 oz., table	15.00	10.00
23 ▸ Tumbler, 15 oz., ftd.		15.00

Accessory Items

	*Pastel	Primary
Tumbler, 12 oz., 4¾", straight stripe		25.00
Bulb bowl, 5½"	15.00	18.00
Cactus pot, 2¼", round		15.00

	*Pastel	Primary
Cactus pot, 2¼", square	20.00	20.00
Flower pot, 3¼"	18.00	15.00
Flower pot, 4", 2 styles	18.00	15.00
Lamp, 7", hurricane	35.00	
Vase, 3¾", 2 styles		10.00
Vase, 5¼", deco	15.00	12.00
6 ▸ Vase, 5¾", ftd.		50.00
Vase, 9", ruffled top	25.00	25.00
Water bottle, 54 oz.	40.00	*40.00

*Add 25% for green   **Jade-ite

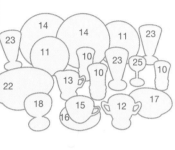

RIPPLE, "CRINOLINE," "PETTICOAT," "PIE CRUST," "LASAGNA," HAZEL-ATLAS GLASS
COMPANY, early 1950s

Colors: Platonite white and white w/blue or pink trim

Hazel-Atlas' Ripple pattern had previously been known by all the names listed above in quote marks until a boxed set divulged the factory name. A reader was considerate enough to share her find with us all. We are often asked how much an original box adds to the value of a set. It depends upon condition, desirability of pattern, and whether the items enclosed are pictured in most cases. However, if the box is a discovery of a pattern name such as that of Ripple (or Gothic previously discussed under "Big Top"), it has more intrinsic value to us as researchers and authors, trying to get the names out there to the collecting public. Naming patterns correctly is important so collectors can identify to others what they are wishing to find.

Ripple presents esthetically by mixing the colors. We purposely contrasted the colors in the picture below to give you an idea of how it looks intermingled. The cup, creamer, and sugar handles come both plain and beaded and the small, shallow dessert bowl remains the most sought piece that some collectors have never found. We have shown both styles of handles in the photo. We see a lot of Ripple in central Florida, but have never encountered one of the shallow bowls for sale. Don't pass by these if you discover one. There is a collector waiting to take it off your hands.

The 10½" serving plate is not turning up in any quantity and they seem to have been seriously used as they are rarely found without scratches and gouges. There was only one of these plates sold per set which made them in much shorter supply than other pieces from the very beginning.

Collectors have discovered at least two different pitcher and tumbler designs that can be used with this set. Both of these sets were made by Anchor Hocking and are found with tumblers in four sizes.

Hazel-Atlas did make a fired-on blue or pink tumbler and mug that could accompany Ripple as accessory pieces. A Hazel-Atlas tumbler with swirled stripes has been found packed in a Ripple set; so there were Hazel-Atlas tumblers made to coordinate with Ripple. One thing we have noticed that is different from other patterns of this era is that it is selling on the Internet. Prices for Ripple are holding up quite well.

		All colors				All colors
13 ▸	Bowl, berry, shallow, 5"	15.00		11 ▸	Saucer, 5⅝"	1.00
2 ▸	Bowl, cereal, deep, 5⅝"	7.00		1 ▸	Sugar	7.50
12 ▸	Creamer	7.50		9 ▸	Tidbit, 3-tier	35.00
10 ▸	Cup	5.00		15 ▸	Tumbler, 5 oz., juice (Hocking)	6.00
3 ▸	Plate, 6⅞", salad	7.00		14 ▸	Tumbler, 6", 16 oz. (Hocking)	7.00
4 ▸	Plate, 8⅞", luncheon	6.00		7 ▸	Tumbler, 6¼", 20 oz. (Hocking)	9.00
5 ▸	Plate, 10½", sandwich	17.50		8 ▸	Tumbler, 12 oz. (Hocking)	9.00
6 ▸	Pitcher, 80 oz. (Hocking)	22.00				

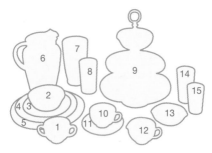

ROMANCE, ETCHING #341, FOSTORIA GLASS COMPANY, 1942 – 1986

Color: crystal

Romance is occasionally confused with Fostoria's June because of the "bow" in the design. Compare the plain round shapes of Romance to those of June, which are found on the optic Fairfax blank. Also, there is a double line etch surrounding June which is not found on Romance. Forty years into this business of buying and selling collectible glassware makes us wonder if sellers look to see if a piece is priced higher in June than Romance, and if it is, then price it as June. Only crystal June is a problem since Romance was not made in color.

Romance was distributed for over 40 years and still has appeal for collectors. We feel some of the allure is in the name itself, but some is apparently from the marvelous garland design; and putting it on the superlative "Sceptre" stemware didn't harm it looks either.

There used to be pricing controversies for Romance. Some dealers have informed us our prices are too high and they can't sell this pattern at those prices; others consider our prices way too low on Romance. Recently, no one has said our prices are too low as Romance is being found in quantities on the Internet to drive the prices way below those of our book. Pricing is something we work harder on than any other aspect of a book. It really is difficult to please everyone when it comes to pricing. We were recently enlightened by a customer at a show, that although they love our books, they were buying another more expensive guide because the prices were higher in it. We strongly believe we need to reflect actual selling prices in today's market and not "hoped for" prices. You can price an item for anything you wish, but if it won't sell for that, what good is that price? However, the prices herein are still only a guide. You alone must ultimately decide what any item is worth to you; and that is your real price. Some people feel their time is more valuable and if they see their needed item even at an inflated value, they buy it to "save time" looking for it.

ROMANCE

	Ashtray, 2⅝", indiv., #2364	20.00
5 ▸	Bowl, 6", baked apple, #2364	16.00
	Bowl, 8", soup, rimmed, #2364	75.00
10 ▸	Bowl, 9", salad, #2364	30.00
	Bowl, 9¼", ftd., blown, #6023	150.00
	Bowl, 10", 2 hndl., #2594	40.00
19 ▸	Bowl, 10½", salad, #2364	40.00
	Bowl, 11", shallow, oblong, #2596	40.00
	Bowl, 12", ftd., #2364	40.00
	Bowl, 12", lily pond, #2364	35.00
	Bowl, 13", fruit, #2364	40.00
	Bowl, 13½", hndl., oval, #2594	45.00
15 ▸	Candlestick, 4", #2324	18.00
	Candlestick, 5", #2596	18.00
	Candlestick, 5½", #2594	18.00
16 ▸	Candlestick, 5½", 2-lite, #6023	20.00
	Candlestick, 8", 3-lite, #2594	35.00
	Candy w/lid, rnd., blown, #2364	90.00
	Cigarette holder, 2", blown, #2364	32.00
	Comport, 3¼", cheese, #2364	22.00
	Comport, 5", #6030	28.00
	Comport, 8", #2364	45.00
20 ▸	Creamer, 3¼", ftd., #2350½	10.00
24 ▸	Cup, ftd., #2350½	7.00
	Ice tub, 4¾", #4132	160.00
	Ladle, mayonnaise, #2364	5.00
	Mayonnaise, 5", #2364	20.00
21 ▸	Pitcher, 8⅞", 53 oz., ftd., #6011	295.00
	Plate, 6", #2337	6.00
	Plate, 6¾", mayonnaise liner, #2364	6.00
6 ▸	Plate, 7½", #2337	6.00
	Plate, 8½", #2337	11.00
	Plate, 9½", #2337	28.00

7 ▸	Plate, 11", sandwich, #2364	24.00
	Plate, 11¼", cracker, #2364	35.00
	Plate, 14", torte, #2364	40.00
	Plate, 16", torte, #2364	75.00
	Plate, crescent salad, #2364	38.00
4 ▸	Relish, 8", pickle, #2364	17.00
18 ▸	Relish, 10", 3-pt., #2364	20.00
14 ▸	Relish, 11", celery, #2364	22.00
22 ▸	Salt & pepper, 2⅝", pr., #2364	35.00
25 ▸	Saucer, #2350	3.00
	Stem, 3⅞", ¾ oz., cordial, #6017	22.00
23 ▸	Stem, 4½", 6 oz., low sherbet, #6017	9.00
8 ▸	Stem, 4⅞", 3½ oz., cocktail, #6017	9.00
9 ▸	Stem, 5½", 3 oz., wine, #6017	16.00
1 ▸	Stem, 5½", 6 oz., champagne, #6017	9.00
2 ▸	Stem, 5⅞", 4 oz., claret, #6017	20.00
	Stem, 7⅜", 9 oz., goblet, #6017	16.00
17 ▸	Sugar, 3⅛", ftd., #2350½	10.00
3 ▸	Tray, 11⅛", ctr. hndl., #2364	23.00
	Tumbler, 3⅝", 4 oz., ftd., oyster cocktail, #6017	10.00
11 ▸	Tumbler, 4¾", 5 oz., ftd., #6017	9.00
12 ▸	Tumbler, 5½", 9 oz., ftd., #6017	12.00
13 ▸	Tumbler, 6", 12 oz., ftd., #6017	20.00
	Vase, 5", #4121	30.00
	Vase, 6", ftd. bud, #6021	30.00
	Vase, 6", ftd., #4143	45.00
	Vase, 6", grnd. bottom, #2619½	45.00
	Vase, 7½", ftd., #4143	55.00
	Vase, 7½", grnd. bottom, #2619½	65.00
	Vase, 9½", grnd. bottom, #2619½	95.00
	Vase, 10", #2614	90.00
	Vase, 10", ftd., #2470	110.00

ROSE, ETCHING #1515 on WAVERLY BLANK #1519, STEM BLANK #5072, A.H. HEISEY & CO., 1949 – 1957

Color: crystal

Heisey Rose is suffering the same fate as its sister pattern, Orchid. Such a copious amount of stems are being found and listed on the Internet auctions that the prices have dropped dramatically. We have been told by several Heisey dealers that they are not buying stems from either pattern because they cannot buy them cheaply enough to resell them. Most Rose is found on the Waverly mould blank and stems are easily recognized with that rose incorporated into it. The very expensive, scarce 10½" dinner plate has a large center with a small border, while the 10½" service plate has a small center and large border. These are being misrepresented on Internet auctions and you need to realize which the real dinner is. Six-inch eper-nettes are rare, as is the hurricane lamp.

	Item	Price		Item	Price
20 ▸	Ashtray, 3"	37.50		Bowl, 10", crimped, floral, Waverly	75.00
	Bell, dinner, #5072	150.00	14 ▸	Bowl, 11", 3-pt., relish, Waverly	60.00
	Bottle, 8 oz., French dressing, blown, #5031	185.00		Bowl, 11", 3-ftd., floral, Waverly	165.00
	Bowl, finger, #3309	100.00		Bowl, 11", floral, Waverly	70.00
	Bowl, 5½", ftd., mint	30.00		Bowl, 11", oval, 4-ftd., Waverly	150.00
	Bowl, 5¾", ftd., mint, Cabochon	80.00		Bowl, 12", crimped, floral, Waverly	50.00
5 ▸	Bowl, 6", ftd., mint, Queen Ann	50.00		Bowl, 13", crimped, floral, Waverly	85.00
	Bowl, 6", jelly, 2 hndl., ftd., Queen Ann	55.00		Bowl, 13", floral, Waverly	85.00
	Bowl, 6", oval, lemon, w/cover, Waverly	695.00		Bowl, 13", gardenia, Waverly	60.00
.15 ▸	Bowl, 6½", 2 pt., oval, dressing, Waverly	70.00	19 ▸	Butter, w/cover, 6", Waverly	100.00
	Bowl, 6½", ftd., honey/cheese, Waverly	50.00	24 ▸	Butter, w/cover, ¼ lb., Cabochon	325.00
	Bowl, 6½", ftd., jelly, Waverly	45.00		Candlestick, 1-lite, #112	45.00
	Bowl, 6½", lemon, w/cover, Queen Ann	250.00		Candlestick, 2-lite, Flame	100.00
	Bowl, 7", ftd., honey, Waverly	60.00		Candlestick, 3-lite, #142, Cascade	85.00
	Bowl, 7", ftd., jelly, Waverly	45.00	9 ▸	Candlestick, 3-lite, Waverly	100.00
	Bowl, 7", lily, Queen Ann	125.00		Candlestick, 5", 2-lite, #134, Trident	75.00
	Bowl, 7", relish, 3-pt., round, Waverly	67.50	8 ▸	Candlestick, 6", epergnette, deep, Waverly	500.00
	Bowl, 7", salad, Waverly	75.00		Candy, w/cover, 5", ftd., Waverly	150.00
	Bowl, 7", salad dressings, Queen Ann	60.00		Candy, w/cover, 6", low, bowknot cover	175.00
	Bowl, 9", ftd., fruit or salad, Waverly	195.00		Candy, w/cover, 6¼", #1951, Cabochon	175.00
	Bowl, 9", salad, Waverly	135.00		Celery tray, 12", Waverly	45.00
	Bowl, 9", 4-pt., rnd, relish, Waverly	80.00		Celery tray, 13", Waverly	60.00
	Bowl, 9½", crimped, floral, Waverly	75.00		Cheese compote, 4½" & cracker (11" plate), Waverly	145.00
	Bowl, 10", gardenia, Waverly	75.00			

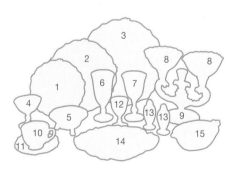

ROSE

	Cheese compote, 5½" & cracker (12" plate), Queen Ann	145.00
	Chocolate, w/cover, 5", Waverly	175.00
	Cigarette holder, #4035	125.00
	Cocktail icer, w/liner, #3304, Universal	350.00
	Cocktail shaker, #4225, Cobel	195.00
18 ▸	Comport, 6½", low ft., Waverly	65.00
	Comport, 7", oval, ftd., Waverly	135.00
17 ▸	Creamer, ftd., Waverly	25.00
22 ▸	Creamer, indiv., Waverly	30.00
10 ▸	Cup, Waverly	45.00
	Decanter, 1-pt., #4036½, #101 stopper	495.00
	Hurricane lamp, w/12" globe, #5080	375.00
	Hurricane lamp, w/12" globe, Plantation	495.00
	Ice bucket, dolphin ft., Queen Ann	325.00
	Ice tub, 2 hndl., Waverly	450.00
	Mayonnaise, 5½", 2 hndl., Waverly	55.00
	Mayonnaise, 5½", div., 1 hndl., Waverly	55.00
	Mayonnaise, 5½", ftd., Waverly	50.00
	Oil, 3 oz., ftd., Waverly	150.00
	Pitcher, 73 oz., #4164	575.00
	Plate, 7", salad, Waverly	25.00
	Plate, 7", mayonnaise, Waverly	20.00
	Plate, 8", salad, Waverly	25.00
1 ▸	Plate, 10½", dinner, Waverly	175.00
2 ▸	Plate, 11", sandwich, Waverly	60.00
	Plate, 11", demi-torte, Waverly	50.00
	Plate, 12", ftd., salver, Waverly	250.00

	Plate, 13½", ftd., cake, Waverly	200.00
3 ▸	Plate, 14", torte, Waverly	65.00
	Plate, 14", sandwich, Waverly	100.00
	Plate, 14", ctr. hndl., sandwich, Waverly	135.00
13 ▸	Salt & pepper, ftd., pr., Waverly	65.00
11 ▸	Saucer, Waverly	6.00
	Stem, #5072, 1 oz., cordial	100.00
12 ▸	Stem, #5072, 3 oz., wine	60.00
	Stem, #5072, 3½ oz., oyster cocktail, ftd.	40.00
	Stem, #5072, 4 oz., claret	90.00
	Stem, #5072, 4 oz., cocktail	35.00
4 ▸	Stem, #5072, 6 oz., sherbet	18.00
	Stem, #5072, 6 oz., saucer champagne	25.00
7 ▸	Stem, #5072, 9 oz., water	34.00
21 ▸	Sugar, indiv., Waverly	30.00
16 ▸	Sugar, ftd., Waverly	25.00
	Tumbler, #5072, 5 oz., ftd., juice	50.00
6 ▸	Tumbler, #5072, 12 oz., ftd., tea	58.00
23 ▸	Tray, indiv. creamer/sugar, Queen Ann	65.00
	Vase, 3½", ftd., violet, Waverly	110.00
	Vase, 4", ftd., violet, Waverly	120.00
	Vase, 7", ftd., fan, Waverly	140.00
	Vase, 8", #4198	175.00
	Vase, 8", sq., ftd., urn	185.00
	Vase, 10", #4198	245.00
	Vase, 10", sq., ftd., urn	250.00
	Vase, 12", sq., ftd., urn	295.00

ROYAL RUBY, ANCHOR HOCKING GLASS COMPANY, 1938 – 1960s; 1977

Color: Royal Ruby

We spotted a Royal Ruby "High Point" #1201 nine-ounce glass for sale misidentified as ruby pattern glass with the name "Sword and Circle" — and priced as though it were rare. We were amused that 1940s glassware has been so misrepresented; this tumbler really wasn't produced in the early 1900s. Royal Ruby is Anchor Hocking's patented name for their red colored glass first produced in 1938 and never before.

Many dealers and collectors incorrectly call all red glass Royal Ruby. Truly, only red glassware manufactured by Anchor-Hocking should be so called. So, flashed red wares produced in recent years on patterns such as Wexford at Anchor-Hocking should not be labeled Royal Ruby either, which we have seen done.

Royal Ruby stickers were attached to each red piece, no matter the pattern. Red "Bubble" or Charm did not mean anything except Royal Ruby to the factory, so don't be shocked when you see a Royal Ruby sticker on Charm or some other identifiable pattern. In this book, Charm and "Bubble" Royal Ruby are covered under those pattern names. Priced on page 212 are only crystal stems with Royal Ruby tops (Berwick) as well as the stems that go with Royal Ruby "Bubble" (Early American Line). See a complete explanation of these stems in "Bubble" on page 17.

Manufacture of Royal Ruby began in the thirties after the merger of Anchor Hocking and Hocking glass companies. A Royal Ruby section in the eighteenth edition of *Collector's Encyclopedia of Depression Glass* covers the pieces made in patterns of the late 1930s. Royal Ruby will continue to be listed in both books since it can clearly be divided into pre and post 1940 productions.

The punch bowl base and the salad bowl with 13¾" underliner are rarely come across in today's market though they are not totally impossible to find. There are two styles of sherbets. The stemmed one seems to be preferred by most collectors. Upright pitchers appear to have multiplied and we see less expensive prices now as compared to a few years ago.

There were six sizes (7, 8, 12 [two styles], 16, and 32 ounces) of beer bottles made in several shapes for Schlitz Beer Company in '49, '50, or '63. The date of manufacture is embossed on the bottom of each bottle. Thousands of these bottles were made, but labeled ones are not often found. Bottle collectors usually find these more charming than Royal Ruby collectors and prices are often higher at bottle shows than at glass shows. The quart size is the most commonly seen.

ROYAL RUBY

	Ashtray, 4½", leaf	5.00
15 ▸	Ashtray, 6", square	8.00
19 ▸	Bank, owl	325.00
17 ▸	Beer bottle, 8 oz.	22.00
	Beer bottle, 12 oz.	65.00
	Beer bottle, 16 oz.	65.00
	Beer bottle, 32 oz.	35.00
10 ▸	Bowl, 4", fruit	6.00
	Bowl, 4¼", round, fruit	5.00
	Bowl, 5¼", popcorn	12.00
8 ▸	Bowl, 6", several styles	12.00
	Bowl, 7½", round, soup	12.00
	Bowl, 8", oval, vegetable	20.00
	Bowl, 8½", round, large berry	15.00
	Bowl, 10", deep, popcorn (same as punch)	35.00
	Bowl, 11½", salad	26.00
14 ▸	Cigarette box/card holder, 6⅛" x 4"	50.00
	Creamer, flat	10.00
11 ▸	Creamer, ftd.	6.00
	Cup, round	4.00
	Goblet, ball stem	12.00
	Ice bucket	50.00
	Lamp	35.00
21 ▸	Marmalade, w/Royal Ruby lid	18.00
	Pitcher, 3 qt., tilted, swirl	50.00
13 ▸	Pitcher, 3 qt., upright	60.00
7 ▸	Pitcher, 24 oz., tilted or straight	30.00
	Plate, 6¼", sherbet, round	3.00
	Plate, 7", salad	4.00
4 ▸	Plate, 7¾", salad, round	5.00
5 ▸	Plate, 9⅛", dinner, round	9.00

	Plate, 13¾"	22.00
	Punch bowl	35.00
	Punch bowl base	30.00
	Punch cup, 5 oz.	2.00
	Saucer, round	2.00
	Sherbet, ftd.	5.00
	Sherbet, stemmed, 6½ oz.	5.00
	*Stem, 3½ oz., cocktail	12.00
	*Stem, 4 oz., juice	14.00
	Stem, 4½ oz., cocktail	14.00
	Stem, 5½ oz., juice	12.50
	Stem, 6 oz., sherbet	8.00
	*Stem, 6 oz., sherbet	10.00
	*Stem, 9 oz., goblet	15.00
	Stem, 9½ oz., goblet	13.00
	Sugar, flat	10.00
9 ▸	Sugar, ftd.	6.00
	Sugar lid	10.00
12 ▸	Tray, 9", relish	15.00
	Tumbler, 2½ oz., ftd., wine	8.00
	Tumbler, 3½ oz., cocktail	9.00
3 ▸	Tumbler, 5 oz., juice, ftd. or flat	3.00
1 ▸	Tumbler, 9 oz., water (several styles)	3.50
	Tumbler, 10 oz., 5", water, ftd.	6.00
	Tumbler, 12 oz., 6" ftd., tea	11.00
2 ▸	Tumbler, 13 oz., iced tea	9.00
16 ▸	Vase, 4", ivy, ball-shaped & others	5.00
20 ▸	Vase, 6", ivy, ball-shaped & others	7.00
6 ▸	Vase, 6⅜", two styles	5.00
18 ▸	Vase, 9", two styles	17.50
	Water bottle (two styles)	225.00

*Berwick or Inspiration

SANDWICH COLORS, ANCHOR HOCKING GLASS COMPANY, 1939 – 1964

Colors: Desert Gold, 1961 – 1964; Forest Green, 1956 – 1960s; pink, 1939 – 1940; Royal Ruby, 1938 – 1939; White/Ivory (opaque), 1957 – 1960s

Sandwich is one of Anchor Hocking's most widely distributed patterns. We had a report via e-mail of a Forest Green cookie with lid, so we asked for a photo. Unhappily, a confirming picture showed a green cookie jar with a crystal lid on it. According to the collector, it was purchased that way, years ago. Maybe it was, but, it was not the first wild goose chase we've encountered regarding a green Sandwich lid. Over 35 years ago I drove 165 miles to examine a lid that had been seen at a flea market near Lexington the previous weekend. When I finally found the dealer's shop, she explained she was looking for a lid and did not have one. The good news was that gas was cheaper then. We'd be willing to bet that most collectors and dealers have at least one similar story. In fact, people are beginning to prod us about writing a book on just our scouting "adventures."

Forest Green Sandwich prices have continued to slow even though items (except for the five little pieces that were packed in Crystal Wedding Oats) remain hard to find. Thousands of those five pieces of Forest Green Sandwich (4⁵⁄₁₆" bowl, custard cup, custard liner, and water and juice tumblers) are available today. You will sometimes see quantities of these five pieces stacked on a shelf display in a mall priced like gold. However, none of the really "golden" pieces of green Sandwich will be among them. Everyone had hot oats for breakfast; thus these pieces accumulated very fast. Prices for other Forest Green pieces have begun to wane as supply (once again) is exceeding demand.

Forest Green pitchers are in short supply. Everyone acquired the juice and water tumblers complimentary among their oats as explained above. Juice and water sets were offered for sale containing a pitcher and six tumblers, but the pitchers were not sold alone. Most everyone already had enough tumblers, so they did not buy sets just to obtain a pitcher. It was a marketing mistake. We understand that the majority of pitcher sets were returned to Anchor Hocking for credit.

Green Sandwich cups are seemingly more prevalent than saucers; as a result, the price of saucers has caught up to the price of cups.

We have priced Royal Ruby Sandwich here, but it is also found in *Collector's Encyclopedia of Depression Glass* in the Royal Ruby section of that book.

A very light pink pitcher was found a few years ago and is pictured on page 215. It is not a vibrant pink, but nothing in pink Sandwich is.

Some collectors are starting to look at amber Sandwich due to its lesser price. However, few are finding footed amber tumblers. That tumbler is cone shaped and like the one shown in crystal. Before you write or e-mail, please look at the crystal one pictured on page 217! If yours is tall and not cone shaped, you have the $4.00 – 5.00 Indiana one, not the rare Anchor Hocking one. The rest of the amber set can be completed with some work and luck. Sadly, there are no pitchers to find in amber.

Ivory punch sets were first promoted in 1957, both plain and trimmed in 22K gold. There is little price distinction today. That set edged in gold seems to be ignored because the gold has a tendency to wear away if ever used. In 1964 and 1965 Marathon gas stations in Ohio and Kentucky sold Ivory gold-trimmed punch bowl sets for $2.89 with an oil change and lubrication. Many of these are still being found in their original boxes.

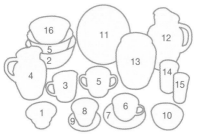

213

SANDWICH COLORS

		Desert Gold	Royal Ruby	Forest Green	Pink	Ivory White
10 ▸	Bowl, 4⁵⁄₁₆", smooth			3.00		
22 ▸	Bowl, 4⅞", smooth	3.00	16.00		4.00	
24 ▸	Bowl, 5¼", scalloped	6.00	20.00		7.00	
	Bowl, 5¼", smooth				7.00	
	Bowl, 6½", smooth	6.00				
16 ▸	Bowl, 6½", scalloped		27.50	65.00		
19 ▸	Bowl, 6¾", cereal	9.00				
20 ▸	Bowl, 7½", scalloped			100.00		
2 ▸	Bowl, 8¼", scalloped		40.00	125.00	27.50	
	Bowl, 9", salad	22.00				
13 ▸	Cookie jar and cover	30.00		*30.00		
3 ▸	Creamer			27.50		
6 ▸	Cup, tea or coffee	3.00		20.00		
8 ▸	Custard cup			3.00		
1 ▸	Custard cup, rolled edge			110.00		
9 ▸	Custard cup liner			2.50		
4 ▸	Pitcher, 6", juice			250.00	495.00	
12 ▸	Pitcher, ½ gal., ice lip			525.00		
18 ▸	Plate, 7", salad	3.00				
11 ▸	Plate, 9", dinner	6.00		95.00		
17 ▸	Plate, 12", sandwich	12.00				
	Punch bowl, 9¾"					12.00
	Punch bowl stand					12.00
	Punch cup					2.00
7 ▸	Saucer	1.00		15.00		
5 ▸	Sugar			*27.50		
15 ▸	Tumbler, 3⁹⁄₁₆", 5 oz., juice			3.00		
14 ▸	Tumbler, 9 oz., water			5.00		
	Tumbler, 9 oz., footed	195.00				

21 ▸ Experimental opalacscent

*no cover

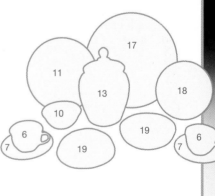

2

22

6

7

4

21

16

2

6

7

2

24

22

16

20

Children's plastic items.

SANDWICH CRYSTAL, ANCHOR HOCKING GLASS COMPANY, 1939 – 1964; 1977

Color: crystal

Anchor Hocking's crystal Sandwich is popular with collectors due to its economical price and availability. We have separated the crystal from the colors to make things easier for our writing and price listings.

Six sizes of tumblers are available in crystal. The nine ounce footed tumbler has never been easy to obtain, and the 3⅜" three-ounce (narrow) juice is missing from most collections. These juice tumblers were regularly found in the New England area. A dealer from Massachusetts tells me they have now disappeared in his area, too. If you noticed the six tumblers, you may not know about the other two sizes found a few years ago unless you have read our *Anchor Hocking Fire-King and More* book where we picture them. There is a 12 ounce cone shaped, footed ice tea which is shaped like the smaller nine ounce water and a 15 ounce footed blown ice tea similar to those found in Mayfair. Just when you think your collection is complete, additional items turn up.

Experimental

The rarely encountered, scalloped top, 6¾" cereal bowl has steadied into a price range of $100.00. Not every collector wants these, which is good, since they are so scarce. Apparently, these scalloped edge pieces were a special order or a trial issue. It is interesting that heretofore unknown pieces continue to appear. Who knows what else will surface as more and more people become aware of the collecting world through the Internet?

We were accurately enlightened by an avid collector that the 9" salad bowl and the punch bowl are not the same bowls as has previously been accepted. The true salad bowl will fit inside the punch bowl and the reason that there is a shortage of punch bowl bases is that there are too many salad bowls masquerading as punch bowls. The salad bowl was listed at 9" in the catalogs and the punch bowl 9¾"; so, if your punch bowl measures only 9" in diameter, you have a salad masquerading as a punch bowl.

Crystal pieces that used to be infrequently found were the regular cereal, 5" crimped dessert bowl, and perfect 12" plates. All those pieces are now being marketed in quantities unknown before due to Internet exposure. The crimped dessert cataloged by Anchor Hocking as 5" only measures 4⅞". Both this dessert and the crimped sherbets are listed only in the 1956 catalog as occasional Sandwich pieces. "Crimped" is Hocking's word to describe these pieces.

Prices are slowly declining for most pieces in this popular Hocking pattern. Amazingly, Sandwich may be the most wanted crystal pattern in this book with the exception of Iris.

Remember that Anchor Hocking reintroduced a crystal cookie jar in the late 1970s that was larger than the old. For a comparison of these cookie jars, see measurements below. The more recent one now sells in the $15.00 range.

Cups, saucers, and 8" plates were giveaways for buying $3.00 (about ten gallons) of gas at Marathon stations in the mid-1960s. The promotion took a minimum of four weeks to obtain cups, saucers, and plates. You could have gotten the crystal punch bowl set for only $2.89 with an oil change and lube. Ah, the good old days. Today, instead of giving you something for buying their product, we are slaves to whatever price they demand. Resourceful minds need to find us tolerable substitutes.

#	Item	Price
29 ▶	Bowl, 4⁵⁄₁₆", smooth	3.00
26 ▶	Bowl, 4⅞", 5", crimped dessert	14.00
	Bowl, 4⅞", smooth	4.00
14 ▶	Bowl, 4⅞", scalloped	5.00
25 ▶	Bowl, 5¼", scalloped	4.00
	Bowl, 6½", smooth	6.00
17 ▶	Bowl, 6½", scalloped, deep	7.00
9 ▶	Bowl, 6¾", cereal	28.00
10 ▶	Bowl, 6¾", cereal, scalloped	120.00
	Bowl, 7", salad	5.00
15 ▶	Bowl, 7⅝", scalloped	8.00
16 ▶	Bowl, 8¼", scalloped	10.00
30 ▶	Bowl, 8⅝", oval	6.00
	Bowl, 9", salad	18.00
31 ▶	Butter dish, low	35.00
	Butter dish bottom	20.00

#	Item	Price
	Butter dish top	15.00
32 ▶	Cookie jar and cover	30.00
34 ▶	Creamer	5.00
18 ▶	Cup, tea or coffee	1.50
12 ▶	Custard cup	3.50
21 ▶	Custard cup, crimped, 5 oz.	10.00
13 ▶	Custard cup liner	15.00
6 ▶	Pitcher, 6", juice	40.00
33 ▶	Pitcher, ½ gal., ice lip	55.00
24 ▶	Plate, 7", dessert	8.00
	Plate, 8"	6.00
20 ▶	Plate, 9", dinner	12.00
27 ▶	Plate, 9", indent for punch cup	4.00
22 ▶	Plate, 12", sandwich	26.00
7 ▶	Punch bowl, 9¾"	18.00
8 ▶	Punch bowl stand	25.00

#	Item	Price
28 ▶	Punch cup	1.50
19 ▶	Saucer	1.00
23 ▶	Sherbet, footed	6.00
35 ▶	Sugar	6.00
36 ▶	Sugar cover	14.00
5 ▶	Tumbler, 3⅜", 3 oz., juice	15.00
3 ▶	Tumbler, 3⁹⁄₁₆", 5 oz., juice	4.00
4 ▶	Tumbler, 9 oz., water	6.00
1 ▶	Tumbler, 9 oz., footed	15.00
2 ▶	Tumbler, 12 oz., ftd.	250.00
11 ▶	Vase, held candle	3.00

COOKIE JARS	NEW	OLD
Height	10¼"	9¾"
Opening width	5½"	4⅞"
Circumference/largest part	22"	19"

1400/5
SERVING BOWL SET

1400/28   LUNCHEON SET

1400/18
SALAD BOWL AND PLATE SET

1400/20   TABLE SET

1400/14   SNACK SET

1400/8
DESSERT DISH SET

1400/26
PUNCH SET

1400/23
FOOTED TUMBLER SERVICE

1400/11
ICE LIP PITCHER

1400/27   LUNCHEON SET

SANDWICH, INDIANA GLASS COMPANY, 1920s – 1980s

Colors: crystal, late 1920s – 1980s; teal blue, 1950s – 1980s; milk white, mid 1950s; amber, late 1920s – 1980s; red, 1933/1970s; Smokey Blue, 1976 – 1977; Bi-Centennial Blue (vivid); Chantilly Green (light); Peach; Spruce Green (dark)

Indiana's Sandwich pattern is an appealing design with a historical basis and was re-made in various colors for Tiara Home Products from the 70s through the 90s. Many dealers and collectors have viewed it with distrust for investment purposes due to the company's penchant for reissuing their glass patterns in older glass colors. This procedure has never allowed the older glassware to gain the status that other companies' older glassware has; but now that they have closed their doors, this could change down the road.

Pink and green Sandwich is priced in the *Collector's Encyclopedia of Depression Glass* since they were made in the 1930s; and although light green (called Chantilly) has been made again, it is a different shade than the original. You can see examples of both greens in the Depression book. The older green Indiana Sandwich will glow vividly under an ultraviolet (black) light while the newer will not. We've had people tell us their green Chantilly glows, but there is a major difference in glowing and reflecting. Please understand that this is not a general test for the age of glass. It is a test for this particular old green Sandwich vs. the new Tiara Chantilly pattern. There is glass made yesterday which will fluoresce under black light especially yellow or Vaseline using the proper chemical formula; and that black light trick is a favorite of unprincipled dealers who portray their new glass as old. Indiana also made a lighter pink in recent years.

Chantilly green was made in dinnerware sets whereas the original green Sandwich was made only in occasional pieces. No dinner plates, cups, saucers, creamers, sugars, or water goblets were made in green until the 1980s. We actually don't care who told you how old these dinnerware items are; they were not made until the early 1980s. We say that because we received a letter from a lady who had taken her green Chantilly pieces to a popular television antiques show, and they explained to her they were from the 1930s; everybody, even the so-called experts make some mistakes.

Tiara Exclusives marketed Sandwich production by Indiana with an offering of red and amber in 1970, Smokey Blue in 1976, and crystal in 1978. Amber, Chantilly green, and crystal were made into the late 1980s.

At a large glassware auction in Cincinnati last fall, a huge Tiara Sandwich collection of over 1,000 amber pieces averaged around $2.00 each. Many items sold for 25¢ and 50¢ and some lots brought even less. The highest price we heard was $25.00 for a canister set and that was a dealer hoping to sell it for more. We presume that a lot more time will have to pass for this to attain collectibility status.

Basically, the price list incorporates the original Sandwich line from the 1920s and the original Tiara listings from the early 1970s. You can probably stock up on Tiara Sandwich pieces at a reasonable price.

The mould for the old wine broke and a new one was designed. Older wines are 2¾" tall and hold three ounces. The newer wines are shown in Tiara catalogs, but no measurements or capacities are given. Teal blue and milk glass are colors distributed in the 1950s; but a teal Sandwich butter dish remade for Tiara as an exclusive hostess gift absolutely destroyed the $200.00 price tag on the 1950s butter dish. This new Tiara one originally sold for approximately $15.00. "New" Sandwich has been heralded to prospective customers as glass that's going to be valuable based on its past; but the company eroded the collectibility of their older glassware by selling new glass copies in like colors. Of all the colors in the spectrum, you'd think they could have found some different shades or dated the later wares. Amber and crystal prices are shown, but you must realize that most of the crystal and all the amber have been made since 1970. Prices reflect the small amounts of these colors that we see at flea markets and malls.

		Amber Crystal	Teal Blue	Red
10 ▸	Ashtrays (club, spade, heart, diamond shapes, ea.)	2.50		
	Basket, 10" high	30.00		
	Bowl, 4¼", berry	2.00		
	Bowl, 6"	2.00		
13 ▸	Bowl, 6", hexagonal	2.00	12.00	
16 ▸	Bowl, 8½"	9.00		
15 ▸	Bowl, 9", console, ftd.	14.00		
	Bowl, 11½", console	15.00		
	Butter dish and cover, domed	16.00	*100.00	
	Butter dish bottom	6.00	15.00	
	Butter dish top	10.00	85.00	
12 ▸	Candlesticks, 3½", pr.	10.00		
	Candlesticks, 7", pr.	20.00		
1 ▸	Creamer	8.00		45.00
8 ▸	Celery, 10½"	12.00		
11 ▸	Creamer and sugar on diamond-shaped tray	16.00	32.00	
	Cruet, 6½ oz., and stopper	20.00	135.00	
6 ▸	Cup	2.00	8.00	30.00
	**Decanter and stopper	22.50		85.00
2 ▸	Goblet, 9 oz.	9.00		45.00

		Amber Crystal	Teal Blue	Red
9 ▸	Mayonnaise, ftd.	13.00		
	Pitcher, 68 oz.	25.00		175.00
	Plate, 6", sherbet	3.00	7.00	
	Plate, 7", bread and butter	4.00		
	Plate, 8", oval, indent for sherbet		6.00	12.00
14 ▸	Plate, 8⅜", luncheon	5.00		20.00
3 ▸	Plate, 10½", dinner	6.00		
	Plate, 13", sandwich	10.00	25.00	35.00
	Puff box	15.00		
	Salt and pepper, pr.	12.00		
	Sandwich server, center handle	18.00		47.50
5 ▸	Saucer	.50	6.00	7.00
4 ▸	Sherbet, 3¼"	3.00	12.00	
7 ▸	Sugar, large	8.00		45.00
	Sugar lid for large size	13.00		
	Tumbler, 3 oz., footed cocktail	7.50		
	Tumbler, 8 oz., footed water	9.00		
	Tumbler, 12 oz., footed tea	10.00		
	Wine, 2¾", 3 oz.	4.00		
	Wine, 3", 4 oz.	4.00		12.50

*Beware, 1980s vintage sells for $25.00
**Stopper half of value

SEASCAPE, #2685 LINE, FOSTORIA GLASS COMPANY, 1954 – 1958

Colors: Opalescent blue and pink

Fostoria's Seascape was added to this book because it was being sought by new collectors and we were tired of seeing this 1950s pattern mistakenly passed off as Duncan and Miller glassware. Seascape was a short-lived pattern and collectors are often attracted to opalescent wares. Both of these reasons make Seascape a pattern to watch.

We have never seen a more conflicting range of prices on any other pattern. Few pieces are advertised for sale; much is priced out of this world as a Duncan and Miller product. The more reasonably priced pieces of Seascape have been bought from dealers who knew what it was, who manufactured it, and when.

Internet auctions show Seascape selling well where properly listed, but in most cases you have to search under 10 or 12 other categories to find a piece. Seascape was produced on Fostoria's Contour (#2666) shapes, but the company gave them different line numbers when they made opalescent. People who collect pink Seascape often purchase pink Contour stemware to use with their sets. These are not opalescent, just pink. You can blend these with pink Seascape, but only crystal Contour ones are possible with the opalescent blue.

By the way, Fostoria's 12" footed salver is usually considered a cake stand in the public's view. You might even find one with an ivy-like design which came from a petite line of about 20 items that Fostoria called Vintage and made in 1955. So, this vine is obviously some designer's idea of a grape leaf. Half the items in #347 Etch Vintage were taken from the Seascape line and used to fetch prices from 20% to 25% higher than the actual Seascape pieces; prices right now for Vintage items seem to depend more on size of the item than rarity. Since these were only made for a year, they should be pretty scarce; still, we see more collectors gathering the non-grape leaf items.

Cathy likes this pattern and has tenaciously hunted it for our photography sessions. Once we have enough pieces for a suitable picture, I have a tendency to get conservative in buying, whereas she believes if we don't have it, we should. You have more pieces to view due to her persistence.

		Item	Price			Item	Price
		Bowl, 4½", pansy	22.00	2 ▶		Preserve, 6½", handled	35.00
3 ▶		Bowl, 8", shallow	40.00	6 ▶		Relish, 9" x 6", two-part	24.00
9 ▶		Bowl, 8¾", ftd.	55.00	4 ▶		Relish, 11¾" x 8½", three-part	40.00
		Bowl, 8¾", square, scalloped	50.00	7 ▶		Salver, 12", ftd.	90.00
		Bowl, 10", salad	50.00			Stem, contour, water	18.00
		Bowl, 11½", shallow	50.00			Stem, contour, sherbet	16.00
8 ▶		Candleholder, 2" high, 4½" diameter	20.00			Stem, contour, wine	20.00
		Creamer, 3⅜"	18.00			Sugar, 2⅝"	18.00
		Creamer, individual	18.00			Sugar, individual	18.00
		Mayonnaise, 3-pc. set	35.00	5 ▶		Tray, 7½", oval, ftd.	40.00
1 ▶		Mint tray, 7½", ftd.	22.00			Tray, individual sug/cr	18.00
		Plate, 14", buffet	75.00				

SHELL PINK MILK GLASS, JEANNETTE GLASS CO., 1957 – 1959

Color: opaque pink

We have condensed Shell Pink from five to three pages. We will continue to show a variety of items, but not everything made. We needed the space for newer patterns and expansion of some others that we have been short changing. More pieces were shown in previous editions should you wish to check them.

Prices for Shell Pink have dropped slightly even though there are some new collectors buying it. All pieces that were seriously priced still are, just not as dearly as they were. The lazy Susan and heavy-bottomed National vase are continuing to outshine all commonly found pieces in price. This fashionable Jeannette pink milk color was made for only a brief time in the late 1950s. It included pieces from several regular Jeannette lines (Anniversary, Baltimore Pear, Floragold, Harp, Holiday, National, and Windsor). Like Anchor Hocking's Royal Ruby and Forest Green colors, pattern was not the important idea, it was the color. Shell Pink was promoted as "a delicate coloring that blends perfectly with all kinds of flowers." That remains as true today as it was then. Shell pink was used extensively by the floral industry. Other pieces were made for "Napco Ceramics, Cleveland, Ohio." The National pattern candy bottom (without lid) was promoted as a vase.

A couple of rarely seen Shell Pink pieces are pictured on page 224, namely, the ashtray and the bird candle holder which was sold with the three-footed pheasant bowl. A Shell Pink Anniversary cake plate was unearthed years ago. Anniversary pin-up vases are being found, though not by us to picture. You can see a duck powder jar in *Very Rare Glassware of the Depression Years, Sixth Series*. We bought a Shell Pink "Genie" bottle that came from the same factory worker's relative who owned the rare duck powder jars. There was no stopper. We have photographed a collector's large Shell Pink plate with the same chevron striped pattern as the punch bowl. It may have been designed as a liner for the punch bowl, but the pattern was underneath where it didn't show. Speaking of the punch bowl reminds me that the original ladle was pink plastic and not colored crystal.

Watch for the Butterfly cigarette box and ashtrays. They have become very popular with collectors, and the price has significantly reduced from those of 10 years ago; so if you wish to own one, now is the time. Be sure to check those butterfly wings. Pieces of those wings have a tendency to "fly off." The price listed is for mint condition butterfly boxes. Out of the $17,000 worth of glassware destroyed when my van was totaled, there were only four pieces damaged but not broken into jigsaw puzzle pieces. One of those was the butterfly cigarette box which had a broken chunk out of the bottom, but amazingly, the lid was intact. The oval, four-footed Lombardi bowls turn up frequently, but those with an embossed design on the inside do not. The difference in price used to be greater; but some collectors feel one oval bowl is enough. The honey jar is easy to spot with its beehive shape, but it has begun to disappear from the market as honey items, per se, are collectible now.

That Harp tray is hard to find; but greater demand for the Harp cake stand, today, almost makes these comparable in price. The five-part, two-handled oval tray, is beginning to catch up with demand. For a while, it was on every collector's want list.

SHELL PINK MILK GLASS

23 ▸	Ashtray, advertising, shell pink	325.00
	Ashtray, butterfly shape	15.00
	Base, for lazy Susan, w/ball bearings	125.00
11 ▸	Bowl, 6½", wedding, w/cover	15.00
	Bowl, 8", Pheasant, ftd.	25.00
10 ▸	Bowl, 8", wedding, w/cover	20.00
13 ▸	Bowl, 9", ftd., fruit stand, Floragold	28.00
	Bowl, 10", Florentine, ftd.	22.00
5 ▸	Bowl, 10½", ftd., Holiday	35.00
	Bowl, 10⅞", 4-ftd., Lombardi, designed center	30.00
1 ▸	Bowl, 10⅞", 4-ftd., Lombardi, plain center	25.00
9 ▸	Bowl, 17½", Gondola fruit	28.00
	Cake plate, Anniversary	295.00
21 ▸	Cake stand, 10", Harp	33.00
	Candleholder, 2-lite, pr.	35.00
20 ▸	Candleholder, Eagle, 3-ftd., pr.	38.00
24 ▸	Candleholder, w/pheasant on side, pr.	350.00
	Candy dish w/cover, 6½" high, square	22.00
2 ▸	Candy dish, 4-ftd., 5¼", Floragold	15.00
12 ▸	Candy jar, 5½", 4-ftd., w/cover, grapes	15.00
	Celery and relish, 12½", 3-part	38.00
	Cigarette box, butterfly finial	160.00
22 ▸	Compote, 6", Windsor	15.00
	Cookie jar w/cover, 6½" high	175.00
	Creamer, Baltimore Pear design	12.00
	Honey jar, beehive shape, notched cover	22.00
	Napco #2249, crosshatch design pot	12.00
	Napco, #2250, ftd. bowl w/berries	12.00
14 ▸	Napco, #2255, ftd. bowl w/sawtooth top	20.00
6 ▸	Napco, #2256, square comport	8.00
	National, candy bottom	8.00
8 ▸	Pitcher, 24 oz., ftd., Thumbprint	30.00

23

24

	Powder jar, 4¾", w/cover	30.00
17 ▸	Punch base, 3½", tall	25.00
18 ▸	Punch bowl, 7½ qt.	110.00
16 ▸	Punch cup, 5 oz. (also fits snack tray)	3.00
19 ▸	Punch ladle, pink plastic	15.00
	Punch set, 15-pc. (bowl, base, 12 cups, ladle)	185.00
	Relish, 12", 4-part, octagonal, Vineyard design	28.00
	Stem, 5 oz., sherbet, Thumbprint	7.00
	Stem, 8 oz., water goblet, Thumbprint	11.00
	Sugar cover	18.00
	Sugar, ftd., Baltimore Pear design	12.00
	Tray, 7¾" x 10", snack w/cup indent	8.00
	Tray, 12½" x 9¾", 2 hndl., Harp	40.00
	Tray, 13½", lazy Susan, 5-part	50.00
3 ▸	Tray, 15¾", 5-part, 2 hndl.	45.00
	Tray, 16½", 6-part, Venetian	22.00
	Tray, lazy Susan complete (w/4 ▸ base)	175.00
7 ▸	Tumbler, 5 oz., juice, ftd., Thumbprint	8.00
15 ▸	Vase, 5", cornucopia	12.00
	Vase, 7"	25.00
	Vase, 9", heavy bottom, National	150.00
	Vase, wall pin-up, Anniversary	335.00

Experimental item.

224

SHIRLEY, FOSTORIA GLASS COMPANY, 1939 – 1957

Color: crystal

Shirley was etched on several major Fostoria mould blanks. All items listed as #2496 refer to the Baroque line and #2545 refer to what is known as "flame." Stems are found on line #6017 which is Sceptre. This is a wide ranging pattern that does not have enough collectors to push the prices upwards. It sells well for us when we find occasional pieces. Stems are around, but not as prevalent as stems in other elegant patterns.

This floral design is often referred to as a poppy which was a popular floral design. Tiffin used Poppies for Flanders and another pattern called Poppy. Cambridge's Gloria is based on a poppy, but Fostoria did poppies proud with etchings of Rogene and Legion besides Shirley.

	Item	Price			Item	Price
	Bonbon, #2496	33.00		4 ▸	Saucer, #2496	5.00
	Bowl, #2496, 5", fruit	22.50			Shaker, #2496, pr.	75.00
	Bowl, #2496, 9½", oval	55.00			Stem, #6017, 3⅜", ¾ oz., cordial	50.00
	Bowl, #2496, 10½", 2-hdld.	60.00			Stem, #6017, 4½", 6 oz., sherbet	18.00
	Bowl, #2496, 12", flared	60.00			Stem, #6017, 4⅞", 3½ oz., cocktail	20.00
	Bowl, #2496, cream soup	35.00			Stem, #6017, 5½", 3 oz., wine	22.50
1 ▸	Bowl, #2496, 3-ftd. nut	35.00			Stem, #6017, 5½", 6 oz., champagne	20.00
	Bowl, #2545, 12½", oval	65.00			Stem, #6017, 5⅞", 4 oz., claret	25.00
	Bowl, #766, finger	25.00		7 ▸	Stem, #6017, 7⅜", 9 oz., water goblet	28.00
	Candelabrum, #2545, 2-lite w/prisms	100.00			Sugar, #2496, ftd.	22.50
	Candlestick, #2496, 4"	30.00			Sugar, #2496, individual	22.50
	Candlestick, #2496, duo	37.50			Sweetmeat, #2496, 6", square	25.00
	Candlestick, #2545, 4½"	32.50			Tray, #2496, individual sugar/cream	25.00
	Candlestick, #2545, duo	72.50			Tumbler, #6017, 3⅝", 4 oz., oyster cocktail	22.50
	Candy w/lid, #2496	95.00			Tumbler, #6017, 4¾", 5 oz., ftd. juice	20.00
	Celery, #2496, 11"	30.00			Tumbler, #6017, 5½", 9 oz., ftd. water	18.00
	Cheese comport, #2496, 4¾"	35.00			Tumbler, #6017, 6", 12 oz., ftd. ice tea	25.00
9 ▸	Comport, #2496, 5½"	27.50			Vase, #2545, 10"	125.00
8 ▸	Creamer, #2496, ftd.	22.50				
	Creamer, #2496, individual	22.50				
4 ▸	Cup, #2496	20.00				
2 ▸	Ice bucket, #2496, w/metal handle	75.00				
	Mayonnaise, #2496, 6½", 2-part	25.00				
	Mayonnaise or sauce dish, #2496, 6½"	35.00				
	Nappy, #2496, flared	20.00				
	Nappy, #2496, round	20.00				
	Nappy, #2496, square	22.50				
	Nappy, #2496, tri-cornered	20.00				
	Pickle, #2496, 8¼"	25.00				
	Pitcher, #6011, ftd.	225.00				
	Plate, #2337, 6"	8.00				
	Plate, #2337, 7"	9.00				
6 ▸	Plate, #2337, 8¼", luncheon	12.50				
	Plate, #2496, 6¼, cream soup liner	8.00				
	Plate, #2496, 9½", dinner	30.00				
	Plate, #2496, 10", cake plate, 2-hdld.	35.00				
5 ▸	Plate, #2496, 10", cracker	35.00				
	Plate, #2496, 14", torte	65.00				
	Platter, #2496, 12"	60.00				
	Relish, #2496, 6", 2-part, square	30.00				
3 ▸	Relish, #2496, 10", 3-part	35.00				

SILVER CREST, FENTON ART GLASS COMPANY, 1943 – present

Color: white with crystal edge

Silver Crest is another Fenton pattern that we borrow for photography. Good friends have a large collection which they bring to the studio in Paducah. We do not buy or sell a lot of Fenton; as a result, we are exceedingly grateful for the help from Fenton collectors and dealers as well as readers who have assisted with listings of Fenton patterns in this book. We appreciate their time and guidance in arriving at price listings for Emerald and Silver Crest.

Fenton's Silver Crest started production in the 1940s and is still in sporadic production today. Each time Fenton has discontinued it, demand and/or financial matters persuade them into re-creating some pieces. There are a number of ways to date your pieces. Before 1958, the white was called opal and had opalescence to it when held to the light. In 1958, a formula change to milk glass made the glass look very white without "fire" in the white. All pieces reintroduced after 1973 will be signed Fenton. Fenton began marking carnival pieces in 1971, and in 1973 they decided to mark all pieces. If you acquire items that have white edging encircling crystal, this is called Crystal Crest and dates from 1942. Many of the very late silver-crested items have violets, roses, or apple blossoms hand painted on the wares and many are signed by the artist painting them. There was also an embossed scrolled design added to pieces in 1968 called Spanish Lace Silver Crest. However, none of these latter decorations can be attained as actual dinnerware sets. Most of the later decorations are specialty items, especially vases.

The pitcher, punch bowl set, tumblers, and hurricane lamps are very hard to acquire, but enjoyable in spite of the price tag. There's a floor lamp shade, which directs the light upward to the ceiling. As with Fenton's Emerald Crest, you will encounter quite a few styles of tidbits using bowls and plates or both.

Some pieces of Silver Crest are assigned two different line numbers. Initially, this line was #36 and all pieces carried that classification. In July 1952, Fenton began issuing a ware number for individual pieces. That is why you see two distinct numbers for many of the items in the price listing.

See page 61 for prices of Emerald Crest. Aqua Crest has a blue edge around the white and prices for it fall between those of Silver Crest and Emerald Crest. Remember that demand and a plentiful supply for Silver Crest is making it one of Fenton's most recognized lines.

	Item	Price
	Basket, 5" hndl. (top hat), #1924	70.00
	Basket, 5", hndl., #680	40.00
	Basket, 6½", hndl., #7336	40.00
	Basket, 7", #7237	40.00
	Basket, 12", #7234	100.00
	Basket, 13", #7233	150.00
	Basket, hndl., #7339	65.00
1 ▸	Basket, hndl., s-divided, #7339	75.00
19 ▸	Bonbon, 5½", #7225	10.00
	Bonbon, 8", #7428	14.00
	Bonbon, 5½", #36	12.00
	Bowl, 5", finger or deep dessert, #680	22.50
	Bowl, 5½", soup, #680	30.00

	Item	Price
	Bowl, 7", #7227	20.00
	Bowl, 8½", #7338	32.50
	Bowl, 8½", flared, #680	32.50
	Bowl, 9½", #682	40.00
32 ▸	Bowl, 10", #7224	50.00
	Bowl, 10", salad, #680	50.00
	Bowl, 11", #5823	55.00
	Bowl, 13", #7223	75.00
	Bowl, 14", #7323	85.00
	Bowl, banana, high ft., w/upturned sides, #7324	60.00
	Bowl, banana, low ftd., #5824	40.00
	Bowl, deep dessert, #7221	32.50
15 ▸	Bowl, dessert, shallow, #680	22.50

	Bowl, finger or dessert, #202	20.00
	Bowl, ftd. (like large, tall comport), #7427	75.00
	Bowl, ftd., tall, square, #7330	75.00
	Bowl, low dessert, #7222	22.50
	Bowl, shallow, #7316	46.00
	Cake plate, 13" high, ftd., #7213	45.00
	Cake plate, low ftd., #5813	40.00
7 ▸	Candleholder, 6" tall w/crest on bottom, pr., #7474	65.00
	Candleholder, bulbous base, pr., #1523	60.00
	Candleholder, cornucopia, pr., #951	65.00
	Candleholder, cornucopia (same as #951), pr., #7274	60.00
	Candleholder, flat saucer base, pr., #680	55.00
8 ▸	Candleholder, low, ruffled, pr., #7271	55.00
31 ▸	Candleholder, ruffled comport style, pr., #7272	95.00
	Candy box, #7280	65.00
36 ▸	Candy box, ftd., tall stem, #7274	85.00
	Chip and dip (low bowl w/mayo in center), #7303	75.00
	Comport, ftd., #7228	22.50
	Comport, ftd., low, #7329	26.00
	Creamer, reeded hndl., #680	26.00
3 ▸	Creamer, reeded hndl. (same as #680), #7201	26.00
6 ▸	Creamer, ruffled top	55.00
	Creamer, straight side, #1924	32.50
	Creamer, threaded hndl., #680	23.00
13 ▸	Cup, reeded hndl., #680	28.00
9 ▸	Cup, threaded look hndl., #7209	22.50
26 ▸	Epergne set, 2-pc. (vase in ftd. bowl), #7202	80.00
	Epergne set, 3-pc., #7200	125.00
	Epergne, 2-pc. set, #7301	120.00
	Epergne, 4-pc., bowl w/3 horn epergnes, #7308	150.00
	Epergne, 5-pc., bowl w/4 horn epergnes, #7305	190.00
	Lamp, hurricane, #7398	125.00
24 ▸	Lamp, floor	150.00
28 ▸	Mayonnaise bowl, #7203	14.00
	Mayonnaise ladle, #7203	6.00
37 ▸	Mayonnaise liner, #7203	28.00
	Mayonnaise set, 3-pc., #7203	60.00
17 ▸	Nut, ftd., #7229	20.00
	Nut, ftd. (flattened sherbet), #680	20.00
14 ▸	Oil bottle, #680	85.00
34 ▸	Pitcher, 70 oz. jug, #7467	275.00
	Plate, 5½", #680	7.00
	Plate, 5½", finger bowl liner, #7218	7.00
	Plate, 6½", #680, #7219	7.50
11 ▸	Plate, 8½", #680, #7217	15.00
	Plate, 10", #680	40.00
12 ▸	Plate, 10½", #7210	55.00
	Plate, 11½", #7212	45.00
	Plate, 12", #680	47.50

	Plate, 12", #682	45.00
	Plate, 12½", #7211	40.00
	Plate, 16", torte, #7216	60.00
21 ▸	Punch bowl, #7306	375.00
22 ▸	Punch bowl base, #7306	110.00
23 ▸	Punch cup, #7306	16.00
	Punch ladle (clear), #7306	25.00
	Punch set, 15-pc., #7306	700.00
	Relish, divided, #7334	35.00
	Relish, heart, hndl., #7333	24.00
10 ▸	Saucer, #680, #7209	5.00
30 ▸	Shaker, pr., #7206	110.00
33 ▸	Shaker, pr. (bowling pin shape), #7305	175.00
	Shaker, pr., #7406	225.00
16 ▸	Sherbet, #680	15.00
	Sherbet, #7226	15.00
	Sugar, reeded hndl., #680	26.00
4 ▸	Sugar, reeded hndl. (same as #680), #7201	26.00
5 ▸	Sugar, ruffled top	55.00
	Sugar, sans hndls., #680	35.00
27 ▸	Tidbit, 2-tier (luncheon/dessert plates), #7296	50.00
25 ▸	Tidbit, 2-tier (luncheon/dinner plates), #7294	50.00
	Tidbit, 2-tier plates, #680	50.00
	Tidbit, 2-tier, ruffled bowl, #7394	75.00
	Tidbit, 3-tier (luncheon/dinner/dessert plates), #7295	65.00
	Tidbit, 3-tier plates, #680	50.00
	Tidbit, 3-tier, ruffled bowl, #7397	85.00
	Tray, sandwich, #7291	40.00
35 ▸	Tumbler, ftd., #7342	60.00
	Vase, 4½", #203	15.00
	Vase, 4½", #7254	15.00
	Vase, 4½", double crimped, #36, #7354	18.00
29 ▸	Vase, 4½", fan, #36	18.00
20 ▸	Vase, 5" (top hat), #1924	25.00
	Vase, 6", #7451	20.00
	Vase, 6", doubled crimped, #7156	19.00
	Vase, 6¼", double crimped, #36, #7356	18.00
	Vase, 6¼", fan, #36	20.00
	Vase, 7", #7455	30.00
	Vase, 8", #7453	27.00
	Vase, 8", bulbous base, #186	35.00
	Vase, 8", doubled crimped, #7258	25.00
	Vase, 8", wheat, #5859	40.00
18 ▸	Vase, 8½", #7338	75.00
2 ▸	Vase, 8½", #7458	80.00
	Vase, 9", #7454	50.00
	Vase, 9", #7459	50.00
	Vase, 10", #7450	115.00
	Vase, 12" (fan topped), #7262	135.00

SILVER CREST

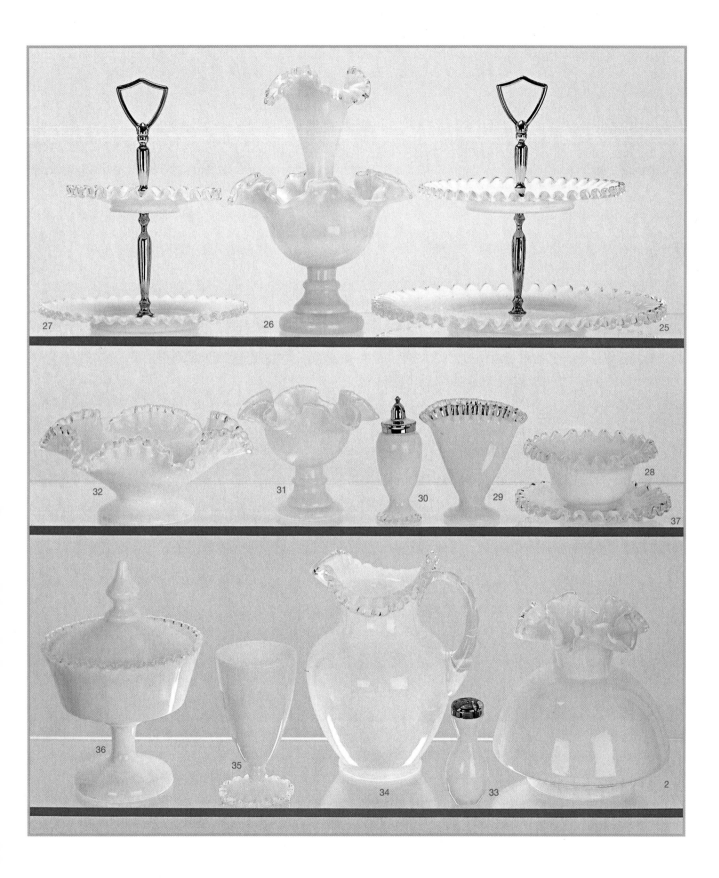

SQUARE, NO. 3797, CAMBRIDGE GLASS COMPANY, 1949 – mid 1950s

Colors: crystal, some red and black

Cambridge Square was initially shown in the 1949 Cambridge catalog as "patent pending." Several of the unused Square pieces photographed here have "patent pending" stickers as well as Cambridge labels. This is one of the few Cambridge patterns that was launched within the time restrictions of this book.

The punch bowl set appears to be one of the more difficult pieces to find in crystal. We don't know if it didn't sell well or Cambridge avoided making large pieces of glassware since they were going into bankruptcy, or both. The icers with inserts are missing from many collections. These were used for shrimp and fruit with ice below, cooling whatever was in the insert.

Square is reasonably priced for a Cambridge pattern; but there are not as many seeking Square as there are other Cambridge wares such as Rose Point or Gloria. Square is heavy and fairly plain which does not excite many collectors. It was made during the financially troubled last years of Cambridge which may mean items are limited even more than we actually know. It may take a few years and more collectors buying it to resolve that. A steady stream of Internet auctions for Square are occurring, but only a limited number of different items are being offered.

A little Square was made in Carmen and Ebony; however, Ruby (Imperial's name) pieces were also made from Cambridge's Square moulds at Imperial in the late 1960s. We're told Carmen pieces by Cambridge are rarely seen; Ruby can be found with some searching. We've also been told that the "old timers" can tell the difference; personally, we don't know how.

We have sold a few pieces over the years, but they do not move very fast unless priced inexpensively. Collectors seemed to love the pieces with "patent pending" or Cambridge labels best; at least they left our booth fairly fast.

		Crystal			Crystal
30 ▸	Ashtray, 3½", #3797/151	6.00		Bowl, 10", shallow, #3797/81	20.00
23 ▸	Ashtray, 6½", #3797/150	9.00		Bowl, 11", salad, #3797/57	22.00
	Bonbon, 7", #3797/164	12.00		Bowl, 12", oval, #3797/65	22.00
24 ▸	Bonbon, 8", #3797/47	18.00		Bowl, 12", shallow, #3797/82	22.00
1 ▸	Bowl, 4½", dessert, #3797/16	8.00		Bowl, punch	60.00
2 ▸	Bowl, 6½", individual salad, #3797/27	10.00		Buffet set, 4-pc. (plate, div. bowl, 2 ladles), #3797/29	35.00
14 ▸	Bowl, 8", oval	15.00		Candleholder, 1¾", block, #3797/492, pr.	18.00
	Bowl, 9", salad, #3797/49	18.00	25 ▸	Candleholder, 2¾", block, #3797/493, pr.	20.00
	Bowl, 10", oval, #3797/48	20.00		Candleholder, 3¾", block, #3797/495, pr.	20.00

	Crystal			Crystal
16 ▸ Candleholder, cupped, #3797/67, pr.	20.00		Stem, #3798, 5 oz., juice	5.00
27 ▸ Candleholder, double, pr.	40.00		Stem, #3798, 12 oz., iced tea	8.00
Candy box and cover, #3797/165	22.00		Stem, #3798, cocktail	12.00
Celery, 11", #3797/103	20.00		Stem, #3798, cordial	15.00
Comport, 6", #3797/54	18.00	13 ▸	Stem, #3798, sherbet	7.00
Creamer, #3797/41	8.00		Stem, #3798, water goblet	8.00
Creamer, individual, #3797/40	8.00		Stem, #3798, wine	12.00
19 ▸ Cup, coffee, open handle, #3797/17	6.00	5 ▸	Sugar, #3797/41	8.00
29 ▸ Cup, tea, open handle, #3797/15	6.00	4 ▸	Sugar, individual, #3797/40	8.00
6 ▸ Decanter, 32 oz., #3797/85	65.00	28 ▸	Tray, 8", oval, for individual sug/cr, #3797/37	10.00
Ice tub, 7½", #3797/34	30.00	31 ▸	Tumbler, #3797, 5 oz., juice	8.00
8 ▸ Icer, cocktail w/liner, #3797/18	35.00		Tumbler, #3797, 14 oz., iced tea	12.00
Lamp, hurricane, 2-pc., #3797/68	35.00		Tumbler, #3797, low cocktail	6.00
12 ▸ Mayonnaise set, 3-pc. (bowl, plate, ladle), #3797/129	22.00	17 ▸	Tumbler, #3797, low cordial	12.00
26 ▸ Oil bottle, 4½ oz., #3797/100	20.00		Tumbler, #3797, low sherbet	6.00
15 ▸ Plate, 6", bread and butter, #3797/20	4.00		Tumbler, #3797, low wine	10.00
9 ▸ Plate, 7", dessert or salad, #3797/23	6.00	7 ▸	*Tumbler, #3797, water goblet	10.00
22 ▸ Plate, 7", salad, #3797/27	8.00	21 ▸	Vase, 3½", heavy	18.00
Plate, 9½", dinner or luncheon, #3797/25	20.00		Vase, 5", belled, #3797/92	15.00
Plate, 9½", tidbit, #3797/24	14.00		Vase, 5½", belled, #3797/91	18.00
Plate, 11½", #3797/26	14.00	10 ▸	Vase, 6", #3797/90	18.00
Plate, 13½", #3797/28	15.00		Vase, 7½", ftd., #3797/77	18.00
20 ▸ Relish, 6½", 2-part, #3797/120	16.00		Vase, 7½", rose bowl, #3797/35	25.00
3 ▸ Relish, 8", 3-part, #3797/125	20.00		Vase, 8", ftd., #3797/80	18.00
Relish, 10", 3-part, #3797/126	20.00		Vase, 9½", ftd., #3797/78	25.00
Salt and pepper, pr., #3797/76	18.00		Vase, 9½", rose bowl, #3797/36	30.00
18 ▸ Saucer, coffee, #3797/17	3.00		Vase, 11", ftd., #3797/79	30.00
Saucer, tea, #3797/15	3.00			

*Crackled $25.00;   Ruffled top $30.00

STAR, FEDERAL GLASS COMPANY, late 1950s – early 1960s

Colors: yellow, crystal, and crystal w/gold trim

Star cups may have slipped past you unless you run across them in a set as we did. The Star cup is plain without a "star" on the bottom as on all Star pieces except the two largest blown pitchers. Due to this, collectors have inadvertently bypassed these when out shopping because they were looking for the telltale star. The cup and saucer were previously shown in yellow. We had to purchase a six-piece setting just to own one cup and saucer; but having finally found a cup made it worth it to us. As yet, we have not come upon a crystal cup or saucer.

Speaking of saucers, they are like the 6³⁄₁₆" plate, but with an indented cup ring. Without a catalog listing for this pattern (except for the pitchers and tumblers), we have had to discover pieces ourselves or depend upon collectors' assistance. So far, only crystal pitchers have been discovered, but there are three sizes of yellow tumblers being found. There is also an 11" round platter which seems to be elusive.

Although there were only a few pieces made, you can put together a small set at a bargain price; and it is eye-catching. Cathy remembers the pitchers being marketed with small colored soaps for the bath. Star pitchers were also sold as a set with Park Avenue tumblers.

You will find frosted, decorated juice pitchers with several designs and matching tumblers. Watch for a similar pitcher with painted flowers matching the red-trimmed Mountain Flowers Petalware. Both frosted and unfrosted pitchers are shown in the new *Collector's Encyclopedia of Depression Glass*. There are several Gay Fad decorations on the juice pitchers that are found with matching Hazel-Atlas tumblers. Several of these sets are shown in our *Hazel-Atlas Glass Identification and Value Guide*.

That whisky (Federal spelling) tumbler is found with labels showing jelly was packaged in them as were those of Park Avenue.

		Yellow	Crystal
2 ▸	Bowl, 4⅝", dessert	7.00	3.00
	Bowl, 5⅜", cereal		5.00
12 ▸	Bowl, 8⅜", vegetable	18.00	9.00
8 ▸	Butter dish, w/lid		90.00
1 ▸	Creamer	10.00	5.00
	Cup	10.00	5.00
4 ▸	Pitcher, 5¾", 36 oz., juice		8.00
5 ▸	Pitcher, 7", 60 oz.		12.00

		Yellow	Crystal
11 ▸	Pitcher, 9¼", 85 oz., ice lip		15.00
6 ▸	Plate, 6³⁄₁₆", salad	5.00	2.50
7 ▸	Plate, 9⅜", dinner	8.00	4.00
	Platter, 11", round	16.00	10.00
	Saucer (indented)	5.00	3.00
10 ▸	Sugar	6.00	5.00
	Sugar lid	14.00	7.00
9 ▸	Tumbler, 2¼", 1½ oz., whisky		3.00
	Tumbler, 3⅜", 4½ oz., juice	10.00	4.00
3 ▸	Tumbler, 3⅞", 9 oz., water	12.00	5.00
	Tumbler, 5⅛", 12 oz., iced tea	16.00	7.00

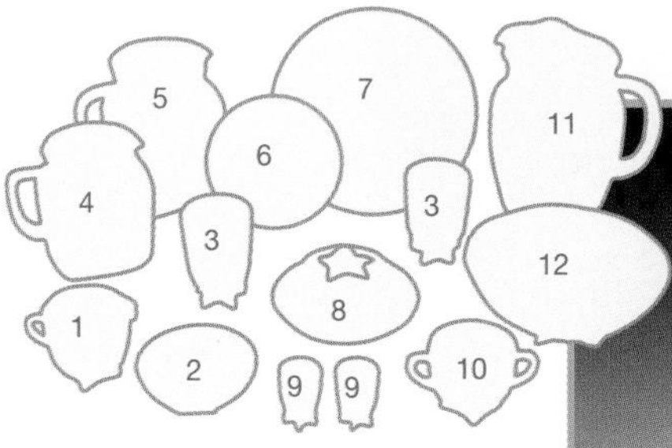

STARS AND STRIPES, ANCHOR HOCKING GLASS GLASS COMPANY, 1942

Color: crystal

Stars and Stripes is another Anchor Hocking pattern that is being erroneously labeled Fire-King. It was issued on its own merit as can be seen by the brochure below.

During World War II, Anchor Hocking modified their Queen Mary moulds and revised them to assemble this small, three-piece dessert set, which could double as a luncheon service. In their ad, pictured below, they deemed it an Early American Design. That eagle motif, emblem of power and authority, has been used by several companies on their wares in the past, the most notable probably being the Dorflinger set cut for Abraham Lincoln in the 1860s. This was Hocking's patriotic acknowledgment of the country's struggle to survive during W.W.II. They were offering people a quick way to wave the flag and sell their glass at the same time.

Collectors have been totally captivated by this small pattern. Prices for tumblers have finally peaked and prices for sherbets and plates have slipped a bit. Note that at least one plate has turned up with red backing over a golden eagle. It may be supposed that a glass and sherbet with like trim could be available. We wish there were more pieces; but three are adequate to do the job for which they were intended; and that may be symbolic as well.

2 ▸	Plate, 8"	12.50
3 ▸	Sherbet	10.00
1 ▸	Tumbler, 5", 10 oz.	45.00

233

SWANKY SWIGS, 1930s – 1950s

Now Internet auctions call any decorated small or large glass a Swanky Swig. It is a problem for which we see no solution forthcoming. Only the Kraft containers usually made by Hazel-Atlas should be so labeled.

Exhibited here are the Swigs sold from the late 1930s into the 1950s. Notice our new format to portray these. Our problem was that we could not come up with every type we pictured in previous books. Grannie Bear collected these and we did not seem to get all of hers we used previously for the book after she died. Smaller size glasses (3¼") and the larger (4½") appear to have been circulated in Canada. The limited distribution of these sizes in the States makes their prices increase more than those consistently found here. With the Internet, these sizes are easier to find than they once were. Earlier Swanky Swigs can be found in *Collector's Encyclopedia of Depression Glass* if you become enamored of collecting each design as many have. Some original lids are pictured which sell for $8.00 up, depending upon condition and the advertisement. Those with Kraft caramels, Miracle Whip, and TV show ads run $20.00 up in great condition.

Posy Jonquil: yellow, 3¼", $20.00 – 25.00; yellow, 4½", $20.00 – 25.00; yellow, 3½", $8.00 – 10.00.

Carnival: yellow and red, $4.00 – 5.00; green, $8.00 – 10.00; blue, $6.00 – 8.00.

Posy Violet: purple, 3½", $8.00 – 9.00; purple, 4½", $20.00 – 25.00; purple with label, 3½", $20.00 – 25.00; purple, 3¼", $20.00 – 25.00.

Posy Tulip: red, 3½", $8.00 – 9.00; red, 4½", $20.00 – 25.00; red, 3¼", $20.00 – 25.00.

Posy Cornflower, No. 1: light blue, 3½", $5.00 – 6.00; light blue, 4½", $15.00 – 20.00; light blue, 3¼", $15.00 – 20.00.

Cornflower No. 2: red, 3¼", $15.00 – 20.00; red, 3½", $2.50 – 3.00; yellow, 3¼", $15.00 – 20.00; yellow, 3½", $2.50 – 3.00.

Forget-me-not: red, 3¼", $15.00 – 20.00; red, 3½", $2.50 – 3.50; light blue with label, 3½", $20.00 – 25.00; light blue, 3½", $2.50 – 3.50; light blue, 3¼", $15.00 – 20.00.

Cornflower No. 2: dark blue, 3½", $2.50 – 3.50; dark blue, 3¼", $15.00 – 20.00; light blue, 3½", $15.00 – 20.00; light blue, 3¼", $2.50 – 3.00.

Forget-me-not: yellow, 3¼", $15.00 – 20.00; yellow, 3½", $2.50 – 3.50; yellow with label, 3½", $20.00 – 25.00; dark blue, 3½", $2.50 – 3.00; dark blue with label, 3½", $10.00 – 12.50; dark blue, 3¼", $15.00 – 20.00.

Daisy: red, white, and green, 3¾", with cheese or label, $20.00 – 25.00.

SWANKY SWIGS

Daisy: red, white, and green, 3¼", $15.00 – 20.00; red, white, and green, 3¾", $2.00 – 3.00; red, white, and green, 4½", $15.00 – 20.00; red and white, 3¾", $25.00 – 30.00; red and white, 3¼", $35.00 – 40.00.

Bustling Betsy: light blue, 3¼", $15.00 – 20.00; light blue, 3¾", $4.00 – 5.00; red, 3¾", $4.00 – 5.00; red, 3¼", $15.00 – 20.00.

Bustling Betsy: green, 3¾", $4.00 – 5.00; green, 3¼", $15.00 – 20.00.

Bustling Betsy: orange, 3¾", $4.00 – 5.00; yellow, 3¾", $4.00 – 5.00; brown, 3¾", $4.00 – 5.00.

Antique Pattern: coffee grinder and plate, green, 3¾", $4.00 – 5.00; lamp and kettle, blue, 3¾", $4.00 – 5.00; spinning wheel and willows, red, 3¾", $4.00 – 5.00.

Antique Pattern: churn and cradle, orange, 3¼", $15.00 – 20.00; churn and cradle, orange, 3¾", $4.00 – 5.00; clock and coal scuttle, brown, 3¾, $4.00 – 5.00; clock and coal scuttle, brown, 3¼", $15.00 – 20.00.

Antique Pattern: lamp and kettle, blue, 3¾", $4.00 – 5.00; coffee pot and trivet, black, 3¼", $15.00 – 20.00.

Kiddie Cup: duck and horse, black, 3¼", $20.00 – 25.00; duck and horse, black, 3¾", $4.00 – 5.00; duck and horse, black with label, 3¾, $20.00 – 25.00; duck and horse, black, 4½", $20.00 – 25.00; dog and rooster, orange, 3¾", $4.00 – 5.00; dog and rooster, orange, 3¼", $20.00 – 25.00.

Kiddie Cup: squirrel and deer, brown, 3¼", $20.00 – 25.00; squirrel and deer, brown, 3¾", $4.00 – 5.00; squirrel and deer, brown, 4½" $20.00 – 25.00; bear and pig, blue, 4½", $20.00 – 25.00; bear and pig with label, blue, 3¾", $20.00 – 25.00; bear and pig, blue, 3¼", $20.00 – 25.00.

Kiddie Cup with label: 3¾", $20.00 – 25.00.

Kiddie Cup: bird and elephant, red, 3¼", $20.00 – 25.00; bird and elephant, red, 3¾", $4.00 – 5.00; bird and elephant with label, red, 3¾" $20.00 – 25.00; cat and rabbit, green, 4½", $20.00 – 25.00; cat and rabbit, green, 3¾", $4.00 – 5.00.

TEARDROP, LINE NO. 1011, INDIANA GLASS COMPANY, 1950 – 1980s

Colors: crystal, crystal decorated, white and white decorated

Indiana's Teardrop is a familiar pattern due to the large quantity of pieces being noticed in the marketplace. Internet auctions rarely offer any crystal pieces other than the cake stand, but the white, sprayed, and carnival finishes abound. Those white comports seem to be everywhere. After we bought one to photograph, we decided that we would not buy another white item. However, when the banana stand was found, we had to relent and pay the price. As with all newly listed patterns, you may find additional pieces.

The decorated white creamer and sugar in the bottom row are well done. The translucent effect shows off the decoration. The opaque white is not as collected as the crystal or decorated crystal.

		*Crystal			*Crystal
16 ▸	Banana stand (white)	30.00	5 ▸	Creamer	6.00
7 ▸	Bowl, 9", 2-handled	18.00	4 ▸	Plate, 11", 2-handled	20.00
6 ▸	Bowl, 10", deep, ftd.	22.00	15 ▸	Plate, 15", punch liner	18.00
11 ▸	Bowl, 13", ftd.	22.00	14 ▸	Punch bowl	28.00
12 ▸	Bowl, 5"	8.00	13 ▸	Punch cup	2.00
9 ▸	Cake stand	22.00		Server, center handled	15.00
2 ▸	Candlestick	12.00	3 ▸	Sugar	6.00
10 ▸	Candy dish w/lid	30.00	8 ▸	Tray, for creamer/sugar	6.00
1 ▸	Comport	10.00			

*decorated add 50%

THISTLE, LA FLO GLASS COMPANY, c. 1960

Color: crystal

This Thistle cutting is almost identical to #1066 Cambridge Thistle. The mould shapes of items differ from those of Cambridge and the Cambridge wares had plain centers whereas these are cut with a starred center. You will note the pieces pictured are not close to any known Cambridge shapes. Cambridge Thistle pieces also had an ovoid shape on the stem cut with bars, which forms a kind of webbing on one part of their stem. To further confuse this issue, Cambridge also had a similar cutting to their Thistle called Silver Maple which had two round, fuzzy balls cut at the base of that three petal flower before the stem.

La Flo Glass Company hired former Cambridge Glass Company employees when Cambridge closed in 1957. This glass was cut with a very-like-Cambridge Thistle pattern from various companies' blanks. We have been able to find a few more La Flo cut items in the last few years, but this does not seem to be widely distributed. We're positive there are other pieces to be found to add to our listing. We'd appreciate being told what you locate.

9 ▶	Bowl, 6", crimped	20.00		11 ▶	Plate, 8", salad	6.00
16 ▶	Bowl, salad, deep, belled	30.00		12 ▶	Plate, 13", torte plate	25.00
8 ▶	Creamer	12.00		2 ▶	Stem, 4⅞", cocktail	15.00
6 ▶	Ice tub	75.00		15 ▶	Stem, 5¼", champagne	12.00
13 ▶	Pitcher, martini	35.00		1 ▶	Stem, 5⅜", wine	18.00
14 ▶	Pitcher, milk	30.00		17 ▶	Stem, 6½", water	18.00
				7 ▶	Sugar	12.00
				10 ▶	Tumbler, 2¼", shot	15.00
				3 ▶	Tumbler, 4½", juice, ftd.	10.00
				4 ▶	Tumbler, 5⅛", sham bottom, tea	12.00
				5 ▶	Tumbler, 6½", ftd., tea	14.00

THOUSAND LINE, "STARS & BARS," "RAINBOW STARS," ANCHOR HOCKING GLASS COMPANY, 1941 – 1960s

Colors: crystal and satinized green

Thousand Line is the line number listed for this pattern in Anchor Hocking's catalogs, but we have heard it called "Stars and Bars" as well as "Rainbow Stars." Both of these collector monikers have charm, but we will stick to the original designation for now. This minor Hocking line is beginning to be noticed by collectors and a few of those are starting collections. All Early American Prescut pieces which are sometimes confused with this pattern have line numbers in the 700s.

You may find some satinized pieces in Thousand Line, and many of these will be color decorated.

Collectors buy the Thousand Line large salad bowl and tray to use today for salads. A glass fork and spoon is regularly found with these. You can find these as reasonably priced as buying newly made glassware items. We were looking through in antique mall recently when the owner asked us to identify for a customer a piece of glass sitting in a booth. It was Thousand Line; so, we showed him the pattern in a copy of our book the shop owner had. He became really excited about that piece he'd found "just like his Mom had." Once again the nostalgia factor at work.

The luncheon plate may be the most elusive item to find in this pattern; bowls seem to be everywhere in the markets; and sugar and creamer sets are just as plentiful. We've now found two large bowls with a ground bottom which might indicate an early production prototype. We have been contacted by a couple of collectors who are wishing to see that bowl. We took the regular bowl and one with the ground bottom to photograph them together to show the different bottoms. However, the instructions were misunderstood and we have a picture of them side by side from the top.

		Crystal				Crystal
1 ▸	Bowl, 6", handled	8.00			Fork	7.50
	Bowl, 7", soup	10.00			Plate, 8", lunch	6.00
	Bowl, 7½" deep	10.00	4 ▸		Plate, 12", sandwich	10.00
2 ▸	Bowl, 8", vegetable	10.00	10 ▸		Relish, 7", three-part, round	8.00
	Bowl, 10½", salad, flat base, 7" ctr.	45.00	5 ▸		Relish, 10", two-handled, oval, 2-part	6.00
	Bowl, 10⅞", vegetable, rim base, 5½" ctr.	12.00	9 ▸		Relish, 12", six-part	15.00
6 ▸	Candle, 4"	4.00			Spoon	7.50
	Candy w/lid	15.00			Sugar, 2½"	4.00
7 ▸	Creamer, 2½"	3.00			Tray, 12½", sandwich	10.00
			3 ▸		Vase, bud	9.00
			8 ▸		Vase, 9", ftd.	15.00

TRADITION, #165, IMPERIAL GLASS COMPANY

Colors: crystal, Nut Brown, Heather, pink, green, Topaz, Bread Green, amber, Ruby, Mustard, Milk Glass, Aquamarine, Blue Mist

Imperial's Tradition is often confused with other patterns including Imperial's Old English and Kemple's Sandwich. Unfortunately, it is also sometimes labeled Cape Cod especially the 72 hole cake plate which is rare in Cape Cod, but not in Tradition. That is understandable to some extent as an early book on Cape Cod made that same mistake. Some collectors never update their books and may still be using that older book. We see Tradition cake plates priced as high as $200.00, but they rarely sell for more than $75.00 on a good day. It is an exceptional piece until you reach 73 and have to retire it from use.

In searching for Tradition, a red footed sugar and creamer were bought early one morning while using a flashlight to see glass in the dark and covered with dew. That purchase started a quest to find what the pattern actually was that is similar to Tradition. It turned out to be Sandwich by Kemple which has an interesting array of pieces itself.

You can accomplish a rainbow collection of water goblets as every color listed above can be found as a goblet. That water goblet was profusely made and given that it is the piece we see most often, you might buy them for a wine tasting party. Today, most people buy older water goblets for their use as wines. Crystal may be the only color in which you can attain a set of any size.

		*Crystal				*Crystal
	Bowl, 4½", finger	10.00		7 ▸	Stem, 3 oz., wine	6.00
6 ▸	Bowl, 6", baked apple	8.00		8 ▸	Stem, 4 oz., cocktail	5.00
	Bowl, 7", shallow	10.00		1 ▸	Stem, 6 oz., sherbet	4.00
	Bowl, 7¾", flared	10.00		5 ▸	Stem, 10 oz., water goblet	10.00
4 ▸	Cake plate, 72-hole birthday	95.00		2 ▸	Tumbler, 9 oz., ftd.	8.00
9 ▸	Pitcher, ice lip, 2 qt.	30.00			Tumbler, 12 oz., tea	10.00
3 ▸	Plate, 8"	4.00				

* add 50% for color

WAKEFIELD, LINE #1932, WESTMORELAND GLASS COMPANY, c. 1932; WATERFORD, 1950s – 1960s; WAKEFIELD w/red trim, c. 1970s and beyond

Colors: crystal, crystal with red

Wakefield, the birth home of George Washington, was so named according to Charles West in his book on Westmoreland, because it originated in the 200th year following Washington's birth. We know there was quite a bit of hoopla surrounding that bicentennial occasion because of glasses honoring the event which survive today. That was also the birth year of our Washington quarter.

In the beginning, Wakefield was produced in crystal of quality materials that cost twice as much as Westmoreland's standard wares. Westmoreland was hoping to put their good crystal in competition with the enormously expensive, imported Waterford and make it inexpensive enough for the common man.

This glassware was re-introduced to the market in the 1950s and once again in the 1960s (with ruby stain) under the Waterford name. In the 1970s and 1980s, before the company's demise, Wakefield was made again with the red trim staining that is so well liked by collectors today. We have a 1963 catalog, which lists the pattern as Waterford with ruby stain instead of Wakefield; we are not exactly sure when the change of name occurred. This applied stain wears easily and will not hold up to washing in the dishwasher. It is a necessity to treat this as the fine crystal it was intended to be and hand wash pieces. It's amusing that the latest issues are the ones sought by collectors, rather than great-grandma's crystal Wakefield without the stain.

Amazingly, in the many catalog references we checked, there were no creamer and sugar sets listed with ruby stain, but you can see them pictured on the next page. In that 1963 price manual accompanying the catalog, the ruby stained wares cost twice what the same piece in crystal cost. If a piece were $5.00 in crystal, it was $10.00 in ruby stain.

Thanks for all the compliments on the layout for this pattern. We did pass those comments along to the editorial staff at Collector Books who were responsible for the great art work. We only find the glass — photography and layout are left to those professionals.

15

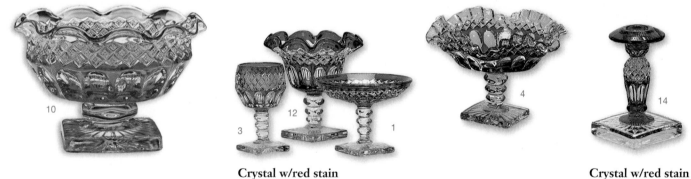

Crystal w/red stain   **Crystal w/red stain**

	Basket, 6"	70.00
	Bonbon, 6", crimped, metal hndl.	35.00
	Bowl, 5", heart, w/hndl.	25.00
	Bowl, 5", nappy, round, w/hndl.	25.00
	Bowl, 6", cupped	22.50
13 ▸	Bowl, 6", heart, w/hndl.	35.00
	Bowl, 8", heart, w/hndl.	80.00
	Bowl, 10½", bell, ftd.	75.00
	Bowl, 11", flat, lipped	65.00
	Bowl, 12", flat, crimped	85.00
	Bowl, 12", ftd., straight edge	70.00
	Bowl, 12", ftd., crimped	90.00
	Bowl, 13", shallow server	70.00
	Cake stand, 12", low ft.	75.00
14 ▸	Candlestick, 6"	40.00
10 ▸	Candy, lipped, open	35.00
	Compote, 5", low ft.	30.00
4 ▸	Compote, 5", low ft., crimped & ruffled	35.00
1 ▸	Compote, 5½", high ft., mint	25.00
	Compote, 5½", high ft., crimped	40.00
	Compote, 7", high ft.	50.00

	Compote, 7", high ft., crimped	75.00
18 ▸	Compote, 8", low ft.	50.00
6 ▸	Compote, 12", low ft. fruit	85.00
16 ▸	Creamer, ftd.	75.00
11 ▸	Fairy lamp, 2-pcs	65.00
	Plate, 6"	12.50
8 ▸	Plate, 8½", luncheon	22.50
	Plate, 10", dinner	65.00
	Plate, 14", torte	75.00
7 ▸	Stem, 1 oz., cordial	50.00
	Stem, 2 oz., wine	32.00
3 ▸	Stem, 3 oz., cocktail	25.00
	Stem, 6 oz., sherbet	18.00
2 ▸	Stem, 10 oz., water	33.00
17 ▸	Sugar	75.00
12 ▸	Sweetmeat, crimped top	35.00
	Tidbit tray, ruffled, metal handle	35.00
5 ▸	Tumbler, 12 oz., ftd. tea	30.00
15 ▸	Urn, w/cover, 11"	60.00
9 ▸	Vase, crimped top	65.00

Colors: crystal; rare in amber

Heisey's Waverly #1519 mould blank is better recognized for the Orchid and Rose etchings occurring on it than for itself, even if it's a superb, stylish blank in its own right.

	Bowl, 6", oval, lemon, w/cover	45.00
6 ▸	Bowl, 6", relish, 2 part, 3 ftd.	10.00
	Bowl, 6½", 2 hdld., ice	75.00
	Bowl, 7", 3 part, relish, oblong	25.00
	Bowl, 7", salad	20.00
	Bowl, 9", 4 part, relish, round	25.00
	Bowl, 9", fruit	25.00
	Bowl, 9", vegetable	30.00
	Bowl, 10", crimped edge	25.00
	Bowl, 10", gardenia	20.00
7 ▸	Bowl, 11", seahorse foot, floral	50.00
	Bowl, 12", crimped edge	30.00
5 ▸	Bowl, 13", gardenia, w/candleholder center	75.00
8 ▸	Box, 5", chocolate, w/cover	80.00
	Box, 5" tall, ftd., w/cover, seahorse hdl.	90.00
1 ▸	Box, 6", candy, w/bowtie knob	45.00

	Box, trinket, lion cover (rare)	700.00
	Butter dish, w/cover, 6", square	45.00
12 ▸	Candleholder, 1-lite, block (rare)	100.00
	Candleholder, 2-lite	35.00
	Candleholder, 2-lite, "flame" center	65.00
2 ▸	Candleholder, 3-lite	65.00
3 ▸	Candle epergnette, 5"	15.00
	Candle epergnette, 6", deep	10.00
	Candle epergnette, 6½"	10.00
	Cheese dish, 5½", ftd.	15.00
	Cigarette holder	50.00
11 ▸	Comport, 6", low ftd.	15.00
10 ▸	Comport, 6½", jelly	20.00
	Comport, 7", low ftd., oval	30.00
	Creamer, ftd.	12.00
	Creamer & sugar, individual, w/tray	40.00

WAVERLY

4 ▶	Cruet, 3 oz., w/#122 stopper	60.00
	Cup	10.00
	Honey dish, 6½", ftd.	45.00
	Mayonnaise, w/liner & ladle, 5½"	40.00
	Plate, 7", salad	9.00
	Plate, 8", luncheon	10.00
	Plate, 10½", dinner	80.00
	Plate, 11", sandwich	20.00
	Plate, 13½", ftd., cake salver	50.00
13 ▶	Plate, 14", center handle, sandwich	55.00
	Plate, 14", sandwich	35.00
	Salt & pepper, pr.	50.00
	Saucer	2.00

	Stem, #5019, 1 oz., cordial	50.00
	Stem, #5019, 3 oz., wine, blown	18.00
	Stem, #5019, 3½ oz., cocktail	12.00
	Stem, #5019, 5½ oz., sherbet/champagne	7.00
	Stem, #5019, 10 oz., blown	18.00
	Sugar, ftd.	12.00
	Tray, 12", celery	18.00
	Tumbler, #5019, 5 oz., ftd., juice, blown	18.00
	Tumbler, #5019, 13 oz., ftd., tea, blown	20.00
14 ▶	Vase, 3½", violet	40.00
9 ▶	Vase, 7", ftd.	30.00
	Vase, 7", ftd., fan shape	35.00

WILD ROSE WITH LEAVES & BERRIES, INDIANA GLASS COMPANY, early 1950s – 1980s

Colors: crystal, crystal satinized, iridescent, milk glass, multicolored blue, green, pink, and yellow; satinized green, pink, and yellow; sprayed green, lavender, and pink

Wild Rose with Leaves & Berries is a small serving ware pattern that growing numbers of collectors are buying. We wish we could find more of the multicolored ware which flies off the table at shows. Even non-collectors have snatched pieces because it is so "pretty" or "neat" or "cool." A rather wide range of colors is available in Wild Rose including some iridescent and satinized items. We have noticed colored sets like the blue pictured in pink, yellow, and lilac. There is a pretty pink seven-piece berry set in a shop near here for $150.00 and they have no idea what it is or who made it. We have been keeping an eye on it and hoping the owner decides to get realistic with the price which so far, hasn't happened.

We have noticed a massive range of prices, some exorbitant on the multicolored pieces. We admit they are nicely colored, but it is not Victorian pattern glass as we once saw it marked. We have enjoyed our multicolored sherbet dishes with fruit, tapioca, and ice cream at many family meals. Those we hand wash for fear that the color will fade in the dishwasher. Using crystal presents no such problem which we do regularly. One collector told me she was using the two-handled tray as a plate so she could set a table with her ware. Collectors are becoming quite innovative in creating table settings.

		Iridescent Crystal Milk Glass Crystal Satinized	Sprayed & Satinized Colors	Multicolored
6 ▸	Bowl, handled sauce	4.00	7.00	15.00
2 ▸	Bowl, 9", large vegetable	10.00	20.00	50.00
4 ▸	Candle	5.00	9.00	25.00
7 ▸	Plate, sherbet	2.00	4.00	12.00
	Relish, handled	7.00	12.00	30.00
5 ▸	Relish, two-part, handled	7.00	10.00	32.00
1 ▸	Sherbet	4.00	6.00	18.00
3 ▸	Tray, two-handled	15.00	20.00	45.00

WILLOW, ETCHING NO. 335, FOSTORIA GLASS COMPANY, 1939 – 1945

Color: crystal with etch

Fostoria's Willow is etched for the most part on Blank #2574 (Raleigh) and on stemware Blank #6023 (Colfax). Willow designs have always been fashionable whether they are on china or glass. Everyone has heard of Blue Willow china if they have been into collecting at all, and this design is based upon similar scenes. There are three sample photos (bridge, house, and willows) so you can identify each of the etched scenes.

What we noticed as we searched for Willow was a lack of knowledge about who made it, although it was acknowledged as an exceptional ware since the prices were seldom reasonable. What you see was purchased a piece or two at a time over several years.

	Bonbon, 5", hdld.	20.00
	Bowl, finger	18.00
	Bowl, 8½", hdld.	22.00
	Bowl, 9", ftd.	55.00
	Bowl, 9½", hdld.	35.00
	Bowl, 12", flared	35.00
	Bowl, 13", fruit	38.00
6 ▶	Celery, 10½"	28.00
	Comport, 5"	30.00
8 ▶	Creamer, ftd.	20.00
	Creamer, individual	20.00
	Cup	20.00
	Ice tub	75.00
	Lemon dish, 6½", hdld.	15.00
	Mayonnaise	22.00
	Mayonnaise plate	8.00
	Oil bottle, 4¼ oz.	75.00
	Olive, 6"	14.00
4 ▶	Pickle, 8"	16.00
	Pitcher, 53 oz., ftd.	195.00
	Plate, 6"	5.00
5 ▶	Plate, 7"	8.00

	Plate, 8"	12.00
	Plate, 9"	28.00
	Plate, 10", cake, 2 hdld.	30.00
	Plate, 14", torte	40.00
	Relish, 10", 3-part	30.00
	Shaker, pr.	60.00
	Saucer	3.00
	Stem, 3⅜", 1 oz., cordial	30.00
	Stem, 3⅝", 4 oz., oyster cocktail	17.50
1 ▶	Stem, 4⅛", low sherbet	9.00
	Stem, 4¾", 4 oz., claret-wine	18.00
	Stem, 4⅜", 3¾ oz., cocktail	12.00
	Stem, 4⅞", 6 oz., saucer champagne	14.00
3 ▶	Stem, 6⅜", 9 oz., water	15.00
7 ▶	Sugar, ftd.	20.00
	Sugar, individual	20.00
	Sweetmeat, 5¼", hdld.	20.00
	Tray, 8", muffin, hdld.	25.00
	Tumbler, 4½", ftd., 5 oz., juice	12.00
	Tumbler, 5⅛", ftd., 9 oz., water	15.00
2 ▶	Tumbler, 5¾", ftd., 12 oz., tea	25.00
	Whip cream, 5", hdld.	33.00

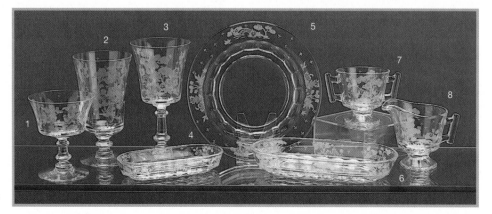

WILLOWMERE, ETCHING NO. 333, FOSTORIA GLASS COMPANY, 1938 – 1968

Color: crystal with etching

Willowmere was listed in Fostoria catalogs for over 30 years; thus many brides chose it as their wedding crystal. We are seeing more and more of this for sale in our travels. Stems and candleholders seem to be prevalent on Internet auctions. Thanks to a generous collector from St. Louis, we are able to show you a variety of pieces. Most Willowmere is etched on Blank #2560 (Coronet); in addition, the stems are etched on Blank #6024 (Cellini).

27 ▸	Bonbon, 5¾", hdld.	20.00
6 ▸	Bonbon, 7¼", 3-toed	20.00
	Bowl, finger	22.00
32 ▸	Bowl, 5⅞", 3-toed nut	22.00
	Bowl, 6", cereal	18.00
34 ▸	Bowl, 8½", hdld.	30.00
	Bowl, 10½", 2-part, salad	50.00
33 ▸	Bowl, 10", salad	50.00
	Bowl, 11½", crimped	30.00
4 ▸	Bowl, 11", hdld.	50.00
	Bowl, 12", flared	50.00
	Bowl, 13", fruit	50.00
	Candlestick, 4½"	20.00
29 ▸	Candlestick, 4", #2560½	18.00
26 ▸•	Candlestick, 5⅛", duo	28.00
8 ▸	Celery, 11"	22.00
	Cheese comport, 3¼"	20.00
	Comport, 6"	40.00
25 ▸	Creamer	15.00
	Creamer, individual	15.00
16 ▸	Cup	8.00
	Ice bucket, 4⅞", ftd.	90.00
5 ▸	Lemon dish, 6¼", hdld.	18.00
30 ▸	Mayonnaise	25.00
28 ▸	Mayonnaise, 2-part	30.00
31 ▸	Mayonnaise plate	7.00
	Oil bottle, 3 oz.	75.00
9 ▸	Olive, 6¾"	22.00
7 ▸	Pickle, 8¾"	20.00
	Pitcher, 32 oz.	195.00
2 ▸	Pitcher, ftd.	295.00
20 ▸	Plate, 6"	5.00
	Plate, 7"	10.00
	Plate, 8"	12.00
18 ▸	Plate, 9", dinner	30.00

	Plate, 11", cracker	20.00
35 ▸	Plate, 11½", cake, hdld.	40.00
24 ▸	Plate, 14", torte	45.00
	Relish, 6½", 2-part, hdld.	20.00
13 ▸	Relish, 10", 3-part, hdld.	30.00
	Relish, 10", 4-part	30.00
1 ▸	Relish, 13¼", 5-part	55.00
	Sani-cut server	295.00
17 ▸	Saucer	3.00
	Shaker, pr.	75.00
	Stem, 3½", 4 oz., oyster cocktail	11.00
15 ▸	Stem, 3¾", 1 oz., cordial	35.00
10 ▸	Stem, 4½", 6 oz., sherbet	10.00
11 ▸	Stem, 4¾", 3½ oz., cocktail	12.00
14 ▸	Stem, 5⅜", 6 oz., saucer champagne	12.00
	Stem, 5⅜", 3½ oz., wine	20.00
	Stem, 5¾", 4 oz., claret	22.00
	Stem, 7⅜", 10 oz., water	16.00
23 ▸	Sugar	15.00
	Sugar, individual	15.00
	Sweetmeat, 5½", hdld.	18.00
	Tidbit, 3-toed	20.00
	Tray, 7½", sugar/creamer	15.00
12 ▸	Tray, 8¼", hdld., muffin	45.00
	Tray, 11", center hdld,. lunch	25.00
21 ▸	Tumbler, 4⅝", ftd., 5 oz., juice	12.00
22 ▸	Tumbler, 5¼", ftd., 9 oz., water	14.00
19 ▸	Tumbler, 5¾", ftd., 12 oz., tea	16.00
	Vase, 6", hdld. (2560)	90.00
	Vase, 7½" (2567)	90.00
	Vase, 9" (2568)	90.00
3 ▸	Vase, 10" (2470)	110.00
	Vase, 10" (5100)	110.00
	Whip cream, 5", hdld.	18.00

WINDSOR, FEDERAL GLASS COMPANY, c. 1974; INDIANA GLASS CO., 1980s – 1990s

Colors: crystal, Aegean blue, Sun Gold, and pink

    Windsor was shown in Federal's 1974 catalog but was not in that of 1979. This gives us fairly accurate dates for Federal's "jewel-like" Windsor. Pink was not listed as a Federal color; so Indiana seems responsible for this color as well as the carnival colors that are prevalent in flea markets today since they acquired the moulds after Federal's ensuing demise.

    We are not sure who assembled the lamp, but if you collect this pattern, it would be a shining piece to own.

		Crystal	Colors			Crystal	Colors
	Ashtray, 6"	2.50	4.00	1 ▸	Marmalade, w/notched lid	4.00	10.00
	Bell	5.00			Pitcher, 18 oz	12.00	
2 ▸	Bowl, 5½"	3.00	5.00		Plate, 6½"	1.50	2.00
14 ▸	Bowl, 6½"	3.50	6.00	3 ▸	Plate, 9¼", snack	2.00	3.00
	Bowl, 10½"	6.00	10.00		Plate, 11"	7.50	12.00
9 ▸	Butter w/cover, ¼ lb.	7.50	12.00	5 ▸	Relish, 8½, divided	3.50	5.00
13 ▸	Cake stand	12.50	22.50		Shaker, pr.	5.00	8.00
8 ▸	Candy dish w/cover	8.00	12.50		Sugar w/cover	4.00	8.00
7 ▸	Cigarette box	6.00	11.00	15 ▸	Sundae, ftd.	3.00	5.00
4 ▸	Coaster/ashtray	3.00	4.50		Tumbler, ftd., water	3.00	5.00
6 ▸	Creamer, 8 oz	3.00	5.00	11 ▸	Tumbler, ftd., tea	3.50	5.50
10 ▸	Cup, 6 oz., snack	2.00	3.00	12 ▸	Tumbler, ftd., juice	2.50	3.50
	Lamp		35.00		Tray, rectangular, 8¼" x 4½"	4.00	6.00

WISTAR, LINE #2620, FOSTORIA GLASS COMPANY, 1941 – 1944; BETSY ROSS, 1958 – 1965

Colors: crystal; white, aqua, and peach milk

Fostoria's Wistar is not being found in quantities to stimulate collecting. Our suspicion is that the lack of cups, saucers, and a dinner-sized plate may have something to do with that as it does in collecting patterns of Depression glass lacking those items. A Wistar is a twining vine with showy clusters of flowers, according to Mr. Webster. Wisteria was named for a C. Wistar, an anatomist who was born in 1760. We became curious about the term when researching a Duncan and Miller stemware with the same name. Up until this revelation, we had thought that Fostoria was doing its part for the country at war by creating a pattern with stars and stripes, on the order of the Stars and Stripes pattern by Hocking.

In 1958, Fostoria rejuvenated this pattern in their milk and colored (pink and blue) milk wares. This revival was renamed Betsy Ross pattern, still a patriotic nod of sorts, whether they originally intended that or not. The stemware and tumblers for Betsy Ross were the Wistar design exactly. However, the other items in Betsy Ross did not have the stars, just the ribbing and vine. This later issue, especially the white, turns up more frequently today than does crystal.

		Crystal	White
	Bowl, 4", sq., hndl.	10.00	
9 ▸	Bowl, 4¼", ftd., round, hndl.	10.00	10.00
1 ▸	Bowl, 4½", triangular, hndl.	13.00	10.00
	Bowl, 5", ftd., hndl.	12.50	
7 ▸	Bowl, 5½", 3-toe, nut	12.50	
11 ▸	Bowl, 6⅝", 3-toe, bonbon	15.00	
	Bowl, 6¾", 3-toe, tri-corner	15.00	
	Bowl, 10", salad	20.00	
	Bowl, 12", lily pond	20.00	
	Bowl, 13", fruit		25.00
5 ▸	Candlestick, 4"	15.00	

		Crystal	White
	Celery, 9½"	20.00	
10 ▸	Creamer, 4", ftd.	10.00	10.00
	Mayonnaise, 2⅞", ftd., w/ladle	30.00	
3 ▸	Plate, 7"	7.50	10.00
4 ▸	Plate, 14", torte	30.00	
	Stem, 6 oz., high sherbet	8.00	10.00
6 ▸	Stem, 9 oz., water	14.00	12.00
8 ▸	Sugar, 3½", ftd.	10.00	10.00
	Tumbler, 5 oz.	10.00	10.00
2 ▸	Tumbler, 12 oz.	14.00	12.00

YORKTOWN, FEDERAL GLASS COMPANY, mid 1950s

Colors: yellow, crystal, white, iridized, and smoke

We added Yorktown to the book to try to eradicate many of the letters and e-mails we receive every year proclaiming that some rare Sahara Heisey Provincial has been discovered that we don't list and wondering how much it's worth and where can they sell it. Heisey's Provincial was not made in yellow; therefore, readers assume that they have found a really rare piece of Heisey. Rare pieces and colors do show up sporadically in various other patterns; but Heisey's colors are extremely well documented and discoveries there are typically 1960s Imperial-made colors from Heisey's moulds.

Crystal Yorktown can be collected within a brief period if you search for it. There are plenty of Internet auctions to aid you if you cannot find enough in your local flea markets. The punch set is easy on the pocket. There is enough yellow around to collect a set, but it will take a bit longer to assemble. We are pricing both colors the same for now, based strictly upon what we have paid or seen priced. We have not paid any more for yellow than crystal. Time will tell if a difference will occur. We see only a few pieces of iridized, mostly the punch bowl, snack sets, and mugs.

All the dark iridized carnival colors are a later Indiana product from Federal's moulds.

		All Colors				All Colors
1 ▸	Bowl, 5½", berry, #2905	4.00		5 ▸	Plate, 11½", #2904	9.00
6 ▸	Bowl, 9½", large berry, #2906	12.00			Punch set, 7 qt., base, 12 cups	30.00
	Bowl, 10", ftd., fruit, #2902	20.00		8 ▸	Saucer, #2911	.50
	Celery tray, 10", #2907	15.00		10 ▸	Sherbet, 2½", 7 oz., #1744	3.00
9 ▸	Creamer, #2908	4.00		2 ▸	Sugar w/lid, #2909	8.00
7 ▸	Cup, #2910	3.00			Tumbler, 3⅞", 6 oz., juice, #1741	4.00
12 ▸	Cup, snack/punch, 6 oz.	2.00		11 ▸	Tumbler, 4¾", 10 oz., water, #1742	6.00
	Mug, 5¹⁄₁₆"	15.00		3 ▸	Tumbler, 5¼", 13 oz., iced tea, #1743	8.00
4 ▸	Plate, 8¼", #2903	4.00			Vase, 8"	12.00
13 ▸	Plate, 10½" x 6¾", snack w/indent	3.00				

OTHER TITLES FROM THE FLORENCES

**FLORENCES' OVENWARE
FROM THE 1920S TO THE PRESENT**
Item #6641 • ISBN: 978-1-57432-449-7 • 8½ x 11 • 208 Pgs. HB • $24.95

**COLLECTOR'S ENCYCLOPEDIA OF DEPRESSION
GLASS, EIGHTEENTH EDITION**
Item #7526 • ISBN: 978-1-57432-559-1 • 8½ x 11 • 256 Pgs. • HB • $19.95

NEWEST EDITION

AMERICAN PATTERN GLASS TABLE SETS
Item #7362 • ISBN: 978-1-57432-546-1 • 8½ x 11 • 192 Pgs. • HB • $24.95

NEWEST RELEASE

**ELEGANT GLASSWARE OF THE DEPRESSION ERA,
TWELFTH EDITION**
Item #7029 • ISBN: 978-1-57432-514-0 • 8½ x 11 • 256 Pgs. • HB • $24.95

**KITCHEN GLASSWARE OF THE DEPRESSION YEARS,
SIXTH EDITION**
Item #5827 • ISBN: 978-1-57432-220-0 • 8½ x 11 • 272 Pgs. • HB • $24.95

**POCKET GUIDE TO DEPRESSION GLASS & MORE,
FIFTEENTH EDITION**
Item #7027 • ISBN: 978-1-57432-512-6 • 5½ x 8½ • 224 Pgs • PB • $12.95

FLORENCES' GLASSWARE
PATTERN IDENTIFICATION GUIDES
Vol. I • Item #5042 • ISBN: 978-1-57432-045-9
8½ x 11 • 176 Pgs. • PB • $18.95
Vol. II • Item #5615 • ISBN: 978-1-57432-177-7
8½ x 11 • 208 Pgs. • PB • $19.95
Vol. III • Item #6142 • ISBN: 978-1-57432-315-3
8½ x 11 • 272 Pgs. • PB • $19.95
Vol. IV • Item #6643 • ISBN: 978-1-57432-451-8
8½ x 11 • 208 Pgs. • PB • $19.95

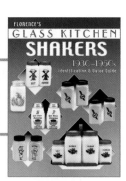

GLASS CANDLESTICKS OF THE DEPRESSION ERA
Vol. 1 • Item #5354 • ISBN: 978-1-57432-136-4 • 8½ x 11 • 176 Pgs. • HB • $24.95
Vol. 2 • Item #6934 • ISBN: 978-1-57432-495-2 • 8½ x 11 • 224 Pgs. • HB • $24.95

ANCHOR HOCKING'S FIRE-KING & MORE,
THIRD EDITION
Item #6930 • ISBN: 978-1-57432-491-4 • 8½ x 11 • 224 Pgs. • HB • $24.95

FLORENCES' GLASS
KITCHEN SHAKERS, 1930 – 1950S
Item #6462 • ISBN: 978-1-57432-389-4 • 8½ x 11 • 160 Pgs • PB • $19.95

FLORENCES' BIG BOOK OF
SALT & PEPPER SHAKERS
Item #5918 • ISBN: 978-1-57432-257-6 • 8½ x 11 • 272 Pgs. • PB • $24.95

UPDATED PRICES

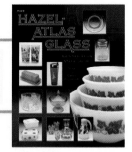

THE HAZEL-ATLAS GLASS
IDENTIFICATION AND VALUE GUIDE
Item #6562 • ISBN: 978-1-57432-420-4 • 8½ x 11 • 224 Pgs. • HB • $24.95